Cosmopolitan dystopia

Manchester University Press

In loving memory
Nada Milić
(1933–2015)

Cosmopolitan dystopia

International intervention and the failure of the West

Philip Cunliffe

Manchester University Press

Published by Manchester University Press
Altrincham Street, Manchester M1 7JA

www.manchesteruniversitypress.co.uk

British Library Cataloguing-in-Publication Data
A catalogue record for this book is available from the British Library

ISBN 978 1 5261 0572 1   hardback

ISBN 978 1 5261 0573 8   paperback

First published 2020

The publisher has no responsibility for the persistence or accuracy of URLs for any external or third-party internet websites referred to in this book, and does not guarantee that any content on such websites is, or will remain, accurate or appropriate.

Typeset in Palatino and Gibson
by R. J. Footring Ltd, Derby
Printed in Great Britain by TJ International Ltd, Padstow

Contents

Figures

Preface and acknowledgements

This is a book about the character of liberal international order over the last thirty years of the post-Cold War era and how it came to be characterised by repetitive military interventions that effectively collapsed into an era of permanent war. There are many ways in which this story could be told. For example, both Emmanuel Todd and Yanis Varoufakis see the era of permanent war as a function of the enormous and abiding US trade deficit. Exemplary conflicts, they argue, were needed to maintain the US position at the centre of the world system, both in supporting confidence in the dollar as the global reserve currency and by way of justifying a system of global 'protection' that ensured other states would provide the necessary inflow of capital that would in turn allow the US to continue consuming more than it produces. Drawing on Greek myth, Varoufakis dubbed the massive scale of US borrowing the 'tribute' that was paid to the Minotaur – the US – at the centre of the international system.[1] John J. Mearsheimer and Stephen M. Walt see permanent war as the outcome of 'liberal hegemony', a catastrophically over-ambitious grand strategy born of US victory in the Cold War and locked into place by a self-serving foreign policy elite.[2] At the grandest level perhaps, it is a tale that could be told in terms of the contradictions of globalisation, which, by spreading growth and development around the world market, has given rise to new challengers who threaten to fragment and undermine that very same global market.

However it is told, it must also at some level be a story about our ideas of international order. In addition to trade talks and global integration and so on, 'liberal international order' encompasses our ideas about the purpose and utility of military force in international affairs, about the structure of political order and authority, about the role and rights of the strong in relation to the weak, and about the possibility and appeal of self-government in both individual and collective terms. This is what merits casting this discussion in terms of international political theory.

To explain, say, the disastrous intervention in Iraq purely as a reverberation of deep, enigmatic structural forces such as a global balance of power being recalibrated or shifts in trade deficits, currency reserves, purchases of US Treasury bonds or the changing pattern of Western states' fossil fuel consumption would not fully capture the awesomely irrational and criminal scale of what happened to that country. Nor would such explanations tell us much about the legacy of political structures and new forms of authority that we will inherit from this era of permanent war. The protracted torment of Iraq reaching back to 1991 seems to me very clearly one of the greatest criminal acts of our times. Yet it is never discussed alongside Rwanda or Srebrenica, both of which are repeatedly (and self-servingly) identified as the worst moments of our era and conveniently seen as sins of omission – morality tales in which the failure of the West to intervene was seen as the most important, overarching aspect of those atrocities. To me, it seemed increasingly clear that military operations which were supposed to have inaugurated either a new supranational global order or alternatively an expansionist American empire built around a 'civilising mission' for democracy and human rights embodied instead a 'de-civilising mission' that led to regression and de-modernisation with the shattering of unitary nation-states that had emerged from the era of Third World revolutions, alongside the dialling back of the markers of secular progress, whether measured in terms of public infrastructure, centralised nationhood, women's rights, secular authority, ethnic and religious pluralism, and so on.

Yet, apparently, sins of commission did not exist. Many scholars, intellectuals and academics have insisted that the 2003 invasion of Iraq had no relationship to the broader pattern of liberal interventions since 1992, while in the next breath insisting that yet another military intervention in yet another Arab state, Libya, was entirely justified and welcome in the very next year after the US formally ended its post-occupation campaign in Iraq. I lost count of how many conferences, panels and academic round-tables I sat through to be reassured not only that, even while the forces of Islamic State were ensconcing themselves on the shores of Tripoli, the NATO bombing campaign had been blessed not only by following the deepest principles of 'just war' theory as enunciated by St Augustine and Thomas Aquinas, but also that the campaign conveniently conformed to the latter-day scriptures of human rights and the writ of UN Security Council resolutions. Exasperated by the blithe self-assurance of those arguing for yet more war, I realised that the recurrent amnesia and casuistry of debates around intervention had to be accounted for and not merely refuted. What was it about these ideas that made it so easy to split apart the most basic questions of cause and effect, to treat every humanitarian crisis as if it were *sui generis*, and to act as if intervention itself had no history? This is the question that I have tried to answer in this book, and it is one that led me to consider contradictions within liberal internationalism itself – contradictions that have given rise, I argue, to a cosmopolitan dystopia.

Books about ideas arguably accrue debts more than other kinds of book. The inspiration for the critique in this book came from engaging with and (I hope) extending the work of several thinkers, namely Jef Huysmans, Anne Orford, Jean Cohen and Samuel Moyn. It was their work that provided the key insights for understanding interventionism in terms of political exceptionalism and anti-utopianism, as well as changing forms of state and sovereign authority, and for contextualising these issues in debates about international order. This enabled me to knot together practical concerns about international security with a theoretical interest in underlying principles of international order. Following in their footsteps I hope to use and expand upon their insights taken from constitutionalist reasoning and international political theory, as I hope to demonstrate over the course of the book that these insights are uniquely well suited to explaining and contextualising certain political outcomes that would otherwise seem aberrational.

Many of the ideas in this book also grow out of earlier work and debates associated with the (now defunct) Sovereignty And Its Discontents working group (SAID) of the British International Studies Association, which I helped to convene and oversee alongside Christopher J. Bickerton and Alex Gourevitch. Whatever insights I can claim in this book also bear their imprint, for which I am very grateful, although needless to say I bear sole responsibility for the arguments in this book, including for any errors of fact and judgement. There were so many round-tables, seminars, workshops, panels and conferences associated with the SAID project, and since, that it seems to churlish to select specific individuals who were particularly influential with respect to the arguments in this book. Nonetheless, I feel obliged to extend a special thanks (in no particular order) to James Heartfield, Michael Savage, David Chandler, R. B. J. Walker, Tara McCormack, Chris Brown, Lee Jones, Ian Zuckerman, Shahar Hameiri, Aidan Hehir, Mervyn Frost, Jonathan Joseph, Peter Ramsay and Jennifer Welsh – all of whom supported the SAID project and/or variously contributed to helping shape the arguments in this book. I also extend my thanks to an anonymous reviewer working on behalf of Manchester University Press. If any of them read the finished product, I hope they find it stimulating and useful even if they do not agree with it. Once again, the fault for any errors is mine alone. A special word of thanks to the charming Marie-Claire Antoine, who initially suggested I write this book, far too many years ago, and was happy to discuss it over a steak and red wine in downtown New York. Another special thanks to Tony Mason, Robert Byron and Jonathan de Peyer, my editors at Manchester University Press, who inherited the project and have shown heroic patience with the book ever since. Last but not least, my grandmother Nada Milić (née Prokić) had a refrain to the effect that if someone asked her for her view about the state of the world, she would happily give them a piece of her mind. When I was little, I promised to give her the opportunity to do so. Hopefully this book goes some way, in a sorely belated and ultimately inadequate manner, to do just that. The book is dedicated to her memory.

Canterbury
December 2019

Introduction: the rise of cosmopolitan dystopia

While I was putting the finishing touches to the manuscript in early 2019, I was in touch via WhatsApp with a journalist who was in Syria, reporting from the front line in the final offensive by the Kurdish-led Syrian Democratic Forces (SDF) against the Baghouz enclave, the last redoubt of Islamic State (IS), near the Syrian border with Iraq. The question of what to do about Western citizens who had joined IS and were now languishing in Kurdish-run refugee camps was also very much in the news: the front cover of this book shows women and children evacuated from Baghouz arriving at a screening centre run by the SDF in the eastern Syrian province of Deir Ezzor in March 2019. All this prompted me to think back to the summer of 2014, the moment when my understanding of liberal intervention shifted decisively. This happened as I read with foreboding the news of the fall of the Iraqi city of Mosul to a new jihadi group. While the fall of Mosul signalled yet another escalation of violent conflict in a country that was already bloody and battered, it was the name of the group, 'Islamic State', that was in many ways more troubling. This strange and sinister name signalled an explicitly political, even geopolitical, ambition and vision on the part of jihadi insurgents – vision and ambition that had hitherto been noticeable by its absence.[1] The desire to establish a new political order that openly challenged the writ of existing nations in the region led me to the conclusion that the rise of Islamic State set the seal on a powerful and pervasive strain of ideas about international affairs – a set of ideas that could be described as political cosmopolitanism, which sought to replace the nation-state with a new, transnational order.

While there was little doubt in my mind that what we were seeing in Iraq in 2014 was the consummation of ideas that I had been discussing in seminar rooms and lecture halls since the late 1990s, I still did not expect the resonances and analogues to be quite so uncannily direct and obvious. While the slave markets, brazen cruelty and fantastical visions of militarised global expansion were all self-evidently and even ostentatiously dystopian, Islamic State was also very clearly cosmopolitan. It was cosmopolitan in the most basic and obvious sense, in that it was multi-ethnic and multinational, comprising many thousands of people from all over the world. These people had descended on two Middle Eastern backwaters, Mosul in Iraq and Raqqa in Syria, in order to join a new political entity that did not aspire to become an independent nation or country in any meaningful sense of the term. Islamic State was thus also cosmopolitan in the broader sense that it rejected the sovereign nation-state. Not only did it seek to overthrow existing nation-states, as when its fighters ejected Iraqi security forces from their bases in the north-west of the country, it rejected the very form of the sovereign nation-state as such. Abu Bakr al-Baghdadi, the late self-styled caliph of the Islamic State, called upon his followers to 'trample' the 'idols' of nationalism and democracy in the sermon with which the caliphate was formally established. He further enjoined all Muslims everywhere to join 'a state where the Arab and non-Arab, the white man and black man, the easterner and westerner are all brothers' and that would enact divine – that is, supranational – justice against its opponents.[2]

Islamic State also made much of its supersession of national borders, as on 30 June 2014, when its militants flamboyantly bulldozed the border posts that formally separated Syria and Iraq, thereby supposedly unifying the territories of the two countries in an integrated new political system that transcended the merely human, secular artefacts of nation-states. Followers of Islamic State renounced their national citizenship on social media and burned their passports, while its fighters saw the world as a single site of battle as they launched terror attacks in cities around the world.[3] At the same time, various Islamist militias and jihadist groups across Africa and Asia, embroiled in their own local conflicts and civil strife, willingly subsumed themselves into this globalised new vision of conflict and supranational order. As a new type of polity, Islamic State claimed legitimacy neither from below (it did not claim to represent any particular nation or group seeking self-determination), nor from above, for Islamic State reached higher than any international law or supranational body when its caliph claimed directly to stand for mankind as such, drawing on nothing less than divine authority to do so.

Travelling to Iraq and Syria for 'humanitarian purposes' may have provided the alibi or initiation for many a Western would-be jihadi, but however pure or impure their motives, however authentic or inauthentic their compassion, it is unsurprising that the logic of humanitarian rescue was entwined with that of violent regime change.[4] After all, while the world bewailed the human rights abuses and atrocities committed by the Syrian government, it was jihadis who were the ones actually fighting the government on the ground, and it was only jihadis who actively, persistently and unambiguously sought to overthrow the Syrian regime. As one reflective would-be jihadi put it, viewing military conquest as a charitable act and feeling entitled to intervene in other countries' civil wars and to rebuild their societies were popular Western ideals more than they were Islamic scripture.[5] In short, humanitarian compassion for distant strangers entwined with transcending nation-states by force if necessary and scorning nationalism through transnational organisation and supra-national authority were familiar themes in world politics. What we were seeing in Iraq and Syria was only a murky mirror, one in which familiar ideals and hopes were being played out in dark and terrible form: permanent war inspired by global ideals in a borderless world.

As J. M. Keynes once noted, 'Madmen in authority, who hear voices in the air, are distilling their frenzy from some academic scribbler of a few years back'. As the spectre of totalitarianism had faded at the end of the Cold War, many international political theorists had turned their scribblings to intellectually subduing that most intensely concentrated, brash and unrestrained form of political power – that institution that recognises peers but has no superiors, the sovereign state. While these scribblings were numerous and varied, many of them shared a similar cast, in that they sought to supersede state sovereignty in various ways. Whether through appealing to global law or vesting their hopes in supranational new regimes and institutions, a common and recurrent concern was to assimilate peoples into new supranational social, legal and political structures – those varied elements that together constituted the 'postnational constellation', as the title of philosopher Jürgen Habermas's book on the matter put it.[6] Vertically, people had to be integrated into new supranational institutions and laws that ramified from regional up to global bodies, and horizontally they had to be blended together, less segmented by national political loyalties.

While many of these changes were often assumed to be a result of the movement of capital and new types of media, globalisation was never merely a matter of spontaneous trade flows or extemporaneous new technologies, but also involved explicitly political projects of integration and reordering to better fit the emergent infrastructure of a new social order. Part of this also involved military force, in which powerful Western states were expected to act as the direct military enforcers and executors of global law, defending individuals' human rights from the depredations of their own negligent and criminal national leaders, arresting war criminals to haul them off before international courts, promoting democracy up to and including the use of force if necessary, and acting to neutralise global security threats – security threats that paradoxically seemed to become more apocalyptically menacing the more globalised Western power became. This was the view of NATO as the 'left hand of God', as per the title of an exultant essay by the philosopher Slavoj Žižek in which he defended the NATO bombing of Yugoslavia in 1999, the North Atlantic alliance cast as the imperfect instrument of a higher justice.[7]

If wars had previously been defined in liberal terms of anti-totalitarianism and anti-communism, they had also been justified in unabashedly national terms too – defending national rights and honour, self-defence and sometimes even plain unadorned national self-interest. In the post-Cold War era, the use of force was still defined in liberal terms but also terms that were at once more cosmopolitan (justified on behalf of others) and humanitarian (protection and alleviating suffering rather than defending liberty). Thus, while in 1999 Habermas acknowledged the 'inevitability of a transitory paternalism'[8] in NATO's invocation of higher right over the rights of sovereign states, he nonetheless welcomed NATO's war against Yugoslavia as embodying 'a leap from the classical international law of states to a cosmopolitan law of a global civil society'.[9] Cosmopolitan political theorist Patrick Hayden saw post-Cold War developments in international security such as the doctrine of the responsibility to protect and the international human security regime as concrete steps towards 'replacing the realist national interest-based security paradigm with a cosmopolitan, person-based paradigm'.[10]

A crucial constituent element of this cosmopolitan vision of politics was human rights. As Perry Anderson observed, for an entire generation of political theorists who had hitherto restricted themselves to theorising politics inside the state during the Cold War, after the Cold War 'human rights became the global trampoline for vaulting over the barriers of national sovereignty, in the name of a better future'.[11] Human rights were to be used to abrade nation-states in order to insert them into new global configurations so that they would fit better alongside new actors such as non-governmental organisations, international courts and supranational bodies. Human rights provided the legal undergirding for cosmopolitan politics, the human face of globalisation. Powerful, evocative and densely layered and distributed across international treaties, conventions, national courts and supranational agencies, human rights have captured the hopes of many millions of people around the world – hopes for justice, social improvement, legal redress and political change. By the same token, human rights have also been widely criticised, not only for the hypocrisy of their defenders but also for an imperious universalism that bleaches out cultural particularism. To be sure, the language of human rights has certainly provided Western states with a supple new discourse of moral superiority to wield over up-start ex-colonies in place of white supremacy. The discourse of human rights also gave an appropriately supranational expression to old European imperial states that had grown habituated to pooling their sovereignty as their individual power waned. There is, though, one element of human rights that has hitherto been overlooked and yet is crucial to understanding both their cosmopolitan character *and* their dystopic results. That element is the post- or counter-utopian character of human rights. Political philosopher John Rawls, for instance, expressly framed his cosmopolitan vision in *The Law of Peoples* as a 'realistic utopia' – that is to say, a vision that was expressly modest, pragmatic and self-restrained rather than being crusading or militant.[12] Juxtapose this with Samuel Moyn's work, which has shown most clearly how human rights could necessarily politically succeed only as a response to thwarted utopianism.[13] It was the failure of New Left hopes for radical transformation in Western democracies – accompanied by the frequently dismal results of Third World and anti-colonial revolutions – that formed the disenchantment that was to provide the basis for human rights as a project. At once modest and fervent, human rights offered a model of politics and activism that was restrained, diffident, circumspect and minimalistic. In place of the radical hopes for drastic improvement to be achieved through the high drama of national politics, the seizure of state power and even revolution, change was to be limited to marginal, incremental but persistent improvement through the alleviation of suffering. Conceived as such, human rights were explicitly anti-political. With human rights targeted à tous azimuts, activists confronted both East and West in the Cold War, championing the rights of dissidents across totalitarian Eastern Europe as well as the rebels imprisoned by fascistic military dictatorships in the Americas, Southern Europe and apartheid South Africa.[14]

Rooted in civil society movements rather than campaigning political parties, human rights activists were uninterested in seizing or wielding state power. Indeed, the human rights movement carried with it the hostility to and suspicion of centralised political authority that would become the core of post-Cold War cosmopolitanism. The advocates of human rights vested their hopes in civil society organisations rather than nationalist movements or political parties. Yet by the same token, nor was the human rights movement anarchist. There was never any intention of abolishing the state as such, for such a vision would, after all, be a political one, involving precisely the kind of ambition and sweep that human rights were defined against. The project never envisaged the dissolution of the state but rather a new kind of state, one in which the mailed fist of state power was softened by the velvet glove of international law, and was to be coordinated with a range of new appendages and prostheses – transnational regimes, new regional bodies, supranational courts, non-governmental organisations, social movements, ethically aware corporations, transnational regulatory agencies and so on.

In political terms, human rights embodied nothing so much as the liberalism of fear – a distinctive strain of post-war liberalism that was cultivated by thinkers such as Isaiah Berlin, Judith Shklar and Raymond Aron.[15] While these thinkers were as suspicious of and as hostile to the utopian totalitarianism that they saw on the other side of the Iron Curtain as any other liberal, they were also wary of grandiose attempts to counter totalitarianism that might risk mimetically replicating its crushing uniformity.[16] Their political vision and hopes for liberalism were thus restricted, with the most that could be hoped for being the cautious, prudent relief of extreme human suffering in a world that was irredeemably conflicted, plural and fallen, beyond redemption. Human rights were the legal and institutional embodiment of this exemplary hope that suffering and injustice could be meliorated while at the same time avoiding the terrible, ineluctable fate of utopians, whose radical passion for sweeping political change inevitably leads to dystopian totalitarianism.

Yet if human rights activists and civil society movements flaunted their lack of interest in political power, political power was certainly interested in them. Human rights rapidly became the dominant ideology of Western states in their foreign affairs, haltingly at first under the Carter and Reagan administrations over the 1970s and 1980s, and then peaking under the Clinton administrations, while remaining firmly entrenched throughout the Bush and Obama era.[17] Widely seen as having provided Czechoslovak, Polish and East German dissidents and activists with the ideological solvent to dissolve the totalitarian permafrost of Eastern Europe, the apolitical, thin but astringent universalism of human rights provided the ideological tonic to exalt Western victory in the Cold War and boost its new military efforts. Human rights became the ideology of post-ideological, multicultural liberal democracies, the moral framework for booming business as capitalism advanced eastwards into Eastern Europe and Asia.

Yet, despite having eschewed the utopian fanaticism of violent rebellion and the seizure of state power, human rights became entwined with war, across Africa, the Balkans and Asia. In the form of humanitarian intervention, democratisation and the responsibility to protect, defending human rights became a necessary component of every Western military intervention as surely as anti-communism had once been during the Cold War.[18] As General Colin Powell, defence secretary in the first administration of US President George W. Bush, put it, non-governmental humanitarian organisations were a 'force multiplier' for the US military.[19] In 1999, as NATO bombed Yugoslavia, Habermas disparaged states' sovereign right to non-interference, arguing that this 'presumption of innocence' built into classical international law was palpably 'absurd' in light of the 'catastrophic history' of the twentieth century.[20] Yet the erosion of the right to non-interference also made all domestic politics directly global. Questions of foreign affairs became instead questions of rights, democracy and government rather than, say, nationally specific institutions and conflicts, a regional balance of power or geopolitical rivalry. Without the presumptive right of non-interference institutionalised in the claims of sovereignty, every domestic crisis becomes a potential vortex that will suck in external powers: at the time of writing, this pattern is repeating with the stand-off in Venezuela between the government and opposition, which is drawing in Brazil and Colombia as well as the US.

After thirty years of perpetual warfare by Western states under the banner of human rights, human rights can no longer claim to be innocent either. Evidently even anti-utopian, cosmopolitan ideals can just as easily succumb to the intoxication of military power and crusading zeal to improve the world. One humanitarian emergency has followed another in which humanitarian intervention is urged even if not enacted, in an unbroken chain reaching back to the no-fly zone established in 1992 over northern Iraq after the end of the first Gulf War and going through the Balkans, East Timor, Somalia, West Africa, Rwanda, Darfur, Iraq, Syria, Kurdistan (not to mention all those instances in which intervention was urged but never materialised – Zimbabwe, Darfur, South Sudan, Myanmar).

More than this, not only have human rights been weaponised, they have also become dystopic. Western interventions have left a chain of shattered states across the Greater Middle East that are locked in perpetual civil strife; Islamic State would never have emerged were it not for the Anglo-American intervention in Iraq of 2003. However much the defenders of human rights may still protest that intervention in Iraq was not an authentic expression of humanitarian ideals,[21] the fact remains that the invasion would never have happened had not the humanitarian suspicion of centralised state power and jurisdictional limits not been normalised by the globalisation of human rights ideology, and had the precedent not been established that humanitarian protection could be invoked to trump the rights of state sovereignty. Cosmopolitan dystopia was thus not restricted to insurgent enclaves in the Middle East: human rights helped to normalise our era of permanent war and with it a new wave of humanitarian occupation.[22] This saw the recreation of trusteeship and a new generation of protectorates sprawling around the world, with a new imperial standard of civilisation, justified on the grounds of the need for prolonged humanitarian protection and oversight. All these together constituted the dystopic involution of liberal internationalism, of which cosmopolitan jihadism and global terror networks were merely the inadvertent progeny.

The centrality of human rights to the political problems of our age is being made increasingly visible in the growing volume of critique directed at the theory and practice of human rights.[23] The entirety of this debate is beyond the scope of this book, and in any case I wish to add only one element to the growing collective critique. This element is to say that it is precisely the counter-utopian character of human rights that makes them dystopian. Negatively defined against the world-historic evils of the twentieth century, human rights cast the alleviation of suffering as the most that can be hoped for. In international affairs at least, this necessarily leads, I argue, to a politics of exceptionalism. This is a politics that is defined by its reaction to exceptional crises, a politics defined against the extreme – halting genocide, massacre, tyranny, starvation, slavery, ethnic cleansing and so on.[24] By having renounced the hope for systemic transformation or radical improvement of the human condition, under the banner of human rights political action *necessarily* becomes increasingly defined by the extreme, with the result that the extreme comes increasingly to define the norm. As the norm and the exception collapse into each other, the need for perpetual redress of recurrent evil that can, by its very nature, never be abolished, only repressed, results in … cosmopolitan dystopia. That is, a world order in which permanent war is normalised by perpetual policing in order to reduce human suffering. The crusading zeal and imperialist aggressiveness of cosmopolitan liberalism are not the results of still being contaminated by lingering traces of revolutionary utopianism, but by an anti-political monism that refuses to countenance a pluralistic international order.

Despite never having set their sights higher than curbing the most extreme human suffering, cosmopolitan liberals have nonetheless produced dystopias in their wake, complete with slave markets, tyrannies, ethnic pogroms, mass murder, massive refugee camps, beleaguered 'safe havens' and 'safe zones', protectorates and permanent war; in more recent times, their efforts have even revived geopolitical rivalries between nuclear-armed states. That their efforts were fated to be dystopic is the core argument of the book, and it is put forward in chapter 3. As well arguing for the dystopic character of cosmopolitan humanitarianism, I also seek to provide a more detailed overview of what cosmopolitan dystopia looks like – to show what an international order built around a dystopic politics of humanitarian emergency looks like. This is done across chapters 1 and 4. Chapter 2 looks at existing critiques of humanitarian intervention and where their limits lie – limits that necessitate a turn towards theorising exceptionalism as the key to understanding humanitarian intervention, the responsibility to protect and cosmopolitan dystopia. Before we review the structure of the argument in more detail, let us briefly define the terms and set the parameters that will operate in the discussion.

Intervening in the intervention debate

Even by academic standards, debates around defining humanitarian intervention tend to be exceptionally knotty. Linked to these definitional problems, much of the debate on intervention has been plagued by what I term the four 'c's – cases, casuistry, causes and concept-stretching – each of which has tended to limit the debate on intervention in various ways. The debate has also been marred by rampant definitional gerrymandering in which the concepts are brazenly fixed in advance in such a way as to ensure desired outcomes, as we shall see below.

The traditional definition of humanitarian intervention was taken as coercive interference in the internal affairs of a sovereign state for humanitarian purposes/to defend human rights. While this classically inspired definition had the benefit of parsimony and focus, it also drastically restricted what counted as such intervention to a handful of cases (Kosovo, Somalia, East Timor – the first of the problematic four 'c's), which were ploughed over and churned up again and again until barren. The prototypical form of this scholarship (in the West at least) was a monograph or edited collection which set out a theoretical overview of how new norms had developed and which then examined and re-examined the same set of cases, with the content of the discussion frequently consumed with poring over the precise wording of UN Security Council resolutions and General Assembly debates to infer evolutionary leaps in international order. The scale of the debate, and the inferences drawn regarding the evolution of international order, tended to grow out of all proportion to the handful of small, poor, marginal and thinly populated territories to which the debate was tethered. The debate thus tended to collapse into casuistry, in which a baroque theoretical superstructure variously buttressed with cosmopolitanism, feminism, constructivism and solidarism sat athwart a narrow set of cases too small to support the elaborate claims being made.

The problem with this narrow definition of intervention was that its interest and relevance was drawn from a wider set of cases and developments that had been defined as irrelevant, even though they shared many characteristics. Thus, for instance, UN and NATO intervention in Bosnia-Herzegovina during that country's civil war in the mid-1990s did not count, as the forces were deployed with the assent of the Bosnian government in Sarajevo, and nor did the NATO intervention in Afghanistan, as that was cast as a case of collective self-defence rather than coercive intervention for humanitarian purposes. Yet both of these episodes drew heavily on humanitarian justifications for their use of force.[25] Thus humanitarian intervention constituted the prototypical form of what Lawrence Freedman called 'liberal wars', in which the use of force was tightly meshed to international law, justified by neo-Wilsonian norms such as promoting peace, extending democracy and ending oppression, typically deployed as an internationally authorised, multinational expeditionary force configured thus in order to disavow national self-interest, with operational tasks that saw the provision of humanitarian aid, protection of human rights and post-conflict reconstruction as integral to the overall military effort.[26] Human rights and humanitarian protection have thus become an integral part of every Western use of force, even when justified by anti-terrorism or other security rationales, further blurring the line between humanitarian intervention as defined by theorists and the actual use of force in Western intervention. It was, after all, with reference to Afghanistan that Colin Powell described the humanitarian efforts of civil society organisations as a 'force multiplier' for the US military.

Humanitarian intervention defined in this way also ignored the vast number of peacekeeping operations that, by definition, were non-coercive, inasmuch as they could operate only with the consent of the state on whose territory they were deployed. Yet, at the same time, peacekeeping has become increasingly coercive, whether measured in operational terms (with increasingly large and more militarised operations involved in battles) or in terms of becoming more humanitarian (increasingly endowed with human protection tasks of varying kinds in the field).[27] Moreover, war itself has been politically and legally crimped, to the extent that it has become intervention, too: with no dynamic towards building economically exclusive imperial zones and with strong norms emplaced against conquest, annexation and territorial revision of borders, the use of force has been structured in such a way that war in general has become intervention by fiat – conceived as limited, discrete, and guided by political aims such as protecting a particular population, changing a government, or suppressing a conflict, rather than strategically annihilating an opponent's forces or bending an enemy to one's will.

The tendency to casuistry was reinforced by definitional gerrymandering in which certain interventions were deemed authentic (e.g., the NATO intervention over Kosovo without a UN mandate) and others inauthentic (e.g., the Anglo-American intervention in Iraq without a UN mandate). Similarly, debates have raged over whether the doctrine of the responsibility to protect is meaningfully different and distinct from humanitarian intervention.[28] Enormous scholarly effort has been invested in drawing and sternly policing these definitional and conceptual boundaries, efforts that seem excessive even by the standards of academic debates, in which so much hinges on definitions. Offensive and pre-emptive campaigns have been launched to insist that Iraq was no humanitarian intervention or to denounce the humanitarian justifications given for Russian interventions in the Caucasus.[29] That such scientific effort has been devoted to shrill exercises in classification is testimony to the bizarre nominalism that has crept into the discipline of International Relations as a result of constructivist theorising, corresponding with the implicit belief that politics can be contained within definitions devised in the library and seminar room. Built around assumptions of the infinite discursive plasticity of the social world, such views tend inevitably to privilege the role of scholars vested in the discursive effort of creating a more humane world.[30]

Indeed, humanitarian theorists vested their faith in the civilising power of discourse: it was argued that the inbuilt rhetorical pressure for consistency and conformity in offering humanitarian justifications for military force would gradually eliminate humanitarian hypocrisy and selectivity, extending and solidifying the protections afforded by the promise of humanitarian intervention to all those threatened by extreme suffering and violence.[31] Ironically for theorists who vested so much hope in entangling political power in their rhetorical webs, they only ended up ensnaring themselves, as non-Western, illiberal and autocratic states availed themselves of that very same well stocked discursive arsenal on which Western states had repeatedly drawn. Russia, Turkey and Saudi Arabia have now found that discursive arsenals have the added advantage that, unlike real arsenals, they can never be depleted.[32] Humanitarian justifications have indeed expanded around the world; this has not made the world humane, and neither has this eliminated hypocrisy or selectivity from the use of force. Such a development was entirely predictable, and would come as a surprise only to those who believe that discourse is the primary driver of social and political life.

The question of authenticity takes us to the third problematic 'c' – causes. If any intervention is deemed problematic or illegitimate for whatever reason, if the Russians do it for instance, or if selfish motives are suspect as contaminating humanitarian altruism, the intervention is discounted and explained away in terms of 'causes', that is, non-humanitarian motivations such as looking to exploit fossil fuel reserves or to maintain hegemony in a particular region. As we shall see in greater detail in chapter 2, the search for or imputation of causes to specific episodes of intervention has persistently bedevilled the critique of intervention. Suffice to say here that to ask what causes or what motivates intervention (not necessarily the same thing) is to misconceive it, because in a given states system the causes and motives of intervention will always fall within a set range. A decentralised political system constituted by the interaction of multiple, partitioned spaces of exclusive political authority will generate not only war but also 'international' intervention as its by-product. Politics cannot, after all, be confined within hermetically sealed containers, and will therefore spill over national boundaries. Thus, inevitably, the pursuit of some combination of national pride, self-interest, strategic advantage, self-defence and ideology will result in states penetrating other states' domains in a variety of forms, including the use of the military force but also often falling far short of it. On the receiving end, what counts as intervention is inherently indeterminate. Whether you think, say, that US President Donald Trump's criticisms in 2018 of the British government's negotiations with the European Union were unwarranted interference in the internal affairs of Britain, or whether they count instead as the invaluable support of an ally, is a political assessment.

To imagine otherwise would be to imagine a world state, or a world without politics. The general class of causes and motives in a system of states will thus always be the same. What will differ will be the precise mix: suppressing instability in a regional neighbourhood, defending client regimes, defending or spreading a particular kind of (ideological) political system, defending compatriots (whether citizens, co-religionists or ethnic kin), shaping the outcome of some cross-border political struggle and so on. All of these motives for intervention have recurred persistently over the course of the modern era. The precise mix of motives will inevitably vary over specific phases of international history and in particular regional sub-systems of the international order. Establishing the precise mix of motives in any particular time or place, or patterns of motives over longer periods, is the task of historians and social scientists. What the search for causes and reasons misses is how the meaning and significance of political power and global order changes and how the cumulative effect of specific kinds of intervention changes the context within which states choose to intervene, as well as how the meaning of intervention itself changes.

For this, we must turn to international political theorists and International Relations (IR) scholars, among whom there has been a long and searching debate about the nature of political order arising from the dilemmas of intervention. The question of intervention cuts to the most basic questions of political order: how to tie together individual rights, political representation and the collective provision of order. Any discussion on sovereignty, whether explicitly or implicitly, is always and everywhere a two-dimensional one, connecting a state's external relations to its internal constitution and relations with its citizens.

The final 'c', 'concept-stretching', reflects the intellectual response to the problems discussed above. In order to broaden the scope of analysis beyond the limitations of the debates identified, some scholars have sought to extend the academic debate on intervention. The contemporary understanding of military intervention lies in the positive international law of the nineteenth century, with intervention cast in the juridical categories of discrete and limited forceful involvements by states in the internal affairs of other states. It was a definition inspired by the imperial penetration of the extra-European world, the prototypical act being the seizure of the customs house to ensure debt collection or enforcing a trade treaty with gunboat diplomacy.[33] As this concept of intervention fails to capture just how far states today in the developing world are integrated into transnational regulatory and governance structures, attempts have been made to extend the concept so that it can assimilate a variety of interactions, such as aid programmes, conflict management, peacebuilding and so on, thereby embedding intervention in wider economic and regulatory processes. Taken to the logical extreme, once the scale and persistence of intrusion in so many post-colonial states is recognised alongside the annexation of core governance functions by international agencies, 'intervention' itself becomes a redundant category.

While these conceptual forays beyond the classical understanding of intervention have been intellectually productive, the end result is that any notion of political transgression involved in intervention is bleached out. Here, military deployments effectively become the extension of aid programmes or merely 'capacity-building' initiatives to improve state functioning – which are indeed the de facto justification for mandates given to peacebuilding operations throughout Africa. At this extreme, any notion of self-determination or even political agency – who is doing what to whom? – has been eclipsed; conceptually, all that we are left with are the spontaneous self-ordering effects of a system of global governance. In order to avoid this, this book retains a core grasp of the classical and political meaning of intervention. As Martha Finnemore has stressed, it is the liminal, transgressive character of intervention that makes it so intellectually intriguing, important and productive.[34] Seeking to show how international order has been transformed as a result of persistent intervention without losing sight of the political intrusion necessarily involved is the purpose of this book.

Instead of stretching the concept of intervention to cover a panoply of different kinds of international interaction, I want, rather, to show how the cumulative weight of repeated post-Cold War interventions has transformed the international order and perversely made certain kinds of intervention less visible. As we shall see, what counts as external interference in the internal affairs of a sovereign state has changed directly as a result of intervention, the practice of which has both moved and changed the markers between what counts as internal politics and what as external politics. For the purposes of this book, humanitarian intervention will be defined as coercive interference in the internal affairs of a state for humanitarian purposes, embedded in a wider category of liberal intervention, meaning the use of force for liberal/neo-Wilsonian ends (such as democratisation or defending human rights). The boundary between the two categories is permeable and, as we shall see, shifts over time – mapping this evolution is part of the purpose of the book.

If the denouement of the story here does not end with the unveiling of the 'real motives' behind intervention, it also takes some new routes. Instead of the usual tales of intervention and post-intervention 'peacebuilding' in Kosovo or Sierra Leone or East Timor, I suggest that the new generation of protectorates need to be examined together, belonging as they do to the same era and global order. Thus Russia's ramshackle new empire in Ukraine and the Caucasus should be considered in comparative context alongside the European Union's clutch of Balkan protectorates, alongside the societies devastated by failed US empire-building, alongside the de facto new trusteeship system managed by the United Nations. All are, after all, the results of military interventions of the post-Cold War era. Another novel theme – and one which is increasingly inescapable for European states – has in fact been present in intervention politics stretching back to the Gulf War of 1991, if not indeed to the US cycle of wars in South East Asia across the 1960 and 1970s – that is, the link between intervention and refugee and asylum politics. Humanitarian intervention is often presented as the enlargement of the sphere of human rights, steadily being pushed outwards to incorporate ever greater layers of humanity within its bounds.[35] Yet the rights claimed by intervening states on behalf of humanity have an inverse relationship with the rights of refugees. An examination of the rights of refugees in light of intervention shows just how naïve and distorting this 'spherical' model of human rights expansion is. A third novel theme in this book is connecting intervention to global jihadism. Much like refugee politics, a connection that seems obvious and inescapable in the context of Iraq and Libya has deeper roots, stretching back to the US sponsorship of the mujahideen in the Bosnian civil war of the early 1990s. It was the 1990s era of humanitarian intervention that globalised counter-revolutionary Wahhabism, helping to turn a Saudi export of the Cold War era into the cosmopolitan jihadism that afflicts the world today. Linking these themes helps us better understand how intervention produced cosmopolitan dystopia.

Outline of the book

Having established the parameters of the discussion, we can now review how the argument is developed over the course of the book. Chapter 1 begins the process of portraying cosmopolitan dystopia by setting up the problem in the book: the involution of the liberal international order. The chapter develops a new perspective on the challenges supposedly confronting the liberal international order today. These challenges are much discussed, and frequently cast as external – authoritarian great powers and regional hegemons or populist revolts that break with liberal norms and institutions, precipitating a new era of nationalist politics and, in the case of Saudi Arabia, Russia and Turkey, military expansionism. In that chapter I argue that the swaying pillars and crumbling masonry of the liberal international order are not the result of a siege by illiberal barbarians, but rather the temple is crumbling because its foundations were mined and the explosives were laid by liberals themselves.

The chapter argues that the problems of the liberal international order today cannot be meaningfully attributed to illiberal challengers such as China, Russia or Turkey seeking to revise the international order to better accommodate their growing power

and divergent interests. Rather – and cutting against the expectations of International Relations theory – the only behaviour that
can be seen as consistent with the theoretical expectations of
revisionism is that of ... Western states. Perhaps for the first time
in modern history, we have status quo powers undermining the
status quo: this was the effect of liberal and humanitarian intervention. Military force was repeatedly used by Western states
to restructure the international order. I suggest this behaviour
requires typifying a new category – inverted revisionism. Yet how
was it that, after having won the Cold War, leading Western states
came to gratuitously squander their victory, actively undermining
the very same international order that they had worked so assidu-
ously to construct over the latter half of the twentieth century?
How can this paradox of self-subversion be explained? This is the
problem that emerges from considering inverted revisionism.

Having shown that liberal intervention subverted the liberal
international order, chapter 2 considers the existing critiques of
intervention and where their limits lie. Several theoretical traditions of anti-interventionist critique are considered, from political
and legal pluralism to strategic traditionalism, and their strengths
and weaknesses are examined. Typically, debates over humanitarian intervention have been cast as extrapolating from underlying
theoretical traditions of understanding international order (the
merits of order versus the imperatives of justice, for instance),
with differing views leading to different outlooks on the merits
of different kinds of intervention in different circumstances. The
problem with this debate is the fact that debates on intervention
themselves are cast as limit points, extreme situations in which
the general precepts break down or do not apply. Thus at some
point all these theoretical debates logically collapse into poring
over particular cases – Burma, East Timor, Libya, Syria and so
on. How different is one crisis from another, that merits an intervention this time? The effect of this conceptual 'close cropping',
so to speak, is to give the impression that all emergencies and

exceptions are essentially the same. This motivates an alternative understanding of intervention – one that attempts to systematically examine it as a politics of exceptionalism. What does the international order look like in which recurrent humanitarian emergencies are entirely normalised? As it is a politics of exceptions, to conceptualise it properly and systematically we need a theory of exceptionalism.

As we shall see in chapter 3, there are different kinds of exceptionalist politics, with profoundly different implications for international order. Adapting a typology developed by Jef Huysmans, I argue that the humanitarian exceptionalism embedded in cosmopolitan liberalism sees human suffering as constitutive of deeper, more authentic forms of human identity and solidarity, with the recurrent transgression of existing political institutions and normative frameworks seen to be a permanent and necessary feature of world order. We also see in chapter 3 that the exceptionalist sovereign is most clearly embodied in the US imperial state, most clearly theoretically expressed in the vision of neoconservative political theorists and jealously and resentfully mimicked by the likes of Russia. Humanitarian exceptionalism cuts across cosmopolitan jihadism, too, as another globalised ideology offering new, more authentic forms of solidarity, defined by hostility to the existing international order and state sovereignty. The destructive consequences of this humanitarian exceptionalism are analysed further, especially the development of humanitarian anti-diplomacy. Anti-diplomacy negates strategic interest and international law founded on sovereign equality, and denies the legitimacy and authenticity of separate political interests and the need to accommodate them. In place of diplomacy considered as political accommodation, it promotes an outlook that necessarily undercuts institutionalised frameworks of international legal and political cooperation.

Finally, in chapter 4 we examine how exceptionalist practices change the character of state sovereignty. The strongest and boldest claim of cosmopolitan legal and political theories was to supersede the parochial nationalism of sovereign states. Perversely, however, humanitarian exceptionalism has neither superseded sovereignty nor the state, but rather reconstituted it, leading to a more hierarchical international order and inflecting a new kind of sovereignty, less defined and restrained by the demands of political representation and lacking any clear limits on its legal jurisdiction and power. This is the paternalistic vision of state power embodied in the doctrine of the responsibility to protect. Instead of treating the responsibility to protect merely as a construct of international law, chapter 4 proposes to treat the doctrine more seriously, giving it its due as a fully fledged theory of political order that recombines international and domestic authority in new ways. The chapter completes the discussion by considering post-intervention dynamics – the state-building and imperial failure that emerged in response to the erosion of centralised authority and political order embodied in cosmopolitan intervention. While much has been made of the strength and insidiousness of the US empire since the end of the Cold War, the reality of cosmopolitan dystopia – in this case, the failure to create enduring forms of centralised political order and the sabotage of the liberal international order – push us to consider the question not of overwhelming imperial power but rather of imperial failure and defeat, not least with the shattered series of nations left behind in Iraq, Libya and Syria.

Chapter 1

Inverted revisionism and the subversion of the liberal international order

The international order is, it is commonly agreed, facing serious challenges. Incipient trade wars are simmering both east and west. While the European Union struggles to maintain its cohesion, the wars in Syria, Afghanistan and the Sahel continue to rage, and geopolitical tensions between Russia and the West continue to escalate. The challenges are grave, not only by virtue of their magnitude but also because they are antithetical to the ideals and institutions of the liberal order.[1] Economic nationalism is eroding multilateral trade and proxy conflicts in Europe and the Middle East are eroding the international peace that has prevailed since the end of the Cold War. In geopolitical terms at least, the fact that authoritarian great powers such as China and Russia, and would-be great powers such as Turkey and Saudi Arabia, seem to exemplify models of self-reliance, strength and stability that are not rooted in liberal democracy exacerbates the sense of crisis. US President Donald Trump's National Security Strategy brands China and Russia 'revisionist powers' and claims that China threatens the sovereignty of states in the Indo-Pacific region.[2]

Russia in particular has been singled out for its military expansionism and interference, from supporting the Syrian regime of Bashar al-Assad to supporting secessionist rebels in eastern Ukraine, reaching back to its intervention in Georgia in 2008, and it was denounced long before Trump took the White House. Richard Haass, president of the US Council on Foreign Relations, insisted that Russia must be dealt with as a 'rogue state' for its interference in the 'internal affairs of others' and its failure to show 'respect for sovereignty', both keystones of the international order for 'centuries', according to Haass.[3] Such sharp denunciation has now become par for the course in East–West diplomacy. In her final statement as US representative to the UN in the closing days of the Obama administration, Samantha Power reiterated how Russia had violated the 'order enshrined in the UN Charter' based on 'a set of rules' that 'included the rule that the borders between sovereign states should be respected'.[4] Obama's secretary of state Jonathan Kerry had weighed in earlier, saying 'You just don't in the 21st century behave in 19th-century fashion by invading another country on completely trumped up pre-text'.[5]

Such rhetoric is shocking and extraordinary on a number of levels, not least in signalling the return of persistent and bitter denunciations between East and West at the United Nations, something largely unknown since the days of the Cold War. More striking still is the insouciance and effrontery of US diplomats accusing other states of manufacturing pretexts for war and violating states' sovereignty. Perhaps most striking of all was the sight of Power, a prolific former activist-academic and journalist who had built a career around campaigning for intervention in civil wars around the world, now condemning Russian intervention. Digging under this hypocrisy is the core aim of this chapter. Inasmuch as the use of force has been used to reshape international relations and has consequently destabilised and aggravated geo-political tensions, this has come from the West – the US, the UK, France and their NATO allies. Such actions were indeed antitheti-cal to quintessentially liberal norms and institutions, undermining self-determination, the sovereign right to non-interference, and subverting the remit and jurisdiction of the UN Security Council. They were also undertaken by liberal powers, states that claimed to stand for the maintenance of the international liberal order and, importantly, cutting against the expectations of International Relations theory. The denunciations of Russia in the same manner in which Russia had criticised the West over the 1990s signals a significant role reversal and, with it, the surest sign yet of the extent to which the constitutive principles of international order have been so thoroughly effaced in international politics that there is no single state or power that can credibly claim to stand for the principled defence of sovereign rights in general.

Before considering the role played by liberal powers in undermining the liberal order, let us consider the role played by authoritarian states and see why it is impossible to attribute the baleful state of international order to their behaviour alone.

Authoritarian great powers such as China and Russia and would-be great powers and regional hegemons such as Turkey, Saudi Arabia and Iran have explicitly cast themselves against the Western-led international order, rejecting democracy and 'Westernisation' and scorning the liberal defence of minority rights and the international human rights regime, proffering in their place national self-assertion, religious traditionalism, social conservatism, political cohesion and social order. What sharpen such political differences are the strategic tensions, military interventions and the projections of political influence: Turkey's intervention in Syria, China's vast investment programmes across Africa and Eurasia and growing assertiveness in the South China Sea, Saudi Arabia's intervention in Bahrain and Yemen, Iran's involvement in Syria and Lebanon and attempt to develop nuclear energy.

Of all these, Russia is seen to be the most militarily assertive and strategically truculent. Russia intervened in Georgia in 2008 as the latter gravitated towards the West, with the former subsequently carving ethnically exclusive protectorates out of Georgian territory and sponsoring their secession – Abkhazia and South Ossetia. More recently and dramatically, Russia annexed

Crimea from Ukraine in 2014 and continues to support secessionist rebels in eastern Ukraine, intervening to defend them from
central government forces in that country's civil war. Before all
of this, Russia had also been heavily involved in a generation
of large and militarily assertive peacekeeping operations across
the ex-Soviet Caucasus and Central Asia throughout the 1990s.
However, it is Russian military intervention in the Syrian civil
war that has arguably been President Putin's most significant
strategic success. Russian intervention in Syria demonstrated the
prowess of Russian arms in rescuing a beleaguered ally, turning
the war in the latter's favour and helping to crush Islamic State
in Syria – in effect, fighting the war on terror more effectively
than Western states themselves. Yet even here, Russian intervention has been limited.[6] The actual numbers of Russian troops
deployed in Syria are low (estimated at between 3,000 and 5,000):
its military successes there amplify the underlying political and
military resilience of the Ba'athist regime in Damascus. At the
same time, Russia has avoided involving itself in the Yemen war,
in which its regional opponents and allies are both involved, and
has declined to involve itself in the US campaign against Islamic
State in Iraq. It has sought to build its new presence in the Middle
East around a conservative vision of defending the political status
quo. Moreover, despite the complexity of the multiple proxy
factions contending the Syrian civil war, Russia has maintained
close, pragmatic relations not only with Iran but also with Turkey
and Israel, and has coordinated strategy with Saudi Arabia in the
OPEC cartel of oil exporters – all this despite Saudi Arabia being
on the opposing side in the Syrian civil war and breaking with the
historic pattern of mutual hostility seen in the Cold War. In short, it
is difficult to see Russian intervention as rampaging or resurgent,
or indeed as merely replicating Cold War geopolitics – Russia
remains, in Viatcheslav Morozov's words, a 'subaltern empire',
whose paradigm of supposedly cunning 'hybrid warfare' reflects
weakness more than strength.[7]

The problem with accounts of the liberal international order that claim it has been subverted by geopolitical rivalry with authoritarian great powers is that it simply doesn't correspond with the facts. Take China. For the last thirty years, the discourse associated with China's economic growth has been that of a 'peaceful rise'.[8] For the first time since the Sino-Vietnamese War of 1979, in 2013 China deployed combat forces abroad when it contributed combat contingents to a UN peacekeeping operation with a counter-terrorism mandate in Mali.[9] On the whole, China has tended to avoid any international military deployments, restricting its overseas presence to logistics and medical units on peacekeeping missions, and even now it deploys military units only with the sanction of the United Nations.[10] In general terms, China's international behaviour has been cautious and restrained. Moreover, aside from issues concerning Taiwan, up until the Syrian civil war at least, China has generally avoided wielding the veto on the UN Security Council, gamely allowing Russia to lead most confrontations with the P3 since the end of the Cold War.[11] Even as recently as 2011, Russia and China abstained from vetoing the NATO campaign against Libya, thereby facilitating the disastrous Western intervention in that country.

For all of Beijing's political caution, of Chinese economic ascent there is no doubt. Russia by contrast remains economically much weaker and correspondingly more politically defensive. Indeed, in many ways Russian assertiveness today is simply a measure of having enjoyed a degree of economic recovery from the nadir of the 1990s: more than any new foreign policy paradigm, Putinism reflects the rising price of oil.[12] Although economically recovered, Russia confronts the same perennial problems stretching as far back as Soviet times: long-term demographic decline, lagging labour productivity and lack of economic diversification. While Russian forces rescued the beleaguered Assad regime, Russia's limited capacity for global power projection was exposed by the smoky *Admiral Kuznetsov* aircraft carrier chugging through the

Mediterranean as if it were a coal-powered nineteenth-century ship. Indeed, the fact that Syria is geographically close to Russia facilitated Russian intervention in the conflict, as Russia was able to launch cruise missiles into Syria from the Caspian Sea to the east. Neither carving tiny ethnic statelets out of Georgia nor annexing the Ukrainian rust belt will make Russia great again, any more than will a Ba'athist victory in the Syrian civil war. In strategic and political terms at least, Russia remains, at most, a regional great power rather than a global superpower. Neither China nor Russia enjoys an alliance system comparable to NATO either to pool their power or to yoke smaller allies to their cause. The closest analogue to such a grouping, the Shanghai Cooperation Organisation, remains much too youthful and geographically and politically diffuse to be either strategically or military cohesive.

Compounded with these limits, neither China nor Russia offers any ideology of systemic transformation.[13] Indeed, quite the opposite. Until recently, Russia and China were both repeatedly castigated not for being too eager to tear up the international order, but rather for being too conservative and attached to the status quo ante! This was the meaning of the charge of being 'Westphalian' powers, the accusation that was repeatedly levelled against China and Russian after the end of the Cold War – they were backwards-looking countries, mulishly attached to outmoded models of politics associated with the non-interference principles of the Westphalian order, established long ago, in the eponymous peace accords of 1648.[14] This Eurocentric framework, so the charge went, was hopelessly redundant in a globalising world which required new political models of interdependence to substitute for the political ego-centrism and self-sufficiency of the old Westphalian order, not least including extensive rights of intervention to stem international problems that welled up within states but spilled over their boundaries.[15] Thus, it was this *refusal* to *change* the supposed status quo, not their alacrity in doing so, for which Russia and China were repeatedly castigated.

Indeed, even as China and Russia have asserted themselves on the international stage, it has still often been while cleaving as closely as possible to the status quo. In the wake of the neo-isolationist nostrums of the Trump administration, China has even gestured at claiming the mantle of global liberal leadership to substitute for that of the US, weaving together multilateral free trade and supporting the institutions of collective security such as the United Nations.[16] To be sure, Russia has been more militarily revanchist than China, yet even so Russia explicitly models its interventions on those of the West. Murderous oppression of Georgia's ethnic minorities was cited in defence of Russia's intervention in Georgia in 2008.[17] The Russian-sponsored unilateral declarations of independence by Abkhazia, South Ossetia and more recently Crimea were all explicit in referring to the precedent of Kosovo's unilateral secession from Serbia in 2008, itself a product of NATO military intervention in 1999 without UN sanction.[18] This reflects, as Morozov argues, the 'normative dependence of the Russian subaltern empire on the West and/or Europe as the only standard against which their own legitimacy is established, domestically as well as internationally'.[19] More broadly, strategically speaking, Russian intervention has persistently been reactive: military operations lashing out at the perceived encroachment of Western influence in the Caucasus and Ukraine.[20] Even in Syria, Russian intervention has been intended to *preserve* one of Russia's few remaining extra-European allies, and to establish a platform for Russia to be considered a geopolitical partner with the West outside of Europe.[21]

To be clear, the point here is not how authentic or plausible we find the justification provided by Russian foreign minister Sergei Lavrov for Russian intervention in Georgia, or how legitimate a Crimean vote for secession could ever be while under occupation by Russian special forces. The only point germane to the argument here is that Russia does not offer any elaborated alternative ideology or political framework to justify its interventions and protectorates, instead cleaving as tightly as possible to whatever legitimacy can be stripped from existing Western precedent and practice: 'it has no sources of legitimacy', argues Morozov, 'other than repeated reference to the universal values of the "civilized world"'.[22] Moreover, Russia continues to criticise Western intervention from the perspective of global multilateralism crowned by the supremacy of the UN Security Council.[23] This cleaving to precedent is true of other instances of intervention by non-Western states. So concerned was the Saudi government to claim humanitarian legitimacy for its intervention in Yemen that it even went to the farcical extent of naming its operation there, Operation Restoring Hope, after the ill-fated US intervention on the other side of the Gulf of Aden, in Somalia, back in the 1990s: 'Operation Restore Hope'. The Saudi intervention has, indeed, been far more inhumane than the US–UN prototype in Somalia. As we have seen, if Russian justifications are hypocritical, the Russians cannot be accused of having a monopoly on hypocrisy. Looking beyond such accusations, though, the fact that Russia has undermined its own credibility as a defender of sovereign rights shows that there is no major state left in the world that can plausibly stand as a consistent and principled exponent of state sovereignty. How could such a thing have come to pass?

Identifying revisionism

If we do look for a revisionist challenge to the international status quo, what do we find? The aggressive use of force, external interference in the internal affairs of sovereign states, an ideology of systemic transformation, the establishment of new international institutions? We do not need to look far: it is obvious that the only contenders for such a role since the end of the Cold War are Western states, principally the US, the UK and France, with varying degrees of support from other Western states both within NATO (Italy, Germany) and outside it (e.g., Australia, New Zealand, Japan, Sweden). That Russian interventions should seem shocking, unprecedented and outrageous only speaks to the extent to which Western intervention has become so normalised and routine as to be utterly unremarkable.

As against Russia's interventions in Tajikistan (1992–1997), Georgia (2008), Ukraine (2014) and Syria (2016), we have Western interventions not only in regional spheres of influence such as the US in Panama (1989) and Haiti (1994, 2004), Australia in East Timor (1999) and the Solomon Islands (2003) and Italy in Albania (1997), but also much further afield – France in Rwanda (1994), Haiti again (2004), Côte d'Ivoire (2004) and Mali (2014), and the UK in Sierra Leone (1998). This is before we even start counting the multiple and notorious major multilateral interventions of the last few decades: namely Somalia (1992), Bosnia-Herzegovina (1994), Yugoslavia/Kosovo (1999), Afghanistan (2001) and of course Iraq (2003) and Libya (2011), as well as Western support for Islamist militias fighting the regime in Syria. Here, we are discounting the enormous scale of UN peacekeeping operations around the world, all tightly controlled through Western patronage and financing of the United Nations, or Western patronage for regional interventions (e.g., US support for Ethiopian and African Union intervention in Somalia from 2007 to the present).[24]

Indeed, part of the reason UN and regional peacekeeping rarely figures in the wider debate on intervention is that it is nominally consensual, as against the classical definition of intervention, that it is forcible interference in a state's internal affairs. Peacekeepers are invited in by governments. Yet peacekeeping involves military power, increasingly on a significant scale: with division-strength complements of armed personnel and the panoply of military violence – tanks, armoured personnel carriers, gunships, even drones and intelligence-gathering capacities – all legally authorised to take offensive and even pre-emptive action under Chapter VII of the UN Charter. All of this is in violation of every classical conception of peacekeeping involving small, lightly armed forces that are permitted to take action in only self-defence. When peacekeeping was conceived during the 1956 Suez Crisis, it was so controversial that the proposed deployment of Canadian peacekeepers for Egypt was rejected on the grounds that their military insignia too closely resembled those of invading British forces, the Egyptians' former imperial overlords. Today, military interventions in the great powers' former colonies – from Italy's 1997 intervention in Albania to France's 2004 intervention in Côte d'Ivoire – pass without public criticism, or else only meet demands for greater efforts – more peacekeepers, backed up with more firepower and political will. Needless to say, neither Washington nor London, nor Paris nor Rome encounter trouble in securing UN backing and forces to support their military efforts, with the UN usually supplying forces from formerly colonised countries to maintain and restore order after Western forces withdraw.[25]

These interventions have left a trail of military bases, 'forward deployments', protectorates, client states or, worse, simply continuous wars in their wake. They were variously justified by the extension of human rights, the defence and extension of democracy, to be reinforced by economic liberalisation and political transformation in the form of post-conflict democratisation and state-building. A dense new infrastructure of international institutions was created to embed these new practices and cushion their effects, from a vast network of non-governmental organisations devoted to post-war reconstruction and humanitarian relief, through international criminal courts established for exemplary punishment of malefactors and criminals, to colossal new international field operations to protect civilians in conflict and distribute medicines, food and shelter on a mass scale, as well as prolonged and elaborate efforts to build up functioning governmental institutions in peacebuilding operations.

Given all the multiple interventions over the last few years – the launch of the campaign against Islamic State forces, simmering discussion in the West over whether to intervene against the Ba'athist regime in Syria, the 2019 Turkish intervention in Syria and so on – it is difficult to recall just how striking and unexpected the 2011 intervention in Libya was.[26] After the bloody outcome of Iraq, the political credibility of intervention was believed to have been poisoned by the geopolitical ambitions and military failures of the US in the Middle East. The fact that the world's most powerful country was unable convincingly to make societies more liberal led to a dramatic curtailing of ambition and hope for the outcomes of intervention – a debate that was splayed out across not only learned journals and scholarly debates but also in the pages of major international media – notably the London *Guardian*, the *New York Times* and the *International Herald Tribune*.[27] Some bemoaned the passing of an era, while others welcomed a supposed new acceptance of prudence, limits and humility in the exercise of Western power abroad.

Yet barely a year after the US-led Operation Iraqi Liberation wound down in 2010, Western powers launched this new Libyan military campaign in the same region where the immediately previous intervention had been so disastrous and controversial, in a region not only steeped in popular scepticism of Western power and imprinted with strong public memories of bloody European imperial raids and occupations – but also in the midst of an unprecedented global economic collapse and a faltering war effort in Afghanistan. Fears of refugee flows across the Mediterranean stemming from the Libyan civil war, the comparative military ease of bombing the Libyan coastal plain compared with bombing the more populous and more geographically dispersed Syrian and Sudanese states, an officer corps in the UK and France looking to deflect budget cutbacks with austerity policies, Colonel Gaddafi's international isolation and lack of significant allies in the region and the wider world, the diversionary appeal of military glory for

British and French politicians ... whatever the precise interlocking of relatively contingent circumstances that explain why military intervention took place in Libya rather than elsewhere, it also shows that the diplomatic and intellectual controversy over the Iraq intervention never cut sufficiently deep to bleed the legitimacy from international intervention.

To be sure, this is not say that intervention is the monopoly of Western states – far from it. It is the cycle of Nigerian interventions in neighbouring civil wars beginning in the early 1990s that inaugurates the era of post-Cold War intervention proper, at least in chronological terms. More recently, Egyptian and Emirati warplanes have replaced British and French jets in the skies over Libya. Looking back earlier, theorists of humanitarian intervention have always been keen to pre-empt charges of Western imperialism by drawing attention to Cold War-era interventions by Third World states: Tanzania's intervention in Idi Amin's Uganda, Vietnam's intervention in Pol Pot's Cambodia, India's intervention in Bangladesh's liberation war against Pakistan.[28] Despite this, intervention by non-Western states in the post-Cold War era were often shaped by Western concerns, if not enjoying explicit Western backing and at Western behest. Ethiopia's intervention in Somalia in 2006 to destroy the Islamic courts saw long-standing national rivalries in the Horn of Africa intersect with the global US war on terror, and fell into the similar pattern of spawning something worse: Al-Shabaab replaced the Islamic courts. Saudi Arabia's interventions in Bahrain and Yemen have been underpinned by US efforts militarily to contain Iranian influence.

The African Union, arguably the single most avowedly interventionist international organisation in the world, is utterly dependent on Western arms and money for its cross-border military efforts. Examples of non-Western military interventions also often occur in circumstances shaped by Western states. Turkey's 2007 intervention in northern Iraq in pursuit of Kurdish separatists was only possible and necessary after the boost to

Kurdish autonomy resulting from the shattering of the Iraqi state by the US invasion of 2003, as are Turkey's more recent interventions in the Syrian civil war in 2015 and 2019. As suggested above, for all their decisiveness and ruthlessness, Putin's unilateral interventions in Ukraine and Georgia were clearly reactive – defensive manoeuvres responding to the expansion of Western institutions multiplying around Russia's borders. Or, more accurately put, Putin's interventions appear decisive and strategic *because* they were defensive, perforce confronting externally imposed limits on Russian power. The contrast with Western military interventions is instructive. As we shall see below, the a-strategic character of Western military escapades reflects the limitless, and therefore incoherent, character of US power.

Unlike smaller states, as a result of their power and wealth Western states are able to reshape international institutions and concerns to better accommodate their interventionist impulses. Vietnam never propagated a doctrine such as that of the 'responsibility to protect', despite confronting a regime in Cambodia more ghoulish and murderous than even that of Hutu Power in Rwanda, let alone the civil wars in Bosnia-Herzegovina and Kosovo. Indeed, how could the Vietnamese hope to offer a new international framework when the US supported the Khmer Rouge against them? Nor did India demand a new conception of sovereignty when it intervened in the Bangladesh liberation war – nor Tanzania when confronting Idi Amin.[29] Even comparatively wealthy developing countries with powerful armies seek Western political patronage for their interventionist escapades, as Nigeria did when it sought (retroactive) legitimation from the UN Security Council for its involvement in the Liberian civil war in the 1990s.

What all this means is that we must look to Western practice if we are to understand revisionist behaviour in international politics today. It is Western states that have explicitly recast international institutions and practices around questions of human rights and intervention, even to the extent of championing a new model of political authority and state power embodied in the doctrine of the 'responsibility to protect'. It is Western states that transformed and militarised UN peacekeeping, hatched a raft of new international laws and generated a whole new network of post-conflict state-building institutions and a dense infrastructure of international criminal institutions, procedures and laws. What sutured together the various elements of this new security paradigm was the suppression of sovereignty, which effectively became increasingly conditional on observance of certain regulated standards of behaviour. This was a de facto new 'standard of civilisation' that inscribed a new hierarchy into international politics, not unlike the imperial hierarchy of the nineteenth century, by which certain states were deemed superior and others inferior.[30] While various conditions were adduced by which it was claimed that sovereign rights could be legitimately revoked – for example, lack of functioning democracy, lack of capacity to respond to natural disasters, possession of nuclear weapons – at the core of this sovereignty-as-responsibility paradigm was the observance of human rights.[31] Some of the most important political philosophers of our era were happy to bless this idea for bringing us closer to nothing less than the Kantian ideal of perpetual peace – a pacific federation of nations.[32]

Theories of Westphalia ...

Let us sum up the preceding discussion before moving on to discuss 'inverted revisionism'. When posed as an issue of political order, the practice of intervening in the internal affairs of states over the last thirty years has typically been cast as pushing past 'Westphalian statehood'. Taken as the paradigm of modern sovereignty, 'Westphalian statehood' is typically understood as the exclusive claim to state authority and control over a given territory and population, with the right to expel any intrusion into its domain. The compact that brought to an end Europe's seventeenth-century wars of religion was the 1648 Peace of Westphalia, and that year is as good a date as any other from which to trace the prototypical forms of political modernity and interaction in international relations. Yet posing the issue of intervention in terms of moving beyond a centuries-old European system of peace treaties is also tendentious, in at least two respects.

First, it is of course child's play to show that no state, no matter how powerful, has complete control over its domain. The state's efforts to resist intrusion are always in vein; thus, even Westphalian states were never properly 'Westphalian'. Yet despite the simplicity of this exercise – or perhaps because of it – scholars instinctively repeat it, begging the question of what drives this ritualistic overthrow of the sovereign state in theory.[33] Once this exercise has been done, it takes only a few short steps to portray sovereignty as an absurd, quasi-totalitarian conceit, a futile attempt to contain fluid societies within notional boundaries in an increasingly globalised world. As we shall see below, the confusion over sovereignty here is total and its consequences, as we have already suggested, disastrous. Perversely, all the theoretical efforts to dissolve the edifice of sovereignty make the error of reifying it, as if sovereignty were a thing that could be dissolved in the first place. If sovereignty is not reified as a thing, then it is treated in a teleological fashion, as an 'institution' that 'evolves' over time.[34] The hidden assumption here is that sovereignty progresses up a ladder of forms, meaning its most recent form – embedded in the paraphernalia of international law, institutions and human rights regimes – is the best and highest.

Yet sovereignty is neither a thing nor an organism that irrevocably 'evolves' into superior species, but rather an institutionalised form of political agency – and agency, by its nature, is flexible. The plasticity of political agency helps explain the theoretical confusion that occludes the status of sovereignty. Once accounted for, however, the inherently plastic character of sovereignty allows us, as we shall see, to better identify political power and hold it to account more consistently. By labelling the state's right to non-interference in its internal affairs as 'Westphalian', any resistance to 'post-Westphalian' politics is pre-emptively indicted as mulish historical backwardness. Even the Nazi jurist Carl Schmitt was able to see through this polemical framing of the issue as early as the 1920s, when he identified how supporters of the League of Nations would castigate state authority 'for purely polemical reasons' as 'the residues of the old "absolutist" states of the seventeenth and eighteenth centuries'.[35]

This is the second problem with the Westphalian/post-Westphalian diptych. In fact, the post-Westphalian world order was ushered in a long time ago and not by NATO jets nor by UN resolutions on human rights, but by the Atlantic revolutions of the late eighteenth to early nineteenth centuries, if not earlier. Properly Westphalian states – that is to say, the pre-revolutionary European states of the *ancien régime* – were not based on principles of popular legitimacy and representation founded in independent nationhood, and nor did they relate to each other through a largely egalitarian system of positive international law. Thus, when analysts of international relations have talked about 'post-Westphalian' statehood across the last thirty years, they are self-evidently not talking about changes to the standing of the Electors of the Holy Roman Empire, quarrels with the Hanseatic League, overthrowing Cardinal Richelieu's design for central Europe, or questioning the status of Catholic minorities in the United Provinces. Whatever has been inherited from the Westphalian treaties of 1648, that legacy had already been upgraded long before, across the last two centuries of global political change. Stripped of the historical anachronism and polemical camouflage, talking about 'post-Westphalian' international relations in the here and now can only mean changes to the status, rights and representative structures of independent nations and the individuals that comprise them.

... and theories of West failure

Once intervention today is accepted as something basically Western in its inspiration and modalities, then it also behoves us to acknowledge the calamitous scale of the failure represented by Western intervention – a calamity that sinks far beneath the dignity accorded to political tragedy. Western states succeeded in the difficult task of making Iraq worse than under Saddam Hussein's dictatorship. In addition to the authoritarian rule endured by Iraqis since the overthrow of Saddam, Western states added constant civil war and sectarian strife, as well as turning the dial back on major developmental indicators such as secularism, public health, women's rights and ethnic and religious pluralism. The tale repeats in Libya. Even if we change the analytical resolution and zoom out, so that the spectacle of human suffering fades from view, the assessment of self-defeating irrationality remains the same. The West has overthrown loyal long-term allies (Saddam) and rounded on eager petitioners (Gaddafi). Western states have helped spawn vast terror networks and armed their own enemies *en masse* with sophisticated modern weaponry. In the Middle East, Western states shattered a regional balance of power in favour of a longstanding rival, Iran, and have stoked an intergenerational sectarian conflict between religious denominations of Shia and Sunni. Western states have antagonised Russia, thereby spurning a potential ally against China in what is likely to be the cockpit of future great-power rivalry in the Asia-Pacific.[36]

What is peculiar about all of this is just how much effort the West has invested in revising the rules and institutions of the international order, not only with such little improvement in aggregate human welfare or the West's strategic position, but also with such little necessity and purpose. The political economist Susan Strange coined the term 'Westfailure system' to describe how the states system was incapable of curbing the forces of global finance. But her moniker would be more apt for the failed project of international intervention, a specifically political rather an economic failure, and a specifically Western one.

Conceptualising revisionism

Thus far, the paradigm and behaviour described would tick the boxes for describing revisionism: use of force to reshape the international order and set new expectations and patterns of legitimate behaviour, the formation of new hierarchies with new standards of behaviour that can be policed with force, the formation of new international institutions, packaged together with an ideology of systemic transformation at both the state and the international levels.... As the label 'revisionism' suggests, revisionist states seek to reshape ('revise') the international order to better fit their political, strategic and economic interests. In Barry Buzan's words, 'Whereas stability is the preferred security solution for status quo states, it defines the essence of the problem for revisionists'.[37] In other words, for revisionist states, stability is restrictive if not outright oppressive. The implications of this view are decidedly materialist and structural – namely, the lack of 'fit' between the material reality of power and the institutional configuration and political dispensation of an actually existing international order, with the resulting friction being driven by long-term processes of change. The systemic grinding of subterranean tectonic plates of economic, social and technological change erupts on the surface in the form of diplomatic crises, jockeying for position and eventually war.

The only surprising element in this picture is that it was core states mounting revisionism: the US and its Western allies and client states, the victors of the Cold War.[38] In his classic study of inter-war international relations, *The Twenty Years' Crisis*, E. H. Carr famously described revisionist states as 'have-nots', with Soviet Russia, Germany, Italy and Japan in mind – states that were variously excluded from the spoils of the peace that was devised in the palaces of France after the First World War and that lavished the UK and France with new territories, enhanced political status embedded in the League of Nations, strategic advantage in the form of privileged alliance systems and restrictions on military competitors, and a trove of new colonial possessions expropriated from defeated powers.[39]

It would be difficult to think of any Western state as a 'have-not' in the aftermath of the Cold War, let alone the US, the UK or France. Not only were these nuclear-armed countries among the wealthiest and most powerful states in the world, not only were they the victors of the Cold War and thus the strategic beneficiaries of the status quo, they were also its architects. They were in various ways at the core of all the various international institutions, laws and organisations that had been built up over the course of the Cold War era and were now no longer restricted by geopolitical rivalry and nuclear stalemate with the Soviets. By any reasonable standard, Western states should have acted as 'status quo states' in the words of Barry Buzan – that is to say, they should have preferred stability. How could the extraordinary revisionist behaviour described above be reconciled with the overwhelming power and prestige of the Western victors of the Cold War?

In his study of international security *People, States and Fear*, Buzan developed a triadic typology of revisionist behaviour, with the extreme ends of the spectrum defined by 'orthodox revisionism' at one end and 'revolutionary revisionism' at the other, with 'radical revisionism' as an indeterminate midway point between the two.[40] All of these behaviours can coexist in any given international system, according to Buzan. Buzan defined orthodox revisionism as the routine jostling for status and position that comes with the dynamic fluidity of power political competition. With its ideal-type expression being the wars of the *ancien régime* states of eighteenth-century Europe, this type of revisionism is defined by its non-ideological character, thereby offering scope for diplomatic adjustment and peaceful settlement of disputes.

Orthodox revisionism does not seem to fit here, as post-Cold War liberal revisionism clearly extended far beyond jockeying for power between peers. Moreover, in the early 1990s, intervention was frequently cooperative, with for example, the US, France and Russia all agreeing to support one another's interventions in their spheres of influence (Haiti, Rwanda and Georgia, respectively). Moreover, humanitarian revisionism explicitly eschewed self-interest in the way it was formulated as being exercised on behalf of others rather than one's own national interest. This was perhaps exemplified in the notion of 'ethical foreign policy' articulated by Tony Blair's first foreign minister, Robin Cook, who notoriously resigned in advance of the intervention in Iraq, in 2003.[41] The classic case of this ethical intervention that explicitly disavows self-interest is perhaps the 1998 British military intervention in Sierra Leone.

On the other end of the Buzanian spectrum, revolutionary revisionism is characterised by the 'challenge to the organising *principle* of the dominant status quo'. It runs deeper than mere jockeying for status and power, and thus it is a struggle that not only concerns the distribution of power but also parlays into domestic values and political structures, involving the 'transnational intrusions of political ideology'.[42] Conflict is correspondingly exacerbated and more liable to polarisation, the archetypal conflict here being the Cold War and, at the regional level, the Middle East after the 1979 Islamic Revolution in Iran.

Revolutionary revisionism would seem closer to the mark here, if we consider the pattern of post-Cold War liberal revisionism. After all, liberal humanitarianism involved the military enforcement of a transnational ideology of human rights on recalcitrant 'rogue' states and criminalised, sub-political insurgents, warlords and militias. The notorious moralisation of conflict pursuant to humanitarian ideology, in which conflict was cast as being between human rights victims on the one hand and murderous regimes and genocidal warlords on the other, risks rendering conflict more intractable – not least when humanitarian enemies may be criminally prosecuted.[43] Marie-Joëlle Zahar, a Canadian professor who has worked with the UN Department of Political Affairs, argues that the moralisation of mediation – particularly with the abandonment of post-conflict amnesties – has helped to precipitate a crisis in conflict management and mediation.[44] The possibility of humanitarian revisionism may even inflame tensions, encouraging would-be insurgents to resort to arms, to prolong fighting or avoid reconciliation in the hope of winning Western support for their cause in the form of air strikes, no-fly zones and military deployments on the ground.[45] Western hostility to the Syrian government and hope for regime change through the proxy of Islamist militias has undoubtedly escalated and prolonged the most lethal civil war of our time.[46] Parlaying international conflict into domestic conflict is also implicit in the transformational agenda built into policies of democratisation, election monitoring, state- and capacity-building and liberal peacebuilding.

The problem with applying the category of 'revolutionary revisionism' to humanitarian intervention is the fact that the international system was *already* liberalised and increasingly democratised, by virtue of Western victory in the Cold War. The withdrawal of Soviet support from the USSR's proxies in various Cold War theatres cleared the way for the spread of liberal peace to countries like Angola, Mozambique, Cambodia, Guatemala and Nicaragua.[47] Economic globalisation provided the powerful undertow for the spread of liberal market capitalism to Eastern Europe and East and South Asia. In such a world, where was the political necessity or strategic imperative to propagate liberal values by escalating the use of force? Buzan notes that in the case of revolutionary revisionism, systemic transformation and ideological diffusion are as much a matter of survival as they are a matter of ideological consistency: the ideological challenge posed by revolutionary transformation at the domestic level necessitates that the new regime at least have allies if not indeed inhabit an entirely transformed system, in order to survive threats by status quo powers. It would be hard to cast any Western intervention of recent times as an attempt at systemic transformation or identify regime-change interventions targeted at neighbouring states that were needed in order to protect beleaguered liberal-democracy or human-rights regimes at the core of the states system.

At some level perhaps, the relentless expansion of UN Security Council power and the growth of intervention could be seen as a neo-imperial counter-revolution, rolling back the political and legal gains made by Third World states in the post-war period as embodied in the UN Charter (a theme we return to in the next chapter). Interventionism could be seen as a reflex revanchism of Western power as the protections afforded to precocious Third World states by the existence of the USSR fell away. Indeed, it was iconic states of the Third World and Non-Aligned Movement that ended up being targeted and dismembered by humanitarian intervention with striking frequency – Libya, Yugoslavia, Iraq and Indonesia. This is the view promoted in various forms and to a greater or lesser degree by a number of authors, such as Frank Füredi, Mohammed Ayoob, David Chandler, Richard Kareem Al-Qaq and Tariq Ali.[48] What makes this image difficult to sustain, however, is the erosion of the place of the UN Security Council as supreme in matters of war and peace.

As the trustee of the powerful, the UN Security Council was conceived as an institutionalised, fully legalised concert system of great-power management. At the end of the Cold War, the Council was ready-made to oversee world order, with the added benefit that it could pre-emptively neutralise systemic rivals or post-Soviet Russian revanchism by dint of already having them integrated into the system through their veto power on the Council. Efforts that have ended up subverting or overextending Council authority have eroded a concrete dispensation of institutionalised political and legal ideals, not merely abstract disembodied principles of order or hoary principles of customary law. Non-intervention was not intended to provide legal and political cover for Third World independence but to safeguard the interests of the permanent five and their regional spheres of influence, and in the end Western revisionism has eroded not only the standing of Third World states, but the institutions of international order itself. Indeed, absent any ideological challenge or competition at the international level, the only principles left for Western revisionists to overthrow were none other than classical liberal internationalist ones – ideals such as national self-determination, sovereign equality, the sovereign right to non-interference, and the supremacy of the UN Security Council in political and legal matters of war and peace. If Western revisionism exemplified the most elemental defining feature of revolutionary revisionism – a challenge to the organising principles of the status quo – it was a challenge that was internal to liberalism, not outside of it.

If Western humanitarian revisionism does not fit the extremes, can we find a place for it on the spectrum between the extremes? Even the less stark category of radical revisionism does not seem to fit. Buzan sees the ideal type of this kind of revisionism as the attempts by the Third World across the 1970s to marshal its members in international organisations to adjust the functioning of the international order without threatening its basic structure – demanding greater economic justice, technology transfer, developmental rights and so on. According to Buzan, as radical revisionism embodies no organised threat to the overall distribution of power and status in the international system, it is most likely to be appropriated by weaker powers, as per the actions of poor developing countries in the 1970s.

With humanitarian liberalism too revolutionary to fit the label of orthodox revisionism, not revolutionary enough for revolutionary revisionism, too radical for radical revisionism, the other element that simply cannot be squeezed into the Buzanian framework is the fact that *all* these categories are supposed to apply to lesser or 'have-not' states, not those perched at the pinnacle of the international system. All of this motivates the need for a fourth category to capture the thirty years of trans-formational liberal humanitarianism that cannot fit into the Buzanian revisionist typology – a species of revisionism that I call 'inverted revisionism'.

As the discussion of Buzan's categories suggests, there is no real precedent for this kind of self-subverting behaviour in International Relations theory. Thomas E. Doyle II considers how John Rawls's 'Law of Peoples' can be sustained in the face of liberal societies that act like the 'outlaw states', which Rawls saw as so threatening to the comity of the international order; but Doyle's account is restricted to US nuclear policies rather than interventionism and in any case is cast in terms of ideal theory rather than seeking explanation.[49] Nuno Monteiro makes the argument that a unipolar order will be prone to conflict, but this an argument about the structure of the international order dictating behaviour rather than capturing the paradoxical character of revisionism.[50]

Hedley Bull veered close to such counter-intuitive reasoning in his 1980 paper about the disintegration of détente entitled 'The great irresponsibles? The United States, the Soviet Union, and world order'.[51] Bull saw the two superpowers undermining their own role as 'nuclear trustees for mankind' through their political blindness and national self-absorption, thereby allowing nuclear arms control agreements to crumble. Written on the cusp of the so-called 'second Cold War', the context for Bull's analysis offers an intriguing historical parallel, as it was also an era in which people had hoped for the Cold War to come to an end through détente. Bull was particularly attentive to the self-defeating action of the superpowers, such as the Soviet military interven-tions throughout the Third World that undercut Soviet claims and credibility to champion the cause of anti-colonial nations.[52] Yet despite some tantalising analysis and intriguing observations,

Bull offers little by way of explanation for the phenomenon, and in any case he clearly sees the competitive dynamics of superpower competition as exacerbating these self-defeating tendencies.

If it was bipolar competition that tore apart the nascent US–Soviet condominium of the détente era, there was no such dynamic of geopolitical rivalry at work that would help explain these fissiparous tendencies in post-Cold War Western hegemony. To be sure, it is important not to underestimate the gravity of contemporary disorder, with some parallels to the second Cold War era, what with sanctions on Russia and crumbling structures of nuclear arms control. Moreover, as stressed by Roland Dannreuther, the Cold War still enjoyed deep structures of nuclear deterrence to stabilise geopolitical rivalry; these are lacking today.[53] Be that as it may, it does not serve as explanation for the major dynamic of subversion.

The consequences of inverted revisionism

I propose the category of 'inverted revisionism' in order to capture the historically unprecedented moment of status quo great powers pathologically gnawing away at the very order that they created – a revisionism that is 'internal' to the status quo (hence 'inverted'). Western states are status quo powers by any reasonable measure. They have confronted little orthodox revisionist jostling for power within their own ranks, and they have successfully faced down both Soviet and radical revisionism from the Third World. Yet over the last thirty years they embarked on challenging the very principles of their own international order in an extraordinary series of military interventions, leaving a slew of protectorates, new international courts and new institutions such as vastly expanded non-governmental organisations and peace-keeping operations in their wake. How might we account for such a historically peculiar outcome? Perhaps inverted revisionism is a pathology of the equally historically unprecedented era of unipolarity, with its destabilising wars explicable in structural terms of a historically rare, if not unique, distribution of international power (although such an account would miss how the politics of state sovereignty have been reorganised as a result of inverted revisionism, as discussed in greater detail in chapter 4).[54]

However one might wish to account for this kind of revisionism, the account provided over subsequent chapters will be cast in terms that seek to capture the shift in political organising principles linked to the extension and militarisation of cosmopolitan liberalism over the post-Cold War period – that is, the political vision that has corresponded with the era of unipolarity. We can define inverted revisionism thus: ideologically charged revisionist behaviour by leading status quo states, including the use of force, in order to alter the organising principles of the international order from which status quo states benefit and/or which they themselves helped to construct, with results that may exacerbate a redistribution of power in the international system.

Let us briefly examine the destructive consequences of this inverted revisionism. There are three obvious tropes to pursue. First, there is the destabilisation that is the usual consequence of the use of force, leading to the normalisation of war. Second, there is the political and legal precedent established by intervention – extending the legitimacy and rationale for other powers to pursue similar policies. Finally, at the most abstract level, there is the erosion of the organising principles of international order – the characteristic that exemplifies inverted revisionism at its most 'revolutionist', to paraphrase Buzan. Let us consider these in more detail.

The normalisation of conflict

That the use of force is bloody and destabilising is, or should be, an obvious truism. Yet even this basic notion seems to have been forgotten in the era of inverted revisionism. Humanitarian and liberal interventions since the end of the Cold War have helped to normalise war, in the very precise sense that they have eroded the substantive normative restraints and institutional barriers built into the architecture of liberal international institutions to restrain the use of force – a theme that we shall return to over the next two chapters.[55] The normalisation of war extends further than this, however: the normalisation of humanitarian force has meant that violence is increasingly seen as an appropriate response to violence. Thus, the problem is not only that the scales of international justice are increasingly weighted towards violence, but that the potentially self-defeating character of this proposition is obscured by the humanitarian purpose of the use of force. The standard by which the use of force is assessed is how far it will alleviate a particular episode of humanitarian suffering, not the overall effects of force in that particular context. This helps explain the strategic blindness of humanitarian force – another theme that we will revisit in the next chapter. It is difficult to understate the degradation of international liberalism that is the consequence of humanitarian intervention: as force has been made legitimate for humanitarian ends, the original Wilsonian goal of gradually eliminating conflict entirely has been substituted with the end of managing conflict, ensuring that it is conducted according to certain standards. In place of building structures of international cooperation to mitigate war and aggression, liberals today have been consumed with debating the relative merits of multilateral military power as opposed to unilateral military power. In place of abolishing war, liberals have normalised it, effectively demanding only that it be conducted according to their standards.

The second pernicious aspect of humanitarian force arises by virtue of the context within which humanitarian and liberal intervention developed. Not only did previous cycles of Western military intervention and counter-insurgency not explicitly challenge sovereign rights – the homage that vice paid to virtue – but they were also directed against anti-imperial nationalist revolts. Typically, these revolts aimed at securing independent nationhood and territorial reunification in the aftermath of colonial legacies of partition and divide-and-rule. Post-Cold War interventions, by contrast, have perforce destroyed the results of these past efforts – in other words, destroyed the state-based modernist paradigm of national unification, secular modernisation and development. The most dramatic exemplars of failure, Iraq and Libya, saw Western military intervention disintegrate fragile and hollowed-out state structures in fragmented and divided societies. Unsurprisingly, the consequences of these interventions have thus frequently been permanent warfare between sub-national, sub-state factions. The opponents in these conflicts are not the classical 'national liberation fronts' of the heroic era of Third World nationalism but, rather, self-consciously ethnic groups or sectarian militias. The most politically ambitious and transnational of such groups, the Islamic State, obviously had no intention of ever integrating into a state-based international order as per the classical paradigm of Third World national revolution.

Doubtless, the lack of any large-scale geopolitical confrontation such as that of the Cold War meant that there was less incentive to discipline strategising and policy with respect to the consequences of such interventions (a point that will be discussed in greater detail in the next chapter). In the cases of Libya, Afghanistan and Iraq, the opportunistic character of intervention – preying on especially fragile states – inevitably meant that the consequences would be disastrous. Military intervention gave both impetus and form to the catastrophic political and social de-modernisation of these countries, with their subsequent retardation into ethnic sectarian strife, religious revivalism and post-secular politics.

One peculiar and overlooked aspect of this politics of chaos is how the Cold War-era alliance between the West and neo-fundamentalist Islam, originally intended as a bulwark against communism and secular nationalism, evolved over the course of the post-Cold War era, as neo-fundamentalism evolved into cosmopolitan jihadism.[56] While the role of the US and the UK in supporting the mujahideen in Afghanistan against the USSR is well known, Western support also helped to globalise the mujahideen after the end of the Cold War by channelling them to the conflicts in Chechnya and the former Yugoslavia and, later, Libya. In Syria in particular, intervention was no longer restricted to multilateral or unilateral state-based efforts, but was devolved to proxy forces and even became a case of individual freelancing, with the phenomenon of the jihadi foreign fighters descending on the country to resist the brutality of the Assad regime.

Any account of post-Cold War cosmopolitanism that does not reckon with cosmopolitan jihadism cannot be said to be complete. After all, the postmodern phenomenon of the dystopic jihadi statelet defended by foreign fighters has most often emerged as a result of intervention by Western states and their allies, whether that be in Iraq, Libya, Mali, Syria or Yemen. Indeed, much of the international history of the post-Cold War era could be written as a story of the waxing and waning of the alliance between the US imperial state and cosmopolitan jihadism, a tale frequently so bizarre, convoluted and self-referential that only a Chestertonian fable could truly do justice to the internal disarray and postmodern machinations of US empire and its clutch of jihadi allies.[57] This alliance has oscillated between tightly meshed interdependence (as in Afghanistan, the Balkans and Caucasus), to estrangement and open conflict when Al-Qaeda went rogue (Sudan, Afghanistan again and Iraq), back to close alliance (the US support for Al-Qaeda and jihadi affiliates in the Libyan, Syrian and Yemeni civil wars).[58]

One final illustration of the unruly shambles and self-defeating character of inverted revisionism and its new paradigms of international security can be identified with respect to the nuclear non-proliferation regime. 'Collateral damage' is a well known trope in debates on humanitarian intervention – an ugly bureaucratic euphemism for civilian casualties that scholars have shamefully allowed to infiltrate their discussions. The unintended consequences of intervention at the regional level, such as destabilising the Middle East and inadvertently boosting Iranian influence in the Gulf, have also become more prominent in contemporary debates. Both of these exemplars of unintended consequences in intervention reflect the parochial character of intervention debates. Yet the repeated interventions have cumulatively had increasingly systemic consequences beyond the effects on regional order. Thus, the NATO intervention in Libya in 2011 following Colonel Gaddafi's abandonment of his country's nuclear weapons programme doubtless spurred North Korea's determination to secure ballistic-capable nuclear warheads.[59] The rapidity and casualness with which Western states switched from a strategy of containing and reintegrating the Gaddafi regime to one of violent overthrow was exceptionally striking. That the doctrine of the 'responsibility to protect' has left Libya in chaos and spread conflict to Mali is incontrovertible. The jihadi statelet of Azawad, which briefly emerged in northern Mali in 2012 before being overrun by French forces and since then occupied by UN blue helmets, was yet another province in the cosmopolitan empire of chaos.[60] That another by-product of the responsibility to protect was damaging the nuclear non-proliferation regime – constructed by Western states – illustrates the self-subverting logic of inverted revisionism, not only overthrowing years of careful diplomacy and commerce in Libya, but disintegrating an entire institutional and treaty architecture built up over decades and designed to preserve a restrictive, mostly Western oligopoly on nuclear weapons.

Precedents for intervention and conflict

Violent disorder is not only an outcome of Western interventions, but also a result of the extension of humanitarian protection norms to other instances of conflict. During the closing phase of his government's nearly three-decades-long civil war against Tamil rebels in the north of the island, the Sri Lankan president, Mahinda Rajapaksa, delivered a major speech in which he declared the military offensive 'an unprecedented humanitarian operation'.[61] It was a remarkable instance of the extension of humanitarian claims to war-making, in this instance not to intervene in another country's civil war, but to extol the close of one. Here, a national leader justified the use of overwhelming force on the grounds of combatting terrorist insurgents and protecting the very civilians that the Sri Lankan government was indiscriminately shelling.

The brutality and indiscriminate violence of the Sri Lankan offensive against a besieged mass of civilians drew widespread condemnation and censure from the human rights institutions of the UN; indeed, it was taken as a failure to implement the 'responsibility to protect' doctrine.[62] The brutality of the Sri Lankan military can be used to expose the humanitarian pretensions of the Sri Lankan government but the follow-on question is: what differentiates Sri Lanka exploiting available international norms for its own military purposes from any other state doing so? Whether or not we are convinced by Rajapaksa's claims of a 'humanitarian operation' is neither here nor there with respect to evaluating the utility and adaptability of international norms in different contexts and with different political purposes.

Sri Lanka is, of course, far from being the only state that sought to exploit humanitarian rationales for warfare. Turkey encountered similar outrage as far back as 2007 when it launched an international intervention in northern Iraq to crush Kurdish secessionists. Saudi Arabia has explicitly sought to invoke humanitarian justifications in its war against Shi'ite Houthi rebels in Yemen. Among all states, Russia perhaps has elevated and systematised the exploitation of humanitarian hypocrisy and interventionist discourses into an entire diplomatic tradition of non-innovation, as we saw above. Russian justifications for intervention drew much criticism – namely, that they were hypocritical, self-evidently self-serving justifications and inapplicable, because their referents were not universal but ethnic compatriots. Yet to seek to arbitrate as to what counts as a legitimate application of such norms by exposing the veracity or humanitarian purity of, say, Russian justifications for intervention in Georgia, or to seek to establish the conceptual and verbal proximity of Russian justifications to pre-existing discourse would be a profound mistake from the point of view of scholarship.

To be clear, the point is about more than hypocrisy or selectivity in the application of norms – criticisms that are always in fact backhanded affirmations of human rights and cosmopolitan norms. For what the case of Sri Lanka and others like it reveals is that the human rights agenda has provided a rationale for warfare, extending the rubric of legitimate war-fighting. Of course, the humanitarian pretensions of the Sri Lankan military could be exposed and contrasted against the reality of the indiscriminate bombing and shelling of trapped civilians, the mass executions of prisoners and subsequent mass disappearances. To question the legitimacy of the application of humanitarian norms in such cases, though, is to be stuck on the horns of a dilemma. Either it is effectively to say that only Western states are entitled to invoke and use humanitarian norms when they use force, in which case the said norms are clearly not universal but particularist, serving the interests of Western power. To say the Sri Lankan offensive was an illegitimate application of humanitarian justifications for warfare would be to suggest, in fact, that humanitarian civilian protection norms are not, properly speaking, norms at all, but an exclusive set of ideas – as narrowly exclusivist as any chauvinistic, nationalistic set of claims justifying a particular war effort. Or, it is to undercut the very notion of international norms to begin with – namely, that they are conceptual, discursive constructs that adapt and evolve precisely by being stretched, adapted and applied to new contexts, pressed into the service of new purposes and interests beyond their original intent.[63] To arbitrate between how far the Russians diverge from authentic implementation of humanitarian norms or to question the authenticity of Russian leaders' humanitarian motives would be to fall prey to the conceit that that evolution of norms is something that could be determined in workshops, conferences and seminars, and not politically. Yet the outraged scholarly reaction to Russian exploitation of humanitarian norms suggested it was almost as if academics themselves held the copyright on these norms.

While there is an entire research agenda built up around studying normative evolution and complexity in international relations, it remains limited by the so-called 'good norm bias' in constructivist research.[64] This is revealed in the implicit weighting towards studying, for example, the spread of 'good governance' standards, the proliferation of human rights, the extirpation of slavery, the demise of the death penalty in countries around the world – all these being the prototypical models for constructivist research on the evolution of norms, and reflecting an inbuilt teleology arcing towards gradual global improvement. That there would be eddies, ebbs and whirlpools in these rising normative tides was overlooked in this research agenda. What was worse was the fact that, say, the Russian exploitation of international norms for its military interventions became a cause of consternation rather than inducing theoretical adjustment, critique and empirical retesting of models against new political realities.

'Normative entanglement' was originally intended to address the problem of humanitarian selectivity. This was the notion that, via the medium of hypocrisy, norms would have a civilising power – as states grew increasingly reliant on humanitarian norms for the use of force, the intrinsic logic of the norm itself would push its enactors to more systematic and consistent application of that norm. Or so the argument went.[65] Yet the theorists of humanitarian norms did not expect themselves to be the ones deceived by their own rhetoric.[66] The notion that norms which had been conceptualised as sociological processes that evolved independently of any individual actor's will could nonetheless evolve in logics independent of theorists themselves, seemed to come as a surprise to academics who denounced Russia's interventions as inhumane and illegitimate.

Yet, at the end of the day, the fact that there was such outrage over the manipulation and debasement of humanitarianism could only betray naïvety over the dynamics of international politics. As was suggested in the introduction to this book, this itself is partly the result of constructivist theorising – theorising that explicitly gave pride of place to academics and policy activists in shaping norms and global discourse, which always inflated the risk of ideological conceit and projection in modelling processes of political change, while underestimating normative flexibility, porousness and adaptability. Here, International Relations scholars of humanitarianism were left in the position of Humpty Dumpty from Lewis Carroll's fable *Through the Looking-Glass*, who scornfully insists to Alice that 'When *I* use a word, it means just what I choose it to mean – neither more nor less'.

It is important to qualify this discussion of normative evolution. Needless to say, norms do not cause or drive military intervention and war, even though they may help to control its conduct and application. Thus, to say that a war might *not* have broken out in the post-imperial periphery of the Caucasus, or that Russia would *not* have intervened militarily in Ukraine without the prior existence of humanitarian norms and the notion of the responsibility to protect – such speculations make for highly implausible counterfactuals. One such thought experiment might, however, illustrate what is at stake in the discussion of international norms and political change. If the Kosovo War broke out today rather than in 1998, would the Russian government have colluded in ending it as it did in 1999 when it pressured the Yugoslav government to accede to NATO demands? Or would Moscow have supported the Serbian counter-insurgency campaign to the hilt, as it has done with the regime of Bashar al-Assad in Syria? Even if Russia had intervened in both Georgia and Ukraine in order to defend its perceived interests in those states in our counter-factual world, in a world without the responsibility to protect and the new humanitarian trusteeship, it is nonetheless difficult to imagine Russia annexing Crimea or sponsoring ethnic secession in the Caucasus to the extent of dismembering Georgia, were it not for the precedent of Kosovo. What is certain, then, is that Western casualness over humanitarian force has contributed to strengthening the new Russian nationalism, providing justification for the paternal authoritarianism of the Putin regime and vindicating its claim to protect Russian interests abroad with military power.

Inverted revisionism and principles of international order

As discussed above, what makes inverted revisionism stand out and go beyond merely 'radical revisionism' is the challenge involved to the organising principles of international order. Indeed, we could even see the destructive consequences and inadvertent effects of humanitarian and liberal intervention as a result of the challenge to the underlying principles of inter-national order – that is to say, not merely the concrete, actually existing institutions of international order, but its constitutive features. Correct identification of the fundamental institutions of international order would make clear the stakes involved in eroding a core institution.

In other words, an account of the chaos in Iraq, Syria and Libya could be given in terms of these countries' ethnic and religious fragmentation, their hollowed-out (Iraq) and decentralised (Libya) state structures lacking democratic legitimacy (Syria), their histories of authoritarian rule and civil strife, and so on. Yet any such explanation would be incomplete if it did not incorporate not only the hammer blows of Western intervention in the case of Iraq and Libya and the immense infusion of political, financial and military support to Syrian jihadis, but also the wider context of an international order in which intervention has been normalised, the right to non-interference rescinded and democratisation by force accepted. A civil war indefinitely prolonged by the chimera of regime change in Syria, as well as states reduced to permanent civil war in Libya and Iraq, should tell us about the character of the international order at least as much as they do about the internal character of these countries themselves. In fact, all the connective tissue of international order – reciprocal expectations, conceptions about future prospects, legitimacy of international agreements and organisation – are knotted together.

In order conceptually to map the destructive consequences of humanitarian and liberal intervention, and in keeping with the Buzanian analysis of revisionism that requires a challenge to underlying principles in order to count as 'radical revisionism', we can identify four organising principles of international order that have been eroded by inverted revisionism. These are: the erosion of the legal and political restraints on war embodied in the UN Security Council; the subversion of the sovereign claim to exclusive and supreme authority within a given territory and of the linked right to non-interference; and with the last, the displacement of sovereign equality by a new hierarchy, founded around a new standard of civilisation. Chaos, destabilisation and precedent are the manifestations of the erosion of these organising principles of international order.

That is to say, we have seen not merely the erosion of concrete institutions of an international order, but its constitutive features, with sovereignty always being the quintessential political institution of the modern international order, given that it defines the very character of international order as such, by binding together its fundamental characteristics. As a claim to supreme secular authority, sovereignty dissolves hierarchically stacked or vertically integrated political structures of suzerain political systems, thereby necessitating homogenised political units and flat, horizontal and therefore egalitarian relations as well as recognitive means of integrating and binding multiple sovereigns together.[67] To erode the character of this institution is necessarily to erode its corollaries of egalitarianism, international decentralisation and exclusive authority within given territories. Doing so has led to new imperial forms, new hierarchies and, within the states whose exclusive authority has been challenged or overthrown, a new Hobbesian war of all against all. That these were necessary consequences of liberal intervention was obscured by the very fact that the post-Cold War era corresponded to the relegation of these theoretical approaches that cleaved tightly to sovereignty as a fundamental category and building block for theory – structural or neo-realist and English School theorising (a theme we return to in the next chapter).

Conclusion

Western states have gone further than merely engaging in intervention or supporting other states' interventionist efforts. Western states championed a new model of intervention built around human rights. Instead of the traditional politics of intervention that saw states flout state sovereignty and international law while denying, disguising or pleading mitigation for their actions, Western states claimed that sovereignty had to be relegated not only in practice but also as a matter of principle: in times of extreme humanitarian duress or crisis, sovereignty had to be trumped by the greater collective claims of humanity, whether human rights or the responsibility to protect. This is the crucial difference with the interventionist politics of the past, and it makes all the difference, because it entails an explicit revision to the principles underpinning the existing political order. It was Western lawyers and scholars who generated the theories to explain and rationalise this new form of international politics, establishing the precedents to which others respond. Russian justifications given for Putin's interventions in Georgia and Ukraine are expertly engineered to outrage liberal opinion by exploiting Western precedents and cosily nestling in the interstices of Western hypocrisy. Western states have pursued this new model of interventionist politics in the face of enormous and abiding diplomatic and legal resistance and scepticism from much of the rest of the world, and often tugging against the indifference, reluctance and scepticism even of their own publics. Western states have pursued interventionist policies to the extent of shattering the post-Cold War harmony of the UN Security Council and even dividing the Western alliance against itself, as happened over the invasion of Iraq.

Cycles of intervention in the Middle East have resulted in an entire generation's worth of violent mayhem and disorder, and in turn provided a new ideological and theoretical armoury to justify warfare. In place of self-determination and sovereign states, the new international liberalism has recreated novel forms of protectorates and trusteeship while degrading states' rights and authority. While nineteenth century and interwar liberals sought to extinguish war through constructing institutional barriers, collective security provisions, through normative transformation and legal restraint, the focus of humanitarianism has shifted the goal from conflict as such to ending mass atrocity crimes rather than ending war itself. The bad faith of such a project is hard to conceal: liberals cannot realistically oppose war given that they believe war is necessary to stop mass atrocities … thereby re-creating the conditions in which mass atrocity is possible.

Western victory in the Cold War did not see the sublimation of the existing international order into a new one. Unlike the two world wars, the previous international order transitioned into a post-Cold War world. In such a world political and ideological renewal could only be achieved by cutting away at existing institutions and inherited frameworks. While the cosmopolitan project offered some kind of future vision, problematic as it was, this quickly withered. The dynamic attempt to recreate international order around individual human rights has resulted in a more disorderly world that is shorter on political ambition and transformation.

Chapter 2

Through the looking-glass: the new critics of intervention

What does it mean to be critical of intervention? After all, any reasonable person would admit that the intervention in Iraq, for example, was a disaster. Even the late unabashedly neo-conservative US senator John McCain, notorious for his unstinting support for the invasion of Iraq and the global war on terror, conceded on the eve of his death that Iraq was 'a mistake'.[1] Both President Obama and President Trump mounted electoral campaigns that criticised the failures and excesses of military operations waged under the administrations of George W. Bush, as well as withdrawing troops from various theatres (notably Iraq). Obama openly admitted that the (entirely predictable) aftermath of the 2011 NATO intervention in Libya was the 'worst mistake' of his administration.[2] Subsequent military interventions implicitly abide by chastened expectations of intervention, as with the 2018 air strikes on Syria that were explicitly restrained in order to avoid any implication of escalation towards regime change.[3] British prime minister Theresa May justified the air strikes on Syria by stressing that they were not intended as an intervention in the civil war, but were purely for the purposes of humanitarian protection – to prevent chemical weapons attacks on civilians.[4] US president Donald Trump bombed Syria, then withdrew US forces, then made to seize Syrian oil fields.[5] If the champions and executors of liberal intervention are so chastened and restrained, is it even possible to muster opposition and critique? Regime change is derided as a policy goal by Western leaders. The liberal peace model of post-conflict reconstruction is vociferously scorned and disparaged in the academy. The bold and open championing of human rights, whether chastened or defiant, is diminished.

Yet despite the withering away of the crusading era of humanitarian intervention, intervention continues unabated, one campaign rolling into the next as seamlessly as bombers refuelling in mid-air. NATO intervened in Libya in 2011 to protect Libyan civilians from Libyan government forces, only one year after US forces had formally withdrawn from Iraq. Then, after Libya, Western forces returned to Iraq as intervention was demanded to protect the Yazidis from the Islamic State offensive on Mount Sinjar in 2014, as well as to protect Kurdish enclaves in Syria. In 2015, the European Union mulled further military intervention in Libya to intercept migrant movements, settling in the end for funding proxy militias instead.[6] Although May's predecessor, David Cameron, had humiliatingly lost a parliamentary vote on intervention in Syria in August 2013, his government nonetheless pursued intervention in Syria two years later.

It was perhaps with the launch of the bombing campaign against the forces of the Islamic State in September 2014 under the Obama administration that the era of military intervention gave way to the era of permanent warfare. Western states have taken their publics past both war fatigue and war enthusiasm to simple, numb indifference in the face of perpetual war. With the launch of new rounds of intervention to redress the problems caused by earlier operations, military intervention has begun to collapse in on itself, each discrete episode disintegrating into one continuous long war in which there is no originary intervention. No longer justified by anything as grand as expanding the reach of human rights, destroying cataclysmic weapons, overthrowing tyrants, defending civilisation or building new global orders, intervention is becoming a crude politics of containment: stemming refugee flows or suppressing new eruptions of insurgency. While Western forces bombed Syria, intervention was demanded to protect the Rohingya fleeing persecution by government forces in Myanmar. At the very least, the fact that military interventions inspired by liberal norms continue should tell us that the critique of such interventions must perforce be inadequate to some degree.[7] Otherwise, how else could the interventions continue?

While it is easy enough to see Iraq as a totemic failure for liberalism, a failure for democratisation, a failure for humanitarian protection, by the same token it would be too easy to dismiss this failure too readily, whether to see it simply as a monument to imperial hubris, the conceits of US nation-building, or as a catastrophic, mutant aberration in the otherwise healthy lineage of liberal intervention and human rights. It is important to understand precisely what Iraq represents the failure of, and what it tells us about the broader pattern of intervention in modern history. A significant scholarly effort has been invested in firewalling the intervention in Iraq from the broader pattern of liberal intervention, in places such as Kosovo, East Timor, Libya.[8] The debate over Iraq helps us to identify the limitations of critical opposition to intervention.

Take the two slogans that embodied the vast popular opposition to the Iraq War in the West – 'no war for oil' and 'not in my name'. The latter was ultimately an apolitical slogan – it did not even make a pretence at seeking to change policy; quite the opposite, it was a signal of withdrawal from the public realm. The sentiment was captured in Ian McEwan's 2005 novel of the era, *Saturday*, in which the protagonist, Henry Pewrone, muses sceptically over the protestors milling about London's streets:

> Don't Attack Iraq. Placards not yet on duty are held at a slope, at rakish angles over shoulders. Not In My Name goes past a dozen times. Its cloying self-regard suggests a bright new world of protest, with the fussy consumers of shampoos and soft drinks demanding to feel good, or nice. Henry prefers the languid, Down With This Sort of Thing.[9]

The idea of 'no war for oil', on the other hand, clearly signalled that another kind of war – say, one for democracy, human rights, humanitarian rescue and so on – *was* legitimate. Both of these sentiments expressed in different ways the basic concern that, in the jargon of political science, human rights had been captured or 'instrumentalised' in justifying the intervention in Iraq – that is, that human rights were used as an instrument to achieve a purpose other than the human rights themselves, for example geopolitical scheming, regional reordering, plundering fossil fuel reserves, neo-liberal democratisation and so on. In other words, the problem was not human rights per se, but something external to human rights – a prosthetic element grafted onto the body. Of course, one might be tempted to ask, what is it about human rights that makes them open to such easy manipulation, that makes them such effective ideological battering rams in imperial expeditions? This latter question is usually avoided, however, forgotten in the pursuit for the real 'reason' behind intervention that sabotaged the noble ideal.

This chapter considers arguments against intervention marshalled from International Relations theory, coming from scholars and schools of thought that were, in various ways, concerned to preserve the international order from what they took to be the powerful solvents of liberal interventionism. I organise these different arguments into several different types that are discussed in turn: pluralist, Charterist, realist and normaliser. The first strand comes from the pluralist wing of English School theorising in International Relations, perhaps the most venerable and influential of anti-interventionist critiques. The second group are those I call 'Charterists' as they are concerned to preserve international law and order, especially as concretely embodied and articulated in the UN Charter. Realists are those scholars who associate with this long-standing school of International Relations theory. It was indeed realists who proved to be the most consistent and vocal critics of recent interventions, either urging restraint on the West (in the case of Ukraine, for example) or offering advance warnings (Libya, Syria). Castigated for a generation in universities across the West, this tradition of thought demonstrated something its critics claimed that it lacked: an intellectual vantage point from which it was possible to criticise world affairs. Indeed, it was precisely realists' focus on military security, geopolitical competition and oscillations in the balance of power that gave realism traction in debates on intervention. Thus, it was intervention that precipitated the move into a looking-glass world in which liberals, supposedly hostile to state power and conflict, sought to usher in the humanitarian millennium through war, while those who were focused on the enduring features of geopolitical struggle and military rivalry – namely, realists – became advocates of restraint, caution and withdrawal. Liberals staked the future of their ideals for international order on battlefield victories, overwhelming air campaigns and alliances with their preferred ethnic militias, while realists, suspicious of attempts to transcend power politics, cautioned against reflex military adventurism. The pacification of realism and the militarisation of (humanitarian) liberalism were perhaps among the strangest of role reversals in this looking-glass world. In a later section of this chapter I cover the 'normalisers', those who, while recognising the destructive consequences of humanitarian liberalism, nonetheless believe it is too deeply embedded in the international order to be excised. Thus their position is that it would be better to adapt the international order so that humanitarian liberalism is less destructive in its effects rather than vainly trying to roll it back. As these scholars wish to integrate the extreme into the norm, I dub this school the 'normalisers'. This is followed by a brief excursus on those who sought to provide a wider perspective on humanitarian liberalism.

There is, needless to say, overlap between these schools (such as the Charterists and the pluralists) – occasionally some of these strands are intertwined in a single argument, and need to be untwined when analysing them more closely. One school of thought opposed to intervention that I have excluded here is that concerned with the impact of intervention on domestic order. This last anti-interventionist argument is motivated by the fear that the use of international force to police peace settlements or protect embattled ethnic minorities in civil wars, or to bring about regime change, will warp spontaneous (perhaps even bloody) indigenous state-building processes. These warping effects will lead in turn to greater disorder and human suffering as a whole over the long run, as there is a failure to build the lasting fundaments of political order. These themes will be addressed in chapter 4.

It is also worth stressing that the purpose of the survey offered in this chapter is to identify strengths and weaknesses of the anti-interventionist critiques in order to lay the foundations for the critique that I offer in subsequent chapters. Although a number of critical responses to intervention are covered here, it would be a mistake to imagine that this betokens some equilibrium in intellectual significance and number between humanitarian liberalism and its critics. The number of scholars, analysts, public intellectuals and 'thought leaders' who were committed to defending and spreading human rights by force consistently outnumbered by a wide margin those opposed or hostile to crusading humanitarian liberalism. Thus some of the debates staged in this chapter are ritual jousts, in that they have too few representatives to carry their ideas into battle – such has been the intellectual fate of English School pluralism for instance, which has few supporters to counter the so-called pro-humanitarian 'solidarists'. Nonetheless, there is a utility to occasionally staging even a mock battle in order to understand what was at stake in these disagreements.

The fraying of international order?
Pluralism and intervention

The most influential strand of anti-interventionist theorising was the pluralist wing of the English School of International Relations theory.[10] As pluralists conceived of international order in a specific way, humanitarian intervention was seen as particularly threatening to that order. Specifically, pluralists conceive of international order as being constituted by the famed international society, but that the fabric of the bonds that constitute this society have been stretched thin and taut. This was the result of these bonds having been repeatedly overextended to cover the influx of new states into the international system over the course of the twentieth century, particularly after decolonisation. In place of the densely woven international society of nineteenth-century Eurocentric international law and diplomacy, what was left in its place was a more threadbare pattern, tautly stretched to loosely bind together a tremendously diverse range of states, which in turn embodied a varied range of political systems, creeds and ethical value systems.[11] The 'content' of this society – or the substance of those connecting threads, to continue the metaphor – was necessarily procedural rather than substantive. That is to say, the connective tissue of international society was all there was to that society, without any broader collective commitment to substantive goals as to what ends states should pursue. Social bonds consisted of norms to regulate interaction and, in so doing, constituted international society itself. Given the diversity of states and global value systems and the thinness of the international society that bound them together, ensuring these connecting strands keep the unruly morass of humanity bound together necessitated respect for the sovereign right to non-interference and the boundaries between different political systems. Enforcing a substantive commitment to specific goals and forms of legal and social organisation – such as human rights or liberal political systems – risked snapping those connecting threads and precipitating international disintegration and wider global disorder. Breaching the thin, protective membrane of sovereignty risked destabilising the global commitment to cultural and social diversity that is tacit in sovereignty, and thereby implicitly threatening a war of all against all.

At first blush, a pluralist outlook would seem to have been strikingly vindicated. Chaos has indeed been the result of repeated rounds of recent intervention in the Middle East, and great-power tensions have been exacerbated by disagreements over intervention in Syria, Ukraine and Georgia. But taken beyond these first impressions, pluralism begins to dissolve as a coherent theoretical perspective on international disorder. Consider the question of sovereignty and political order. In the pluralist view, the institution of state sovereignty is a thin crust layered over the magma of cultural, ethnic, national and religious diversity. The implications here are that conflict and disorder result primarily from the clash of value systems and beliefs, and that international order is an intrinsically fragile form of political life, with generalised disorder and chaos ever-present – views perhaps reflecting the inspiration of English School theorising in Europe's now historically remote wars of religion. Here, sovereignty is valued on the grounds that it helps to demarcate different human groups from each other, thereby helping to preserve social order by avoiding interminable conflict over fundamental values. The value of sovereignty is thus both instrumental (in that it facilitates common human interaction between varied groups) and also intrinsic (in that it helps the flourishing of human cultural diversity).

Yet such assumptions are difficult to sustain in light of modern history – assumptions about the origin and nature of conflict, about the extent of human diversity in a globalised world, about the risks of generalised chaos. There have been sufficient rounds of military intervention since the end of the Cold War to test the validity of these assumptions, and they do not hold up. With the exception of the peculiarly prolonged and lethal Syrian civil war, violent conflict has tended, on the whole, to decline, despite the best efforts of Western liberals to propagate humanitarian militarism.[12] What is more, many of these interventions have been nominally or formally consensual, legitimated by the institution that is, by the pluralists' own reckoning, the highest organ of international society: the UN Security Council. How can peace-keeping operations – which are, after all, forms of direct military intervention – weigh in the scales of pluralist theorising, given that such operations work at the express behest of governments? Many interventions have also been intra-regional – within Europe, Africa or the former Soviet Union – making the assumption of global cultural clashes less tenable. Nor has this integration been merely economic or Western-centred: some of the most ardent supporters of thickening human rights regimes and post-national forms of integration have been, for example, African states.[13] There has also been a trend towards regional devolution of inter-vention – as seen with efforts by the African Union in Somalia, and the Gulf Arab dictatorships intervening in Yemen, Syria and even as far afield as Libya. So, clearly, there is a dynamic of small states abrogating rights of intervention to themselves, partly in order to respond to the aftermath of earlier interventions by extra-regional/Western powers. Yet such decisions also reflect strategic decisions made by the US, too, and they would not take place without US connivance and tacit, if not explicit, support.

In other words, a story of attenuated international social links at the global level does not provide a satisfactory picture of the dynamics of regional intervention. While there has been a degradation of international order flowing from the growing proclivity to override sovereignty, this is not an uncontrolled, fissile chain reaction blowing apart the international order (as the pluralist outlook might lead us to believe), but rather involves specific political decisions in concrete regional contexts.

The dynamics of international integration – technological, economic, communications – cannot be discounted so easily in the face of easy generalisations about human cultural diversity. While disputes over intervention have certainly been damaging to post-Cold War political consensus, the pattern of disagree-ment has been less protean, cultural and values-based so much as political and strategic – clashes over how far to extend, permit and legitimate intervention encroaching on states' rights, perceived spheres of influence, geopolitical interests or allies (for example, the Anglo-French disputes over intervention in central Africa in the 1990s).

If we take the political maelstrom in the Middle East that has resulted from intervention there – in Syria, Iraq, Libya, Yemen – it would be hard to attribute this directly to a clash of value systems per se. After all, the NATO humanitarian intervention was explicitly invited into Libya by the anti-Gaddafi rebels and sanctioned by the regional body, the League of Arab States. Generalised disorder has resulted from the shattering of central state institutions and authorities, the collapse of the political project of Arab nationalist modernisation, and from the failure and involution of brutal counter-insurgency campaigns and shifts in the regional balance of power. Again, the disorder resulting from intervention in the Middle East is *intra*-regional, and to the extent that it is a clash of competing value systems at all, it is intra-religious (between the Sunnis of the Gulf monarchies and the Shi'ite Arabs backed by Iran). It is not, as a pluralist outlook would lead us to expect, a protean clash between different civilisational value systems at the global level.

Finally, in the pluralists' view, institutions of international society are essentially mimetically disseminated – that is to say, they are weak copies of each other, each one being a paler imitation of the European original. Yet this view underestimates the extent to which the institutions of social and political modernity have percolated throughout the world, and the extent to which these institutions and values have greater depth and traction in modernising societies than the logic of pluralism would suggest. Turkey's 2019 intervention in northern Syria for instance is driven by the need to suppress the threat of Kurdish nationalism – indicating the enduring resilience of modern nationalism outside of the West, and which it would be unwise to dissolve away into a generic fable about cultural atavism.

It was English School concepts that proved to be the most intellectually fruitful in relation to the issues associated with humanitarian intervention in its early phases. Yet it was also humanitarian intervention and, later, the responsibility to protect that motivated the need to craft new, more counter-pluralist, 'solidaristic' perspectives on global order, ascribing greater global cohesion around a vision of international liberalism. This was matched by a multiplication of theoretical categories. To Hedley Bull's originary five fundamental institutions of international society, Kal Holsti added an extra three, dividing their functioning into constitutive and regulative, while Barry Buzan distinguished between primary and secondary institutions, the latter being 'deposits' of primary institutions, with most major English School theorists now holding to the idea that secondary institutions have a 'reticular' character, in the words of Torbjørn Knutsen, so that they can affect primary institutions: in this case that the responsibility to protect can reshape the fundamental institution of sovereignty.[14] If this extended intellectual canopy of new institutions made the overall theoretical structure of the English School more impressive, it has also made its theoretical referent points more concrete, embodying them in actually existing institutions, obscuring originary and fundamental institutions behind the foliage of secondary institutions. The net result is perhaps that the erosion of fundamental institutions is less obvious and noteworthy: change can be understood in terms of the evolution of concrete institutions rather than the evaporation of more abstract underlying primary or fundamental institutions. Thus, the evolution of the English School into solidaristic views has obscured some of the significant originary contributions of the English School on questions of sovereignty and order – but, as we have seen, pluralism cannot motivate or sustain a defence of sovereignty once it is ensnared in the thickets and brambles of solidarism.

The limits of Charterism

Closely flanking pluralism in the phalanx of opposition to liberal and humanitarian intervention was a doctrine that, when its various elements are compounded, is, I suggest, best described as 'Charterism'. Much like pluralism, Charterism was concerned with the overall integrity of international order, but with a more explicit focus on the specific laws, norms, provisions and concrete institutions associated with the UN Charter and UN organisation as instantiated in and developed since 1945 (with a focus, as we shall see, on one article of the Charter in particular).[15]

From the view of Charterism, the growing proclivity for intervention threatened the sovereign right to non-interference enshrined in Article 2(4) of the Charter and, with it, the norm of non-aggression. The debate around Charterism was most intense at the turn of the century, following the 1999 NATO intervention in Yugoslavia in order to halt the Yugoslav counter-insurgency campaign against separatists in the province of Kosovo. Although the Kosovo War was far from the first Western-led military operation to invoke humanitarian justification for force, unlike previous interventions in Somalia or Bosnia-Herzegovina, this took place without the sanction of the UN Security Council or the state in question (Yugoslavia).

There were a number of inter-related concerns here. First, Article 2(4) of the UN Charter articulated the sovereign state as enjoying a presumptive right to non-interference in its internal affairs, and thus this article was seen as being part of the normative architecture of the post-war international system that impeded the waging of war. This article was an integral part of the post-war achievement of international law in establishing legal barriers to war, removing a possible justification for opportunistic cross-border meddling and conflict that could conceivably escalate into a general war. What was at stake here was the extent to which the UN system had succeeded in delegitimising international war

74

by restricting possible legal justifications for it. By invoking a higher right to defend suffering humanity within the borders of sovereign states, humanitarian intervention directly contravened this article, as did liberal intervention in claiming that it was legitimate and necessary to improve a state's internal political structures and governing institutions by coercion if necessary.

Defending this article of the UN Charter involved more than merely conservative legal positivism, a stubborn clinging to the precise wording of black-letter international law. International lawyers and legal theorists did not discount the possibility of innovation and change, but they pointed to the fact that there was simply insufficient agreement within international society to credibly claim that customary international law had evolved to a point of acceptance of a new discretionary norm of intervention.[16] Here the concern was that, whatever the justice of humanitarian concerns and however cogent the interpretations of various human rights treaties, to be properly woven into the fabric of international law such innovations had to be consistently accepted by a wide majority of states. This was a sharp and clear criterion of 'legal legitimacy', as it were, but also one that humanitarian intervention never met, as both the doctrine and instances of humanitarian intervention were consistently and resolutely opposed by a majority of states. This was conceded even by the so-called Independent International Commission on Kosovo established by the Swedish government in 1999 to resolve legal and political issues pertaining to the intervention. Despite being established by a NATO-allied country and with the majority of its members hailing from NATO member states, the Commission's conclusion was that the intervention was illegal but nonetheless legitimate.[17] This accepted the fact that neither positive nor customary international law had changed with respect to a so-called right of humanitarian intervention.

Despite this, the Charterist defence of the right of non-intervention was problematic on a number of fronts. First, there was never any clear or justifiable reason to give normative or legal priority to Article 2(4) of the Charter over the commitment to human rights in the Charter's preamble or other human rights regimes and treaties embedded in the UN system through repeat and multiple affirmations of both the Council and the General Assembly. This was, indeed, the challenge mounted by the defenders of humanitarian intervention – that there was a legal and normative basis within the Charter and its wider, ramified system that gave scope for humanitarian intervention at least, if not liberal intervention. That Article 2(4) had been given de facto priority over much of the period of the Charter's existence, as a result of the Cold War deadlock on the Council, produced the mistaken impression of de jure priority – which never existed. During the Cold War, Article 2(4) enjoyed normative apprecia- tion as superpowers excluded rivals and challengers from their respective spheres of influence among client states and allies – a disposition that was further strengthened by the rapid multiplica- tion of newly independent states, which had strong interests in preserving their freshly won independence from encroachment.

Whatever its legal cogency and principled commitments, by harking back to the Cold War-era Charter, Charterism was always defensive and conservative, its strength and appeal diminishing the further the Cold War receded into history until it was eventu- ally eclipsed by the doctrine of responsibility to protect. Charterism was also fatally flawed beyond this as the UN Charter only ever provided the slenderest of defences for state sovereignty. For at the same time as the Charter articulates a right to non-intervention, it also assimilates another classical sovereign right, the right to wage war, to the highest authority within the United Nations, the Security Council. Traditionally, the right to wage war was the ultimate prerogative of the sovereign state, but the UN Charter spliced it in two, limiting it to the right of self-defence for states, and concentrating everything else in the hands of the UN Security Council, which in turn, by dint of the veto, meant concentrating the right to wage war in the hands of the five permanent members. So sweeping was this power that the UN Security Council even abrogated to itself the right to *override* claims to self-defence by any sovereign state. Thus, the ultimate legality of any conflict, even that of self-defence, depends on the decision of the Council.

That the Council abrogated the rights to wage war to itself while also enshrining a right to non-intervention seems less paradoxical if the historical context within which the Charter was drafted is considered. Conceived in a world in which the European imperial powers were hankering to restore their colonial empires in Asia, and the US and the USSR were seeking to sequester their respective spheres of influence, the principle of non-interference was conceived less to provide shelter for (as-yet virtually non-existent) Third World states but, rather, to protect the sovereignty of the victors and their client states. Viewed in the context of the larger complex of wartime and post-war innovations and institutions in which the UN system was born, the 'norm against aggressive war' subsequently enshrined at the UN war crimes trials in Nuremburg and Tokyo was supposed to freeze the status quo ante before the revisionist challenge mounted by the Axis powers.[18] Trusteeship – that is to say, political tutelage and oversight – was the political model the UN conceived for those states emerging from empire.

In short, the most consistent and logical way to interpret how the Charter aligns the powers of the Council and the rights accorded to sovereign states is as a means for the permanent five to preserve their interests from encroachments by each other, while reserving the right to police all other member states. What the origins of the legal and political system of the Charter tell us is that it offers few protections and guarantees for smaller states, while also rescinding certain traditional sovereign rights – notably, the right to wage war – in return for membership of the world body.

The Charter thus embodied an extraordinarily dense and extensive concentration of power in the hands of the UN

Security Council – a 'trusteeship of the powerful', as conceived by US president Franklin Delano Roosevelt.[19] The fact that the UN did not evolve in line with its constitutional powers and design reflected not its benevolence towards the sovereignty of newly independent member states joining the organisation, but the deadlocks of the Cold War era. Article 2(4) offers no defence against the higher rights of the Council to decide what constitutes a threat to international peace and security. Indeed, any matter can be deigned a threat to international peace and security, and that decision overrides any putative right to non-interference. This is the basis on which the Council has drastically expanded its remit, which now extends to matters internal to the state – and it is precisely this power that the Council has used extensively since the end of the Cold War to designate a growing range of internal conflicts as threats to international peace and security, thereby legitimating the relentless expansion of intervention in the internal affairs of states.[20] The Charter system was designed to institutionalise and legitimate the 'trusteeship of the powerful', with the human rights of the preamble and the preceding Atlantic Charter supplying a thin sugar coating to the bitter pill of hard power, self-consciously constructed to avoid what were seen as the idealist aspirations of the failed League of Nations.[21]

Council power and authority asides, how far could we say that humanitarian intervention has re-legitimated the use of military force in a way that the prosecutors at Nuremburg had sought to dispel? Answering this question is partly an issue of correctly locating the stakes involved in this claim, and where they matter. The concern over the erosion of normative restraints on warfare is understandable, and indeed an important role has been attributed to normative and legal progress in contributing to the global decline in violent conflict.[22] The origins of legal attempts to criminalise war reach back to the notorious Kellogg–Briand Pact of 1928. Given the wars that followed this ill-fated accord, it would seem that if there is a relationship between international norms and mass political violence, it is clearly not a direct or unidirectional one. Norms against wars did not stop the massive violence of Cold War-era post-colonial and anti-colonial wars, or prevent the superpowers waging their own wars, whether overt or covert. The assumption that the erosion of such norms makes war easier or more likely would suggest that conflict is directly proportional to the strength and number of legal fetters in which it is bound. Yet there is no widely accepted explanation of conflict that attributes its causes simply to lack of legal restraint at the international level. Nor did the norm of non-intervention necessitate particularly costly or complex legal and political manoeuvres to circumvent it. Calling upon the 'support' of allies legally allowed client regimes to involve their superpower patrons within their own internal affairs. For instance, the Soviet puppet leader in Afghanistan, Babrak Karmal, 'requested' Soviet intervention in December 1979 in a radio message broadcast on the frequency of Radio Kabul from within the USSR![23]

Cutting away at the thin strands of international law that restrict the waging of war is unlikely to be particularly significant in this regard. To understand the stakes resulting from the greater likelihood and normative acceptability of military force requires us to shift our perspective away from international law. Given the role of the UN Charter in international law and the power that it gave to the Council, there was precious little space from which to criticise Council choices. However states may have politically justified their actions to themselves, the Charter provided the Council with the necessary powers to follow through on great-power choices. Thus, here too, international law fell prey to its reliance on Charter principles. In the end, international law rooted in the Charter provided few resources with which to counter the claims made for humanitarian intervention, whether from the viewpoint of non-aggression or that of defending the claims of customary law.

Political realism: strategic traditionalism versus ethical imperatives

As indicated in the introduction to this chapter, one of the strangest outcomes of the era of intervention has been the theoretical resurgence of the realist theoretical tradition in International Relations.[24] This has happened not so much in a burst of new scholarship, theoretical breakthroughs and conceptual innovation, nor any remarkable increase in predictive power and empirical accuracy on the part of realist analyses, the work of Nuno Monteiro notwithstanding.[25] Rather, by virtue of consistently reapplying the same intellectual framework over a protracted period, realists succeeded in performing the one thing that had been denied to them by an entire generation of scholars: their capacity to be critical. A whole generation of post-Cold War International Relations scholars, particularly in the British academy, have built up their authority on re-enacting the ritual slaughter of theoretical realism at the beginning of their courses, textbooks and monographs. An entire generation of students have been taught that the discipline has surpassed the narrow orthodoxies of a failed tradition, which was castigated for being rigid, dogmatic, positivistic *and* unscientific, and, worse, militaristic. In light of the destructive consequences of inverted revisionism, we are left wondering how it was that critical International Relations theorists undercut their capacity for critical responses to Western interventionism, so that the stale orthodoxies appeared critical once again. Unfortunately, such questions are beyond the scope of this chapter. As we shall see, however, while realists may have proved more critical than their liberal and critical peers, their accounts of humanitarian liberalism are also incomplete.

The nature of the anti-interventionist critique from the political realist vantage point is structured somewhat differently to that of pluralism and Charterism. Whereas the latter two are concerned with preserving a peaceful, law-governed international order, realists are less concerned with avoiding war, as they accept it not only as a tragic inevitability but as part of the routine functioning of an anarchic political system – an international system lacking centralised authority. What realists have taken issue with is the type of conflict involved in humanitarian and liberal interventions, and the blunders and overstretch that have resulted from what Mearsheimer and Walt term 'liberal hegemony'. Here, political realists and strategic traditionalists criticised humanitarian intervention for running the risks of conflict with its unpredictable outcomes and possibilities for escalation, but without being offset by strategic gains or payoffs.[26] This was the result of adventurist foreign policy and fighting for the wrong (humanitarian) reasons, lacking the strategic focus that would result from a grasp of core interests, and being inattentive to the dynamics of power at the international level. Thus, the intervention in Iraq is seen to have inadvertently boosted the power of Iran by virtue of destabilising the regional balance of power, while the intervention in Ukraine is seen as alienating Russia, a potential ally in constructing a viable balance of power against a rising China. The damage identified by the realist critique of humanitarian and liberal intervention comes not from conflict per se so much as the *type* of conflict that humanitarian military intervention represents. Let us consider three different types of realist critique – a structural critique, a critique from the viewpoint of strategic traditionalism and a classical realist critique.

Realist scholars Mearsheimer and Walt have launched a two-pronged attack on liberal hegemony, which is underpinned, as they see it, by the notion of the US as an 'indispensable nation'. Even this intensely condensed precis of the argument betrays the contradiction in which a traditional structural realist such as Mearsheimer finds himself in, as he is left having to explain international order by reference to the behaviour of a single state (the US), rather than the international system. Structural realism is predicated on a strict conceptual separation between domestic and international politics, the latter realm having to be explained in holistic terms. In a unipolar world, Mearsheimer at least feels justified in compressing this conceptual distinction, as an international system in which there is only one centre of power means that inside-out accounts of US behaviour are theoretically consistent with the premise of the structural approach.[27] Thus, the pathological, repetitive failure of liberal hegemony is explained in sociological terms as the result of a foreign policy establishment that carries a bipartisan consensus on 'liberal hegemony'. It is ultimately a critique of international order provided in terms of the sociology of the 'Beltway', the circumferential road around the US capital. This micro-focus is justified by reference to a unipolar distribution of power. Walt offers a cutting but ultimately familiar and pedestrian critique of a 'power elite' ensconced in an imperial capital.[28]

The ideology of the Beltway is then explained in terms of a progressive liberalism that necessitates a meddlesome globalism which ultimately provides employment for the foreign policy elite and their offshoots. While Walt and Mearsheimer's scepticism about the ideas and motivations of the Beltway foreign policy 'experts' may well be justified, it is insufficient as an account of the contradictions within liberal international order or indeed liberal interventionism. An explanation cast in terms of the sociology of the Beltway would have difficultly accounting for the humanitarian leadership assumed by British prime minister Tony Blair over the Kosovo intervention, or indeed over Iraq, or French intervention in Libya and Mali. Moreover, why is it necessary for the 'progressive liberalism' identified by Mearsheimer to set itself against sovereignty and the nation-state? That is to say, a meddlesome globalism could conceivably operate without needing expressly to delegitimise the notion of state sovereignty, or to gravitate towards supranational and transnational political forms and institutions. Many opportunities for direct intervention by Western states were avoided – in places such as Liberia,

Sudan and Congo. Yet transnational military interventions *were* pursued – by multinational armies of blue helmets, deployed not only under the expectation of curbing conflict (the old concern of liberal internationalism), but also of humanitarian protection for refugees and civilians (the new liberal humanitarian hope). Understanding developments such as these requires a wider scope than Beltway politics. Even in the era of unipolarity, international order cannot be explained entirely in terms of US foreign policy or the workings of the US elite.

Notwithstanding this limit, with their insistence on the priority to be given to core interests, realists have found plenty of targets among humanitarian arguments for war. Yet they nonetheless have tended to underestimate the extent to which liberal internationalism has been propelled into supranational forms of politics that depart from classical ideals such as international cooperation, global trade and self-determination. By the same token, Mearsheimer also tends to overestimate the forces of modern nationalism, which is noticeable by its absence in the bloodlands of global cosmopolitanism. For example, there are no national liberation fronts resisting outside interveners in Libya, Iraq, Afghanistan, Haiti or South Sudan. Indeed, as we saw in the introduction to this book, Islamic State was explicitly cosmopolitan rather than nationalistic. For those states that have been reduced to permanent warfare, cosmopolitan global order is no longer hospitable for the unification projects of Third World nation-building.

It is not only structural realism that has enjoyed a revival as a result of liberal interventionism, but also classical realism. Drawing on the work of Thucydides, among others, Richard Ned Lebow has set out a 'tragic vision' of international politics in which policies of over-reach and hubris lead to the fragmentation of alliances and the hollowing out of international cooperation and moral authority, eventually resulting in downfall of the great power.[29] He sees this kind of anomic unilateralism as visible long before the intervention in Iraq, stretching across the US withdrawal from the Anti-Ballistic Missile Treaty in 2001, through refusing to join the International Criminal Court, to disavowing the Kyoto Protocol in 1997 – among other policies.[30]

Yet, as beguiling and inescapable as tragedy appears to be in accounting for the grand questions of international order, it is limited in providing a complete or even a satisfactory picture of international order during the cosmopolitan era. While the US does indeed have a long pattern of unilateralism, the intervention in Iraq was the culmination of interventionism more than it was culmination of US foreign policy with respect to climate change or nuclear arms control agreements. Moreover, as we have seen, this was a pattern of interventionism that swept up Western states as a whole, including those that had maintained distance from NATO such as Sweden and France, yet had nonetheless also become more interventionist. Until Iraq, interventionism helped to solidify the Western alliance more than to fray it, and that pattern resumed after the diplomatic fracas over Iraq subsided. Indeed, Lebow himself tends to conflate the Western alliance system with international order *tout court*. Yet Iraq is not Syracuse, and while the Sicilian expedition of 415–413 BC may have brought Athens low in its war with Sparta, unlike Syracuse, Iraq was devastated by the US invasion, and however disappointing the strategic payoff of US firepower proved to be, it will not precipitate the end of US supremacy, but only signal a relative erosion of its lead over other nations. There will be no cosmic justice enacted against the US, and perhaps this essential lack of nemesis is a bitter and more tragic proposition to accept than the pattern of *elpis, atē, hamartia* and *nemesis* that structured Greek tragic drama.[31]

Thus, Lebow casts US unilateralism as anomic conceit and pathology, a turning away from cooperative ties within which its moral authority and self-identity are ultimately nested. In other words, US unilateralism as manifested in interventionism is a tragic deviation from international order. The problem with this is that the problems of international order are explained by reference to the anomic behaviour of the US – and this would be insufficient to explain the spread of interventionism, the rise of responsible sovereignty as a paradigm of government, or humanitarianism as an ideology of international order. In short, while tragedy may or may not be a useful prism for understanding world politics, it is not sufficient to understand either the origins or the effects of an interventionist international order.

Finally, if we turn to consider the argument for strategic traditionalism against humanitarian altruism, it is all too easy to be trapped in dichotomies between altruism and self-interest. However pragmatic, practical and hard-headed humanitarians have wished to seem, by its very nature the case for humanitarian responses to conflict *has* to be based on claims that stretch beyond self-interest, grounded in ethical claims to relieve human suffering. As Roland Paris notes, 'In the absence of altruism, it is simply "war"'.[32] The principles of just war have been invoked to mediate this dilemma, one of those principles being that a military intervention that risks sparking greater conflict, and thus greater harm, cannot be said to be just.[33] Thus, Libya, isolated and without great-power patrons (abandoned by its Western allies), and with thin air defences, was seen as a viable target, unlike the more heavily populated Syria, which enjoyed Russian military backing and stronger air defences to boot. At the same time, to be in any way meaningfully valid or logically self-consistent, there is no avoiding the fact that humanitarianism has, to some extent at least, been a-strategic – it cannot be driven purely by self-interest.[34] Thus, liberal interventionists have been buffeted between demands for ethical stringency and consistency, on the one hand, and, on the other, for pragmatic opportunism, to rescue imperilled and suffering humanity wherever they can (as exemplified in the contrast between Syria and Libya). This was indeed the first line of defence for liberal interventionists seeking to insulate their ideas from contamination with respect to the US intervention in Iraq. Here the claim was that whatever claims may have been made for human rights, the US intervention in Iraq was *too* strategic, too concerned with geopolitics and extraneous political concerns to be meaningfully humanitarian. At the core of the attempt to defend humanitarian intervention from contamination by the toxic legacy of the Iraq intervention was the claim that it was insufficiently altruistic.

To be sure, the use of force for humanitarian ends always requires a degree of political will, which in turn implies some degree of self-interest as a basic precondition. US intervention in Haiti, for example, melded an unwillingness to accept Haitian refugees fleeing military dictatorship alongside the opportunistic attempts of the Clinton administration to ingratiate itself with the Congressional Black Caucus.[35] Even in the case of the 1999 Kosovo intervention, inflated into nothing less than a cosmic clash of good and evil in the rhetoric of British prime minister Tony Blair, interests could still be discerned. The failure of the Serbian counter-insurgency campaign in the then breakaway province of Kosovo threatened to destabilise the regional post-war settlement that the Western powers had struck only four years earlier, and in which they were deeply invested, with peacekeeping forces deployed both in neighbouring Bosnia-Herzegovina and in Macedonia. That said, whatever the failures and brutality of the Yugoslav counter-insurgency campaign against Kosovar secessionists, it was clearly not a threat to core Western interests any more than it was a manifestation of cosmic evil. This was reflected in the conduct of the NATO air campaign, which, aside from its own infliction of civilian casualties, exposed the lack of strategy at the core of the operation: aimless, tactically ineffective against Serbian counter-measures, bombing with no credible threat of the use of ground forces, it eventually evolved into a rolling campaign of devastating civilian infrastructure with no purpose.[36]

For all that strategic traditionalists have inveighed against humanitarian drift in the use of force, it would be wrong to forget that, at a basic level, crafting strategy is hard.[37] The post-Cold War era has no monopoly on calamitous strategic failures, any more than the Cold War has a monopoly on cool, rational strategic pragmatism – one need only think of Vietnam, which was famously criticised by realists at the time for its crusading aspects and strategic blindness.[38] The problem with strategic traditionalism in inveighing against the strategic and political ineptitude of liberal intervention and humanitarian warfare is failing to explain it properly, instead of merely criticising it, or relying on explanation simply by contrast with the Cold War, the latter elevated into a higher plane of supremely confident statecraft.[39] The issue, then, is not so much that of greater or lesser strategising or fixating on what the genuine strategic aim or goal is or should be behind any particular intervention – but, rather, to locate military intervention as practice in an overall political context. Certainly, the nature of the Cold War endowed particular military interventions in the developing world with geopolitical interest that they otherwise might not have had. The fact that in the Cold War there was a political challenge in the form of Soviet communism and a military balance of power involving nuclear weapons would doubtless have sharpened thinking and strategic calculations about the stakes involved in military intervention, whether overt or covert. One need only think of the Soviet premier Nikita Khrushchev's menacing of London and Paris with atomic rockets following the Anglo-French intervention in Egypt in 1956, or the knowledge that Western military intervention in support of the 1956 Hungarian uprising would have precipitated a third world war.[40]

In other words, the absence of any limit to Western power – at least until the Russian intervention in the Syrian civil war – inflated by globalist ideologies of the redundancy and irrelevance of sovereign borders in the post-Cold War era, helps explain the lack of limits and the lack of clear objectives in the new liberal interventions. More than the presence or absence of strategic interests, this inflation of power also speaks to the changed character of the stakes in conflicts. Given that the stakes are lower in intervention today, and that there are fewer limits on power projection, taken together such circumstances discourage hard-headed thinking about political and strategic costs, trade-offs or even the clear identification of strategic goals. All of this makes the leeway for opportunistic moralising with military power all the greater. The strategic problems associated with intervention are embedded and contextual, therefore, not merely reducible to the errant feeble-mindedness of a particular generation of political leaders and policy planners, nor to a lapse of strategic rigour among the bureaucratic and military cadre of the state. Finally, it is also worth noting that the era of liberal humanitarianism did not emerge *ex nihilo* but has its roots in the earlier era of Wilsonianism, which stretches across the twentieth century.[41] Strategic traditionalists who hark back to the putative clarity of the Cold War era can hardly be surprised to confront a world in which war against constant, low-level global insurgencies and the US appetite for global leadership have become embedded.

The normalisers

Here we turn to one final set of critics of intervention who have specifically taken issue with the political and legal character of post-Cold War intervention. Their critique is rooted in thinking through the constitutional structure of international order and its legal and political characteristics.[42] As with the thinkers discussed above, the 'normalisers', too, are concerned with the damaging impact of intervention on international order. Their concern, though, is less with how the bonds of international order may be frayed, or how regional balances of power may be disrupted or military quagmires fester, but rather with how recurrent interventions have created legal and political precedents that are at odds with the existing constitutional structures and institutions of international order. It is a more holistic vision of international order than Charterism, seeking to go beyond merely contrasting one part of the Charter with the other. In particular, these thinkers focus on the exceptionalist character of intervention – how intervention has created an ad hoc alternative international regime, marking a break with the ordinary functioning of international politics. Their response has been to neutralise the destabilising impact of these exceptionalist politics by elaborating a new, more conceptually integrated regime, either through accepting a parallel regime of 'legitimate illegality' or instead recasting the international order as a whole so that it can accommodate the new humanitarianism. Their hope is that this conceptual reconciliation will provide the basis for an orderly evolution of international politics. Let us examine these two responses a little more closely.

In the first case, in his seminal legal study of modern interventionism *Just War or Just Peace?* Simon Chesterman criticised the recurrent exceptionalist justifications for intervention given by the UN Security Council – that is, the way in which each intervention was treated as an exception, governed by alternative rules and principles distinct from the ordinary and routine functioning of the United Nations.[43] Chesterman argued that not only did this accumulation of alternative justifications and precedents degrade the legal framework of the Charter, it also degraded the institutional structures of the UN, as the opportunism of the permanent five in persistently legislating on new 'threats to international peace and security' led to the inflation of the scope and substance of UN Security Council authority. The image that emerges from Chesterman's analysis is of a drastically unbalanced, top-heavy UN, straining under the weight of a resurgent and domineering Security Council, which was shredding the normative restraints on warfare embedded in the international legal order by repeatedly extending its legal recognition to various interventions.

Yet Chesterman had little means of constraining the enormous power of the permanent five within the legal resources provided by the Charter system, and saw that there was no political alternative to a concert with a collective interest in expanding and legitimating its power. Recognising the inevitability of intervention and concerned to preserve the Charter system from the interventionist canker at its core, Chesterman suggested a model of 'exceptional illegality'. Instead of the gradual legalisation of intervention that eroded the right to non-interference in the internal affairs of sovereign states, Chesterman suggested that the burden of justification be shifted away from a justification for non-intervention by states being intervened in, to a justification for intervention by the intervening states. In Chesterman's view, this would resurrect the normative presumption against war built into the Charter while also granting scope for the forceful relief of humanitarian suffering where possible.[44]

Chesterman's position is criticised by Jennifer Welsh as being unviable – on the grounds that the international order has already having been extensively reconfigured around interventionism.[45] Jean Cohen echoes similar concerns about Chesterman's model of exceptionalist illegality, arguing that there can be no return to a pre-interventionary era, and offers a different solution. Cohen is far more exercised than Chesterman about the challenge of humanitarian liberalism. She fiercely criticises the 'new security paradigm' that sees

> the seemingly arbitrary redefinition of domestic rights violations as a threat to international peace and security, and the selective imposition of debilitating sanctions, military invasions, and authoritarian occupation administrations by the [Security Council] or by states acting unilaterally ... framed as 'enforcement' of the values of the international community....[46]

Cohen is admirably clear that the human rights agenda and even more so the theorists of humanitarian intervention have contributed decisively to this new security paradigm. Indeed, Cohen sees the immensely powerful Security Council as modest and restrained in its legal innovations and exercise of political discretion when compared with the fierce demands for unilateral intervention emanating from theorists of humanitarian intervention.[47] She sees this as a shift in the human rights agenda, from the global civil society project of constitutional transformation and anti-authoritarian activism in Eastern Europe and Latin America to what she terms an 'enforcement model' focused on state-led projects of coercion through the imposition of sanctions regimes and military intervention. Here, Cohen sees the Security Council and hegemonic states as having hijacked the civil society regime of human rights and in so doing having undermined the Charter framework, usurping the interests and representative 'constituent power' of the international community at large with an imperial condominium. Whereas Chesterman takes his cue from the UN Charter in making his primary concern not sovereignty or self-determination but rather international peace, Cohen is particularly sensitive to the snuffing out of sovereign rights as the overarching framework for political autonomy. She identifies three moves in particular: the substitution of human for state security; the conceptualisation of human rights in terms of security; and what she terms the 'functionalisation' of sovereignty. She argues:

> By undermining respect for sovereignty as a principle of legal and political autonomy, the ideological discourse that accompanied the enforcement model [of human rights] paved the way for the present global security regime that is now threatening human rights, sovereign equality, and constitutionalism, domestically and internationally.[48]

Cohen's response to the degradation of international order is two-pronged. One prong is political and other legal, while the pole-arm is based around the European Union (EU). For Cohen, the EU needs to be strengthened, not only to act as a viable counter-hegemon to the US, but also as part of a process of global constitutionalism to sublimate the problems of the 'new security paradigm' in a world order that is simultaneously more politically pluralist *and* more legally integrated. In short, Cohen's response to the Council over-reaching its power is to proceed with solidifying legal and political power at the global level in more democratic and legitimate structures, deriving from an explicitly constitutionalist reading of the Charter that allows for legal supranationalism and devolved constitutional pluralism.

Cohen's global reformism is addressed to larger problems than military intervention and what she sees as the usurpation of human rights, so the full sweep of her ambitious and intriguing vision of global confederalism is beyond the scope of this chapter. Nonetheless, some critical observations can be made regarding the ultimate compatibility of interventionism and global confederalism. First, many of the concrete reforms proposed by Cohen amount to seeking to regulate, capture and crimp Council and unilateral practice rather than reversing or opposing it. She frankly acknowledges the limited character of such efforts – although an 'important step in the right direction', such limited efforts 'may be as good as it gets for the foreseeable future'.[49] Indeed, some of Cohen's specific proposals are remarkably close to the traits associated with humanitarian exceptionalism that she denounces. On the one hand, the constitutionalisation of the international order envisaged by Cohen involves curbing the veto and restructuring the Security Council. On the other, Cohen envisages a 'guarantor of international right and international law – a state powerful enough to ensure that others play by the rules to which it also subscribes' – language that is uncannily close to the discourse of the 'indispensable nation' promulgated by Madeleine Albright, US representative to the UN under the Clinton administration.[50] In seeking to avoid the Scylla of traditional sovereignty and the Charybdis of imperial cosmopolitanism, Cohen's pluralism ends up looking fairly similar to our current world order.

Cohen's project for global politics envisages an international order in which sovereign autonomy is preserved alongside enforceable human rights standards through the constitutional device of a Bund – a transnational political structure that is mid-way between a federation and confederation.[51] She is explicit that constitutional pluralism at the domestic and regional levels would substitute for the concept of sovereign equality in a globalised world order, made redundant under the new interventionist security paradigm.[52] While the constitutional device of the Bund may help to resolve questions of sovereignty and enforceable rights standards in a way that is at least legally consistent and rooted in a tradition of constitutional theorising and practice, it is difficult to see how it dispels the dilemma posed by political emergencies – whether humanitarian or otherwise.

A global Bund seeking to preserve a pluralistic, transnational order of political self-determination across a variety of states would mean that Cohen's Bund could not realistically rely on a standing army, as this would be too centralising and federal. *Without* a standing army, however, a global Bund system would be no more effective in collectively resolving when to enforce community standards of human rights than our current more centrifugal and decentralised global political system. A global Bund would face the same problems as the United Nations does: when, where and by whom would human rights be legitimately enforced across self-determining political entities? The effort to maintain such standards across states would inevitably result in such a Bund fissuring between those dedicated to maintaining human rights standards and those subjected to them, in turn reflecting and consolidating underlying hierarchies of power and inequalities of wealth. In other words, the same kinds of exceptional humanitarian crises that bedevil the UN would also tear apart a global Bund, and would rapidly disintegrate the buttresses that Cohen suggests could be used to bolster such a structure (Cohen lists reflexivity, tolerance, 'an internal attitude toward global law and willingness to justify legal interpretations in universal rather than parochial terms', as well as 'political legitimacy and prudence'[53]). Indeed, the attempt to normalise humanitarian intervention through a Bund could conceivably end up being even more destructive than it already has been in our current world order, not unlike the way in which Rawls envisaged any possible world state as 'a fragile empire torn by frequent civil war'.[54] We can see already how the centrifugal pressures of intervention and proxy wars in Syria and Ukraine have sharpened tensions between East and West at the global level; such tensions could conceivably be amplified in direct proportion to the world order being more institutionalised and integrated as it would be in a Bund.

Excursus: humanitarian liberalism as legitimation crisis

If we were to take a broader view of the international order, what might we say was the political and ideological significance of the 'new interventionism'? Most theories of humanitarian intervention cast it as part of a teleological story in which human rights continue to radiate outwards, expanding, diffusing and thickening around the world – and the removal of geopolitical rivalry on the UN Security Council facilitated this historic decompression of individual rights at the global level. The real story is more complex. The change in the global balance of power was clearly a precondition for greater Western military involvement in formerly non-aligned, ex-colonial and Third World states, but to see intervention as a spontaneous by-product of a shift in the balance of power would be to take such a high level of resolution as to be virtually meaningless. On closer inspection, what is important to note is that the new military humanitarianism was the result of a geopolitical contest which the West had won.

One of the few attempts to connect the growth of human rights in the international sphere to wider political changes at the end of the Cold War was provided by David Chandler. Chandler's argument was original and important in two respects: he was not afraid of drawing explanatory connections across the analytical and disciplinary divide between the international and domestic spheres of politics, and, more importantly, he also provided a wider political framework in which to contextualise the growth of human rights militarism rather than falling back onto the secularised gospel stories of human rights, the latter casting the growth of human rights as one of slowly expanding and densifying normative progress washing over the world. Chandler argued that human rights militarism grew not only out of an international transformation but also out of a domestic political transformation, which in turn required seeing the end of the Cold War not just as a shuffling about of bloc politics and international alliances but also involving a domestic political transformation – the ideological compression of the political spectrum, exacerbating the demassification of politics, and coinciding with the slow decay and fragmentation of party political systems that were rooted in Cold War ideological divisions – all themes, indeed, that have only grown more important in discussion of European political systems since then. In this context, Chandler argued that the legitimation crisis and deficit of Western, or at least Anglo-American, domestic political systems and parties prompted a search for moral boosterism, looking to renew political authority through military adventurism abroad. It is the legitimacy deficit that Chandler offers as the closest to a causal explanation of the 'new interventionism', occasionally even suggesting that electoral fortunes track episodes of intervention.

The logic of Chandler's analysis here resolves itself into an examination of electoral politics and foreign policy in Western states, for which, however, no evidence is presented and for which, of course, no evidence is available. The UK Labour Party won the 2005 election with Tony Blair at its head, despite the UK having joined the US in the enormously unpopular invasion of Iraq in 2003. The notion that a deficit of domestic legitimacy causes intervention has no predictive power; that is, it fails to explain why one particular intervention should happen rather than another, or to account for the expansion of the new interventionism, which has no obvious or immediate domestic political payoff for Western elites. Another problem for this line of analysis is the centrality of the US, whose post-Cold War domestic political evolution has followed a very different path from that of European political parties, the majority of which have ancillary rather than leading roles in propelling the new interventionism.

What we can take from Chandler is an acceptance that there certainly is a relationship between the post-Cold War decay of Western political systems and the new interventionism, but with the caveat that it is not likely to be an immediately causal or unilinear one. US political leaders in particular had already experimented with human rights as a substitute legitimating system for global leadership in place of anti-communism in the détente phase of the Cold War. In Europe, human rights had developed as a substitute for imperial power. With communism gone, human rights were already in place as a new power framework. The global context mattered because it transformed the significance of human rights – the circumstance of an ideological triumph was a historic vindication of Western political systems. This story is a familiar one – with the end of the USSR, the option of a possible epochal and systemic transformation of social order was eliminated. Among the post-historical theorists, it was accepted that there was a peripheral rump of disorder and misrule in the Third World and inner cities that would need to be controlled and managed, but the only remaining historic task of political transformation was no longer innovation but dissemination.

This new context gave a specific inflection to human rights, rendering them post-political or post-ideological: Western politics was no longer an ideological system whose historic claims were subject to dispute, which required the justification or active extraction of affirmative consent in order to function. In this context, the use of military force justified by reference to human rights was thus a vindication of Western political systems, an affirmation that the best societies in the world and in human history required no meaningful or systemic improvement – and every effort militarily to disseminate human rights affirmed this notion. Much as the 'small wars' of the late Victorian era provided the suitable backdrop to the halcyon era of nineteenth-century European bourgeois civilisation, so the 'small wars' of the 1990s and early 2000s – Kosovo, Sierra Leone, East Timor – provided the backdrop to Western victory in the Cold War, global prosperity and economic expansion.

Conclusion

Opponents of humanitarian wars have been subjected to remarkable calumny. Despite the appalling record of violent death and destruction and authoritarianism flowing from humanitarian and liberal interventions, opponents are still frequently cast as being inhumane, moral relativists, supporters of fascism and dictatorship, with no concern or regard for basic decency, let alone human flourishing. Yet even at their most modest, in a mild conservative concern for maintaining a degree of international order as opposed to driving through reckless change justified by liberal democracy and human rights, the anti-interventionists have been vindicated – if not in the annals of the discipline or in university seminar rooms, then in the devastation wrought across the Middle East. Collectively, the anti-interventionist critique of humanitarian militarism offers a salutary reminder of the importance of political order for human flourishing, and the fact that the circumstances of war itself, with its violent mayhem and disorder, create maximal opportunity for the very abuses humanitarianism seeks to curtail. The arguments of anti-interventionism concerning the need to preserve a stable international order have frequently demonstrated greater consistency and principle than those of humanitarian liberals.

Nonetheless, as we have seen, these various counter-arguments to humanitarian liberalism exhibit persistent weaknesses. Indeed, their failure is partly manifest in the fact that humanitarian liberalism itself persists as a justificatory discourse for war. Instead of expiring in the deserts of Iraq, humanitarian liberalism continues to provide pretexts for military intervention and even regime change, as we have seen subsequently in places as varied as Libya, Syria and Côte d'Ivoire.[55]

Part of the problem is that a consistent anti-interventionism is ultimately unviable – defined negatively in opposition to humanitarian liberalism, it cannot be sustained in a world of competing sovereign states. Or, another way of saying the same thing, anti-interventionism is beholden to exceptions. The arguments against humanitarian intervention immediately dissolve when confronted with the casuistry of humanitarian emergency, in which the experience of past interventions does not apply or the rules are seen to be redundant in the face of a new moral emergency of extreme human suffering. Post-hoc criticisms of the collapse of state institutions fade when held up against the prospect of imminent massacre, as when Colonel Gaddafi's forces descended on Benghazi, or when Syrian government forces use chemical attacks in densely populated civilian areas. In such circumstances, the question of whether or not to intervene inevitably recurs.

Given the enduring commitment to adventurist intervention displayed by a broad range of governments across the West and beyond, as well as the growing use of intervention by non-Western states, it is not difficult to see why people could claim intervention is now an embedded aspect of international order. At the same time, it would be wrong to overstate either the geopolitical conditions underpinning a more interventionist order, or the permissive domestic political conditions that make it possible. Similarly, it would be wrong to subscribe to an evolutionist or teleological view of the international order, making the mistake of restricting the notion of sovereignty to a fixed, arbitrary limit. More than this, the real mistake is to imagine that interventionism is capable of settling into a stable new order, in which interventionism is built into the ordinary functioning of the international normative and legal framework. To imagine this as a possible future is to misconstrue the character of intervention and political exceptionalism.

Instead of being trapped in these skewed debates around speculative counterfactuals (how many would die if we didn't intervene?), or the juxtaposition of known outcomes in Iraq and Libya against unknown unknowns (what would be the consequences of further intervention in Syria?), it is useful to shift our perspective to think through emergencies themselves as a mode of political action – how and why is humanitarian liberalism constructed around exceptional scenarios?

Chapter 3

What should we do? The politics of humanitarian exceptionalism

What should we do? There is a genocide, a civil war, a conflict, a natural disaster, atrocities, an oppressive government threatening a beleaguered population somewhere in the world, posing the question of how we should respond. It is a question that has consumed debate over Western foreign policy for a generation. Yet, despite a cumulative toll of many hundreds of thousands dead,[1] renewed great-power tensions between nuclear-armed states, a series of shattered societies and a growing assortment of protectorates, the eruption of every new humanitarian crisis is still subjected to the same set of amnesiac's questions. Should we 'go in'? Should we do something? Should we at least launch air strikes, if not put 'boots on the ground'? Do we need to establish safe havens, buffer zones or aid corridors? Does humanitarian relief need military protection? Can special forces be deployed? Is a UN mandate legally necessary or merely politically expedient? Or can we dispense with the UN entirely? Is partnership with a regional organisation required? When should peacekeepers be deployed?

The compulsive resort to force followed by recurrent amnesia about its consequences repeats across countries, governments and parties of both left and right – and it has lasted for thirty years, protracted under governments whose democratic pledges have included criticism of interventionism – notably the Obama and Trump administrations. Such pathological behaviour cannot be explained merely by the strategic ineptitude or crusading zeal of particular individuals or governments, and it is too systematic and strange to be accounted for merely by the logic of unintended consequences. Nor can it be explained by attributing uncanny powers of mass hypnosis, nefarious scheming or public seduction to our reigning elites. Rather, the pathological recurrence of failed policy on this scale suggests an underlying political paradigm at work – a paradigm in which we are all, to some degree, complicit. As a political paradigm, it involves an extensive and interlocking framework of ideas, institutions and policies as well as a constellation of political and intellectual elites that together reproduce the same outcomes in the face of contradiction, breakdown and failure. Given the cumulative scale of catastrophe, it is now no less urgent that we wrench ourselves out of this paradigm defined by the repetitive logic of disaster and rescue, and disaster again.

Part of the reason why this paradigm continues to function so effectively as a justification for military intervention is that it is based on the premise of overriding and highly specific humanitarian emergencies, which by definition nullify precedent and historical experience, and necessitate overriding other considerations. The issue was framed most succinctly by the late Kofi Annan, the former UN secretary-general: 'if humanitarian intervention is, indeed, an unacceptable assault on sovereignty, how should we respond to a Rwanda, to a Srebrenica – to gross and systematic violations of human rights that affect every precept of our common humanity?'[2] Yet, as we shall see, this poignant and pointed question, seemingly so simple, is also deceptively coercive and multilayered. The emergency hypothetical contains within it a number of assumptions and implications that channel thinking and ultimately political outcomes in particular directions. As we saw in previous chapters, military intervention continues unabated despite the fact that it seems to lack strong partisans and in the midst of general disenchantment and disillusionment with its outcomes and effects. This is, I suggest, the result of intervention being framed in the terms of political exceptionalism:

action in response to the most extreme circumstances that require violation of existing norms and institutions.

Interventions are regarded as aberrations defined by their anomalous character in response to extreme events – events that 'shock the conscience of mankind' in the words of the United Nations, terminology which has since become the standard adopted in international political theory. The exceptionalist cast of Annan's statement is evident. On the one hand, he accepts the importance of sovereignty as a *Grundnorm* of international order, while also implying that there are circumstances in which subverting sovereignty may be necessary. Annan is suggesting, implicitly at least, that while we may disagree about the legitimacy of particular interventions or even dispute the validity of humanitarian intervention in general, there are clearly circumstances in which everyone could reasonably be expected to agree to take action in response to human rights atrocities. Annan's statement here is thus clearly exceptionalist, that is, Annan's 'gross and systematic violations of human rights that affect every precept of our common humanity' necessitate, in the words of Ian Zuckerman, 'forms of action forbidden by general rules'.[3] In this case, it may necessitate an (otherwise) 'unacceptable assault on sovereignty'.

These gross and systematic offences against every precept of our common humanity could include events such as the Islamic State offensive against Mount Sinjar to enslave and exterminate the Yazidi people in 2014, the lassitude and incompetence of the Burmese government following the devastation of Cyclone Nargis in 2008, or the murderous brutality with which the Burmese military persecuted and expelled the Rohingya peoples of western Myanmar in late 2017. They could also plausibly include the recurrent use of gas against defenceless civilians over the course of the Syrian civil war, the massacre of captured prisoners at Srebrenica in 1995, and so on. Just as these are shocking, extreme events, so too are the humanitarian counter-responses understood to be aberrational. As we shall see below, the internationally sanctioned doctrine of the responsibility to protect sees international intervention as relevant only where states fail in their duties to provide protection – a final resort.

Even before the responsibility to protect formalised intervention as an exceptionalist measure in the international order, Nicholas Wheeler had already adopted the Churchillian discourse of world war in order to capture what was at stake in debates over the humanitarian use of force – in Wheeler's words what justified intervention was a 'supreme humanitarian emergency'.[4] Thus in this formulation the politics of humanitarian intervention was explicitly exceptional, that is to say, a politics that in the words of Zuckerman again, necessitated 'a suspension, break, or transformation of all or part of the fundamental formal or informal laws governing a political order'.[5]

It is worth pausing here to briefly emphasise the contrast between the contexts across which Wheeler transplants these exceptionalist claims. For an emergency to be an emergency, it has to fulfil three criteria, namely, temporal (the emergency has to be immediate), epistemic (it has to have been unexpected) and existential (it has to constitute a fundamental threat).[6] Churchill's original discourse, subsequently theorised by just-war theorist Michael Walzer in terms of a 'supreme emergency',[7] sought to rally the British nation to counter the existential threat posed by Nazi Germany to the autonomy and survival of the British state in the early 1940s. Transplanted to the context of a grave *humanitarian* emergency, there are some changes to the framing of the issue, with significant political implications. For a start, who is entitled to decide what constitutes a supreme *humanitarian* emergency? Clearly, any particular country has a right to decide for itself if it is existentially threatened, but what entitles a country to claim the *moral equivalent* of a national threat to its *own* survival, located in *another* state that poses no such actual, existential threat? Who decides when the conscience of humankind has been shocked?

Who can legitimately claim to speak for humanity and authentically represent humankind? Nonetheless, in circumstances of extremity, such questions are all too frequently put aside, and perhaps legitimately so – the situations are, after all, extreme.

Framed in this way, debate about intervention is obviously truncated. Indeed, the entire character of intervention and its different possible forms speaks to the fact that it is understood to be limited in scope and restricted in its aims in a way that, say, war was (traditionally at least) not supposed to be. Intervention is not cast as a general rule or ordering principle but, rather, it is about urgent expedient action to save human life and relieve or halt extreme suffering – and from such a perspective, other considerations are necessarily less important if not in fact redundant or illegitimate by default. If it is established that we are, indeed, confronted by a supreme humanitarian emergency, the relevant issues are immediately collapsed into questions of immediate efficacy, not general principle. Intervention is about remedial means of humanitarian redress: safe havens, humanitarian aid corridors, peacekeeper deployments, aid drops, ceasefires, bombing campaigns, deployment of special forces, refugee camps. It is not about a clash of competing visions for political and social order. Humanitarian intervention was never envisioned by its partisans as part of a single, integrated campaign of incremental global conquest to replace independent nations with a new transnational order, nor was it legitimised as an effort to substitute the sovereign state with new political structures. Even those who did not shrink from neo-imperialism and openly called for the globalisation of new forms of humanitarian trusteeship as the necessary post-war complement to humanitarian intervention saw the suppression of national autonomy as a temporary measure (hence the need for trusteeship), with political independence of sovereign states to be restored at some future point.[8] In other words, even in its most developed formulations, humanitarian intervention was always seen as a temporary break with the ordinary functioning of the international order, an exceptional, corrective use of force in response to an exceptional crisis.

Given that the problems of humanitarianism are formulated in these terms of emergency and extreme specificity, what does it mean to be for or against military intervention in such cases? We may disagree about the merits of a particular intervention. One may believe, say, that bombing Syrian government forces may be unwise because it may antagonise the Syrian government's patrons in Moscow and thereby precipitate an even worse conflict. At the same time, one could also consistently believe that we should support intervention in Libya, whose government was abandoned by its erstwhile allies in London and Rome, because in this latter case humanitarian redress could be successfully effected without precipitating a great-power conflict. Even the arch-exponents of intervention frequently disagree as to the cases in which intervention is or is not merited.

The point is this: however conservative, reluctant or cautious one may be about any particular humanitarian crisis or its possible resolution, *in principle* there will be some permutation of circumstances in which any rational person will concede that intervention is, on balance, justifiable, however anti-imperialist or isolationist that person may be. Even John Stuart Mill in his renowned 1859 essay 'A few words on non-intervention' – still the single best short critique of intervention – concedes that there are certain specific, exceptional circumstances in which overriding the sovereign right to non-interference may be merited (and this is to say nothing of Mill's embrace of imperial conquest against peoples that he deemed incapable of sovereignty).[9] Even were one to disagree with every single instance of liberal intervention stretching back to nineteenth-century European interventions to defend Christians in the Ottoman empire, through to NATO interventions in the current era, one cannot rationally and consistently be against *all* interventions in principle, as this would only be to say that one refuses to acknowledge that exceptional times exist – itself an inconsistent position. When every case is at least potentially a supreme humanitarian emergency – that is, by definition atypical, extreme, urgent – what does it mean to be for or against intervention in general? How is it possible to form any kind of general view on intervention in such circumstances, given that intervention itself is *not* taken to be a general principle?

The most elaborate and sophisticated structures of theoretical reasoning or models of world order may give way or legitimately be put to one side when confronting circumstances of extreme human suffering that are aberrational or extreme and, indeed, this putting to one side can be done without necessarily undermining general rules. Supreme humanitarian emergencies thus neutralise and override critical concerns and opposition. Every issue becomes one of expediency rather than political right: is it possible to relieve human suffering in these circumstances? Yet if the theory and discourse of supreme humanitarian emergency can effectively neutralise dissent, scepticism and opposition by transforming every consideration into one of simple humanitarian effectiveness, there is one issue that cannot be neutralised in terms that are consistent with the discourse. Namely, how can it be that extreme crises demanding such exceptional responses are so routine and recurrent? What does an international order look like in which the extreme of human suffering has become normalised, routine, even banal, and exceptionalist responses so persistent? This requires us to consider the politics of exceptionalism as such, and what it might mean in the international realm.

The politics of exceptionalism: domestic and international

Exceptionalism is a familiar trope in domestic politics, most typically associated with states of emergency that interrupt ordinary national political functioning. The problems of domestic exceptionalism are well established in law and politics: the risks of executive power usurping legislative, consensual and representative power; the distorting effects of the exercise of discretionary, executive power on the functioning of law, the danger of tilting the balance of constitutional order to the imperative of security over the preservation of liberty. Exceptionalism is frequently associated with creeping authoritarianism, as executive command displaces the influence of the mediated representation of civil society in the state, eroding the practice of democratic deliberation, empowering security agencies and the bureaucracies of the deep state, with supposedly temporary powers becoming entrenched, thereby permanently truncating certain civic and political freedoms and deflecting the trajectory of political development over the long run in sinister directions.

For exceptionalism to count, we need to be able to differentiate normality from the extreme, and this presupposes that there is a country of sufficient power and solidity that it can institutionalise a state of emergency in response to specific threats. Exceptionalism as a type of politics thus presupposes a nominally rational, secure, centralised and normatively stabilised and institutionalised political order. In other words, exceptionalism presupposes precisely that institution – the sovereign state – whose *absence* is said to define the realm of international politics as opposed to that of domestic politics. How, then, can exceptionalist politics be applied to the international realm?

Indeed, there is a whole tradition of theorising about international politics that takes the *absence* of security to define international politics in such a way that it could *all* be said to be exceptionalist, by its very nature. That is to say, this view would see the international realm as that political domain, characterised by command, force and the exercise of executive power against extreme threats, that prevents any possibility of long-term normative deliberation or legal institutionalisation that would enable the demands of security to be displaced by higher concerns and thereby transformed into a rational, predictable order. From this perspective of political realism, international politics is the realm in which exceptionalism is taken to such an extreme that it morphs into something that in fact constitutes the international realm.[10]

Even those traditions of liberal political theorising that self-consciously define themselves against realism presuppose the constitutive exceptionalism of the international sphere, precisely in the fact that they seek to 'domesticate' the international realm. That is to say, they seek to subdue its exceptional character by transplanting modified versions of domestic politics into the international realm in the forms of international law, institutions of cooperation and deliberation, and collective decision-making, for example with parliamentary-style international organisations such as the UN General Assembly.[11] Although liberals might see greater chance of domestication in international politics, they too begin from the premise that international politics is structured by exceptionalism, with the implication that all the legal and institutional achievements of international politics remain more fragile as a result. Exceptionalism, the capacity and will of the state to adopt emergency provisions that erode or transform the hitherto ordinary functioning of domestic politics, presupposes, then, a boundary between politics that happens inside and a politics that happens outside.

This returns us to the question that began this section: if it makes sense to characterise humanitarian intervention as exceptionalism, how can we graft the category of exceptionalism from domestic politics onto the international realm? Yet, as pointed out by Jef Huysmans, the very 'fact that one can transpose legal theories focusing on the state and domestic politics to international relations is not surprising, given that theories of the state are also theories of the political more generally'.[12] It is possible to concede that the international and domestic constitute two separate political systems without having to deny that exceptionalist politics might apply to both. After all, the exceptionalist claim of humanitarian intervention is to break down the barrier between the domestic and the international – it is to say that the domestic political system is unable legitimately to sustain its ordinary functioning, requiring international intrusion to restore security or to mitigate human suffering. For these reasons, we can be confident that we can graft theoretical concepts from one domain on to the other without worrying that they will not sink roots in the new soil.

In practice, of course, international relations has its own constitutional orders and eras, even if it has no central government – think of the 1648 Peace of Westphalia, the 1815 Congress of Vienna, the 1919 League of Nations and 1945 United Nations – all attempts to establish the principles of order and routine to enable predictable and stable interaction. Indeed, if the premise of liberal internationalism and institutionalism is to seek to 'domesticate' the international realm by reproducing the prototypical features of domestic rule at the international level, then, by the same token, we could just as easily transplant the politics of exceptionalism to the international sphere too, which is what might happen when a concrete, putative order of laws and norms faces extraordinary challenges that fall outside its reach, purview or capability to address. These eras crumble when they are incapable of dealing with new threats or challenges – exceptions or emergencies that disrupt the ordinary functioning of any given order.

Indeed, exceptional scenarios are constantly invoked as threatening to shatter the current UN order and to precipitate its collapse, thereby mirroring the lifecycle of the League of Nations. So US president George W. Bush warned of the threat presented by rogue states and the proliferation of weapons of mass destruction, and that, if the UN were unable to confront these challenges, it would go the way of the League.[13] As the example of Bush suggests, domestic order is usually based upon and imbricated with international order – particular eras of domestic governance across states correspond to particular eras of international governance, and extreme threats that justify exceptionalism in the domestic realm often emanate from the international realm and presage threats or challenges to that order.

To take one notorious example, the era of 'El Stanato' in Paraguay saw Alfredo Stroessner rule as an autocrat under a rolling thirty-year-long state of emergency in which Paraguay's fairly liberal and progressive constitution was in a permanent state of suspension, an act justified by the threat posed by the alleged global communist insurgency.[14] Or, to use a more recent example, domestic counter-terror legislation has expanded state surveillance in Western countries and has been justified by reference to the threat of global jihadist insurrection, which in turn motivates extraordinary wars – Afghanistan, Iraq, Syria. The extraordinary threat posed by jihadism has justified the normalisation of the state of emergency in France. President Emmanuel Macron changed the French constitution to incorporate the temporary provisions of the state of emergency originally passed by his predecessor, François Hollande, in response to the terror attacks of 2015, with the result that the powers of the police have now been enhanced.[15]

How much weight or emphasis any observer would care to place on the role of international norms, laws or institutions in integrating these international orders will differ according to individual inclination, theoretical bent and so on. Yet few would deny that international political history can be meaningfully partitioned into different eras governed by different patterns of institutional interaction that are not entirely reducible to, say, the underlying distribution of power or economic development. Even those of a realist theoretical bent, and thus typically sceptical of the viability of any normative project to restrain the exercise of state power in international politics, would still likely see a routine pattern of order, such as that of the 1815–1848 Concert era, built on stabilised, reciprocal expectations of great-power behaviour and self-conscious balancing.[16] Accepting that international interactions have some degree of routine underpinned by constitutive ordering principles, and that the international sphere enjoys a degree of normative institutionalisation, need not commit us to naïve liberal idealism about international politics.

Having established the possibility of discussing exceptionalism in the international domain, let us return to the question of humanitarian intervention – in what way is it exceptionalist, and what does it matter? As we shall see below as I adapt a typology devised by Jef Huysmans, there are different kinds of exceptionalist politics, with significantly different implications for international order.

Typifying international exceptionalism

If humanitarian intervention is indeed a form of exceptionalist politics as I have argued above, then why has it become normalised? How can exceptionalist politics be seen both as aberrational and extreme, and as recurrent, necessitating the repeated use of military force. How do we account for the schizophrenia of humanitarian politics? We also know that humanitarian and liberal intervention has involved not just violating or undermining state sovereignty, but also flouting international law as expressed in the UN Charter (Article 2[4], as discussed in chapter 2), as well as ignoring or subverting the will of the UN Security Council (Kosovo, Iraq, Georgia, Syria) and overextending it in almost every other case of intervention. To understand this apparent contradiction, we need to distinguish between different types of political exceptionalism. Jef Huysmans develops a typology of international exceptionalism in which he divides it into two essential types – what he calls *normative* and *existential* exceptionalism. Let us briefly consider each in turn, the better to understand the character of humanitarian exceptionalism.

Exceptionalist politics always involves political power transgressing an existing normative order – whether the norms be legal or political – when expediency and necessity are deemed to trump these norms. We have already seen that different theoretical perspectives would lead analysts to grant different weight to the role of norms, institutions and laws in the international sphere, as per the traditional realist/liberal divide in international politics. Nonetheless, however much views of international norms may differ, depending on where one is on the theoretical spectrum, normative exceptionalists will hold to the idea that politics exists in a dialectic with law. In this view, politics can be captured to greater or lesser degrees through the institutions of law, international regulatory regimes and agreements, organisations, treaty systems, and so on. Realists might discount the capacity of these kinds of institution in the international sphere but accept that they do apply in the domestic sphere. At the same time, however, even those realists who entirely discount the validity of international norms and institutions would see state restraint in international politics as a rational political choice rather than being effected by international legal and institutional restrictions. At the liberal end of the spectrum, the commitment to institutions may be sociological more than normative, in that liberals could see international organisations and governance regimes as a concrete means of embedding, regulating and institutionalising political decision-making without reference to the content or aspiration of normative codes.

With normative exceptionalism, the rationale for transgression will vary with where one sits on this spectrum. A liberal may make the case for exceptionalism by seeing that a specific concrete normative order is redundant, necessitating political discretion and innovation in creating a new normative order. An example of this would be, say, the US during and after the Second World War, when the Atlantic, Bretton Woods and San Francisco conferences inaugurated the United Nations order to substitute for that of the League, and the war itself represented a de facto normative and institutional interregnum between the two eras. This would correspond with that most basic and intuitive definition of political exceptionalism, in which norms are temporarily suspended in the interests of necessity or for some putative greater good. Alternatively, if exceptionalism is not seen as a burst of political creation needed to generate an entirely new order out of a normative interregnum, then exceptionalism could be justified in breaking the letter of the law in order to preserve its spirit, or as a plea for mitigation, in which the transgression is accepted but justified. This latter case could perhaps be seen in the example of India's justification for its intervention in East Pakistan in 1971 during the Bangladeshi war of independence.[17]

By the same token, on the realist end of the spectrum, where the least significance is given to legal or institutional structures and international politics is seen as being more defined by political expedience and necessity, the risks of transgression are different, less in damaging norms and laws as much as, say, undermining a country's international status, leadership role, credibility as an ally, or perhaps destabilising the balance of power and prompting countervailing balancing that will limit one state's room for manoeuvre in the international system. Whatever the varied emphasis given to the efficacy and role of institutions and laws, on this spectrum exceptional politics is seen to be limited in scope and time, and not in itself transformative or defining a political order. Pluralism underpins this view, in the sense that it is accepted by all on this spectrum that the interaction, coordination and organisation of multiple actors with potentially conflicting interests are the baseline of international politics.

In contrast to this normativist vision of exceptionalism, the other possible vision is existential according to Huysmans' classification. In this view, exceptions are seen as *defining* the political order and this is rendered meaningful through the transformation of the political identity of the actors involved. The extreme is seen to be as defining identity. This type of exceptionalist politics is 'existential' because the breakdown or rupture of a given set of norms or institutions is imbued with a deeper significance and seen to have potentially transformative effects. Huysmans describes this kind of response as 'political inwardness' – in which political identity is less defined through interaction with others, but rather through projections of collective self-renewal from the inside-out, a self-projection that requires the reassertion of political identity through the erosion or overturning of external, objective constraints on the expression of identity. As identity is emphasised, so political mediation is de-emphasised, whether that be horizontal interaction with other political actors, or vertical integration into supranational and transnational regimes, whether this be eroding the constraints of international law or spurning allies.

Again, linking the extreme to political identity is independent of the relative weight one might grant to the role of political power and decision-making as opposed to institutions and laws in the international arena. As with normative exceptionalism, so here, too, existential exceptionalism can be expressed in different ways, depending on whether one tends more towards realism or liberalism. Huysmans dubs these 'ultrapolitical realism' and 'ultrapolitical liberalism'. Within realist approaches to international politics, the intensification of existential exceptionalism, the assertion of internal renewal and self-assertion independent of others militate against a traditional realpolitik, which, even though it may countenance the radical expression of power politics beyond normative restraints, nonetheless accepts structured interaction and synthesis of other actors' interests through strategic coordination, alliance formation, balancing, and so on – all the traditional behaviours associated with classical diplomacy and power politics. In contrast to classical realpolitik, ultrapolitical realism justifies an 'extremely aggressive security policy that seeks to secure the political community by deleting difference and thus the need for its diplomatic mediation'.[18] Far from conceding the reality of political difference and conflicting interests, anti-diplomacy becomes the organising principle of ultrapolitical realism, a projection of political identity that requires the suppression of political pluralism and the homogenisation of different political actors (as with democratisation by force).

Huysmans sees Blairism in its crusading mode – the era of prime minister Tony Blair's 2003 Labour Party conference speech – as exemplifying this ultrapolitical realism, as well as the neoconservative policies of the first George W. Bush administration, in which expressions of US political identity were intensified through the invocation of an exceptionalist discourse of order and chaos, swirling with apocalyptic themes of globalised terror, rampant rogue states, irrational dictators and weapons of mass destruction:

> An example of [such] policies in the wake of 9/11 ... is a foreign policy that links assertions of an apocalyptic era with a policy of aggressively democratising the world through unilateral military intervention and that substitutes a universal assertion of moral values for institutional deliberation.[19]

As the war on terror introduced exceptionalism to the domestic political arena with the vast expansion of surveillance, curtailment of civil liberties and an empowered security apparatus, so this played out on the international stage through the subversion of existing norms and institutions with respect to prisoners' rights, a new globalised regime of torture and extraordinary rendition, as well as the subversion of international law and the UN in Iraq.

To schematise the above discussion: it matters a great deal how exceptionalist politics is conducted and envisioned. Looking at Figure 3.1, quadrants 1, 2 and 3 are more easily visible in the practice of international politics. Indeed, Huysmans' own work was primarily concerned with the international crisis precipitated by the 2003 Anglo-American invasion of Iraq and neoconservative visions of militarised global democratisation. In Huysmans' typology, quadrant 4 is the empty, mysterious, unmapped part of the grid – that of 'ultrapolitical liberalism'. In his words, 'The political position in Quadrant 4 is the most difficult to explain, because it combines an assertion of a normative order with cutting

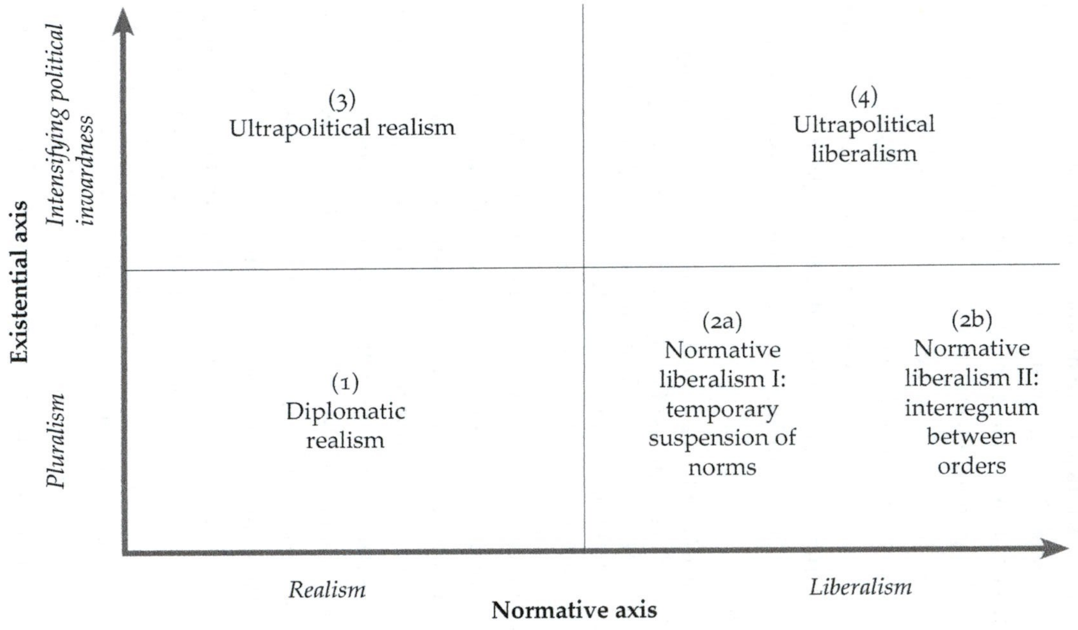

Figure 3.1: Mapping international exceptionalism. Adapted from Huysmans, 'International politics of insecurity' (2006)

off of common ground for symbolic interaction. Is this position possible?'[20] After all, if existential politics is established by slicing away the external constraints and mediating links that impede the renewal and self-assertion of political identity, how is such 'political inwardness' compatible with the international infrastructure – legal, institutional, normative, global – usually associated with liberalism? Although Huysmans argues that this seems to be 'a particularly powerful strand in the Western debate, about international politics after the end of the Cold War', he pleads lack of space to fully develop the argument, with the only example that he can give of such ultrapolitical liberalism being that of 'humanitarian intervention without the backing of the UN'.[21]

Arguing with and against Huysmans, I want to put the case here that post-Cold War, Western-led humanitarian intervention and the responsibility to protect are the embodiment of this 'ultrapolitical liberalism', or, better, 'cosmopolitan liberalism' (see Figure 3.2, p. 132). Going by Annan's statement, the threat is to our identity as human beings as such – our common humanity is *revealed* in the process of being threatened by 'gross and systematic violations of human rights'. This highly interventionist cosmopolitan liberalism bears all the hallmarks of existential exceptionalism, in which extreme challenges prompt the cultivation of new political identity, and which has involved the transformation of traditional, positive international law into a postmodern version of a new system of natural law centred on human rights.[22] The UN itself is correspondingly shifted from its state-centric focus based around mediating the pluralism that is internal to the society of states into becoming the direct institutional embodiment of cosmopolitan humanity, empowered to oversee individual rights and universal ethics at the global level, with the interests of state security deprioritised in favour of 'human security'. The doctrine of the responsibility to protect, I argue, represents the normalisation of this new order of cosmopolitan exceptionalism. Far from being the 'most difficult to explain' of the different varieties of international exceptionalism, I want to show that cosmopolitan liberalism and humanitarian exceptionalism are in fact the archetypes of international exceptionalism as practised by Western states since the end of the Cold War.

Before exploring specific attributes of cosmopolitan exceptionalism, we need to establish how exceptionalism is embedded at the core of international politics through the doctrine of the responsibility to protect.

Norming the exception: the responsibility to protect

The doctrine of the responsibility to protect has significant consequences for the structure of state authority and legitimacy, as we shall see in the next chapter. Here, we can trace the international consequences of responsibility on the global constitution, such as it is. As we saw in the introduction to the chapter, the bold era of humanitarian intervention would seem to be over – yet military intervention is as common as ever, still justified by humanitarian terms: witness the Western cruise missile strike against Syria as punishment for the use of chemical weapons against civilians in April 2018. In the Middle East, bombing campaigns, drones, 'military advisers' and special forces have replaced large occupying armies. Yet many diplomats, scholars, theorists and activists of various stripes loudly lament the lack of meaningful intervention in the Syrian civil war, and particularly the failure to abide by the promises of the responsibility-to-protect doctrine.[23] Identifying the shifting politics of exceptionalism at the core of the responsibility to protect will help us to understand how the doctrine can be pervasive while intervention itself always falls short of its proponents' hopes. To see this, we need to understand first how the doctrine was conceived as a response to the problems resulting from humanitarian intervention – the solution to which was to *institutionalise* the exceptionalist politics present in the earlier doctrine of humanitarian intervention.

Humanitarian intervention could never be easily absorbed into international society: as a claim to enact a higher right over that of the sovereign state, but which could only ever be exercised by sovereign states against each other, it was inevitable not only that such a doctrine would lead to clashes, but also that it could also be accommodated only by drastically distorting the political and legal principles that governed a decentralised, pluralistic and (in legal terms at least) largely egalitarian international order. That the language of human rights echoed so strongly the discourse of Christian altruism and moral righteousness that powered imperial expansion in the nineteenth century only inflamed the suspicions of those in the developing world. As Ramesh Thakur pointedly noted, 'in many non-Western minds', humanitarian intervention 'conjures up ... historical memories of the strong imposing their will on the weak in the name of human rights'.[24]

Perhaps even more importantly, however, it was inevitable that strong states claiming rights of intervention against weaker states would end up disagreeing as to where this principle could be legitimately applied, particularly if they began to encroach on each other's respective spheres of influence and allies. Humanitarian intervention in Somalia, a country without a governing state and an orphan from the Cold War, was very different from intervention in Yugoslavia in 1999, the latter a regime linked to Russia and whose conflicts mirrored those in which Russia found itself mired after the disintegration of the USSR. These in turn were different from the intervention in Georgia in 2008, the latter a US-allied regime bordering Russia and seeking integration into transatlantic security structures.

Although claiming inspiration from Rwanda, the doctrine of the responsibility to protect was crafted in 2000, following NATO's Kosovo intervention, and not following Rwanda's civil war of 1994. In other words, it was the breakdown in the great-power concert on the UN Security Council that prompted the turn to the responsibility to protect, and not the scale of human suffering: the Kosovo intervention took place without authorisation of the UN Security Council. This took the form of a report by an eminent international commission, sponsored by the Canadian government: the International Commission on Intervention and State Sovereignty (ICISS). The Commission consulted widely around the world, including in anti-interventionist capitals and cities – Beijing, St Petersburg and Cairo – before publishing its report. The ethos of that report was conciliatory, pragmatic and modest, generously acknowledging criticism such as the fact that the very language of 'humanitarian intervention' problematically 'loads the dice in favour of intervention before the argument has even begun, by tending to label and delegitimise dissent as anti-humanitarian'.[25] The report even acknowledged the fact that free-floating rights of intervention could prompt opportunistic insurgent movements to pursue destructive strategies of securing outside support, and that post-conflict reconstruction efforts should not degrade substantive autonomy by avoiding the creation of external political and financial dependence.

Although the report contained little that was substantively or conceptually new, it was, nonetheless, a remarkable document, at least by the standards of such reports.[26] Lucid and elegant, it effectively synthesised many themes of international conflict management – mediation, peacekeeping, conflict pre-emption, post-conflict reconstruction – and systematised them, conceptually integrating them as concatenations of a new paradigm of sovereignty that would become pervasive over the first decades of the twenty-first century, the modest and reasonable-sounding notion of 'sovereignty as responsibility'.

The report sought to allay fears of promiscuous intervention and human rights imperialism by restricting the remit of intervention. This was accomplished by emphasising the extreme, exceptional character of circumstances in which intervention was legitimate, and the legitimacy for such intervention was claimed through a brilliant sleight of hand. This involved claiming that the responsibility to protect belonged primarily to states, and it was only in the exceptional case of the failure to abide by this responsibility that intervention would be legitimate. The sleight of hand lay in shifting from the unarguable claim that states are bound to provide the public good of security to the claim that the failure to do so necessitates that the international community substitute for the incumbent state. With this sleight of hand, the commissioners warped the whole conceptual structure of modern political authority and representation – as we shall see in the next chapter. What needs to be noted here is that exceptionalism lies at the core of this doctrine – indeed, its claims to be an improvement on the doctrine of humanitarian intervention are motivated by exceptionalism. To ward off fears of opportunistic or predatory interventionism, the report emphasised that only the most extreme cases of human suffering legitimated intervention. Thus, the doctrine of the responsibility to protect emerged as a means of reconciling conflicting priorities of international law and order, and this was achieved through the attempt to norm the exception: identifying a set of extreme circumstances in which the authority of a state may be substituted by the international community (these became systematised as genocide, ethnic cleansing, war crimes and crimes against humanity – the four mass atrocity crimes).

Published only a few months after the terror attacks against New York and Washington, DC, in September 2001, the new doctrine was not born in propitious circumstances. As the US responded to the terror attacks, it seems that the high tide of humanitarianism would recede before the new tide of reinvigorated state security. Yet against all expectations, the responsibility to protect became in this same era an international consensus, even an orthodoxy. Not only did the doctrine survive over a decade of the war on terror, it also survived the invasion of Iraq, when many feared that the Anglo-US exploitation of humanitarian arguments to justify the invasion would poison the humanitarian well.[27] Only a year after the US withdrew from Iraq, the UN Security Council legitimated another war, which proceeded as if it had been scripted by the ICISS, complete with a Sino-Russian abstention from vetoing the NATO campaign against Libya on the grounds that they had no core interests to protect in that country. The doctrine of the responsibility to protect has sunk deep roots in international relations, and developed a canopy of UN special advisers, reports and resolutions, and a network of institutions dedicated to propagating the doctrine, as well as a dense foliage of theories, analyses and frameworks.

With all this unexpected success and hot-house growth, there has been much debate about how far the doctrine has been contaminated by the compromises needed for it to secure global approval. Indeed, at times it would seem that the doctrine was primarily designed to generate academic publications and workshops more than actual political outcomes. Endless controversy has roiled attempts to understand the doctrine. What is its precise status? Is it a form of 'soft law', a nascent form of customary international law, or an actual duty?[28] Does it apply to peacekeeping operations, and what about the other so-called 'pillars' of the doctrine – prevention and post-conflict reconstruction?[29]

Yet public debates on the expediency and necessity of military intervention draw little distinction between humanitarian intervention of the 1990s and supposedly transformed issues of the 'responsibility to protect' in the twenty-first century. One of the ICISS commissioners, Ramesh Thakur, fulminates against those who fail to appreciate the fine points of distinction between the doctrine of the responsibility to protect (R2P) and humanitarian intervention: 'it is difficult to know if the continued employment of "humanitarian intervention" in the academic world as synonymous with R2P is due to intellectual hubris, laziness or incompetence'.[30] However vociferously academics insist on the arcania of the R2P doctrine, political reality differs. In his memoirs, former British prime minister Tony Blair draws no distinction, seeing his own 1999 'doctrine of the international community' in which he justified intervention over Kosovo as lying on a continuum with the responsibility to protect.[31] Nor are all academics embarrassed to claim that the responsibility to protect essentially extends the ideas and practices of humanitarian intervention, as made clear by Mary Kaldor in her book on the topic.[32]

We can sidestep these debates among the proponents of the doctrine, because for those with no stake in propagating that doctrine, the issue to be accounted for is this very chimerical character. The responsibility to protect is at once quasi-legal, semi-institutionalised and politically insubstantial, yet with a very real legacy of war and destruction behind it. The chimerical character of the doctrine can be evaded by extrapolating into the future, seeing it as an 'emerging norm' that will consolidate itself in the fullness of time.[33] Instead, I would suggest that its chimerical character reflects the fact that it represents an attempt to normalise and embed the exceptionalist doctrine of humanitarian intervention into the structures of international society – and it is *this* that explains its unstable, shifting character. Thus, what matters for our purposes here is that what was already an exceptionalist doctrine, humanitarian intervention, was supposedly superseded in the form of the responsibility to protect through an attempt to embed exceptionalism, by claiming, in effect, that sovereignty *already was* exceptionalist, one sovereign state being interchangeable with another in the duty of providing protection. What we need to understand are the implications for global order of this attempt to norm the exception.

Beyond all the academic debates about how wide or narrow the scope for intervention is or should be, or how the doctrine addresses other aspects of military intervention, what is clear is that all permutations of the responsibility to protect retain its exceptionalist core: the claim that intervention should be restricted to the most extreme cases of human suffering resulting from state neglect or oppression, those cases that 'truly shock the conscience of mankind'. Understanding the exceptionalism of the doctrine also helps us to understand how the doctrine can be assimilated into state practice and international diplomacy so rapidly, while manifesting so little in terms of measurable improvements to conflict reduction or actual attempts at intervention.[34] The sceptics of the doctrine see this as expressing the bad faith and compromising of the doctrine, but this is only because they misunderstand how the doctrine actually functions. Once understood as a type of political exceptionalism, it becomes clear why so much political life can be reorganised around the principle of *potential* military intervention without manifesting any more *actual* military interventions. For what exceptionalism tells us is that it is about boosting discretionary political power, not restricting it. While the responsibility to protect has certainly made intervention legally easier and more politically legitimate for powerful states, for all those being victimised by state dysfunction, neglect and oppression, the responsibility to protect offers explicitly nothing except vague hopes and promises. So what kind of exceptionalism is it? Where would the responsibility to protect fit in the typology developed by Jef Huysmans, laid out in Figure 3.1 above?

Exceptionalism and universal sovereignty

The first point to stress is that the doctrine is built around the immanence of humanitarian emergency in international order – that is, the likelihood of its repetitive recurrence. If we go back to the question posed so poignantly by Kofi Annan at the beginning of the chapter, then we see that the massacres in Srebrenica and Rwanda constituted supreme humanitarian emergencies and that this is implicit in Annan's statement. Yet it is also evident that Annan is not talking either about the small Bosnian town, nor the central African country wracked by apocalyptic violence in 1994. Instead, Annan is talking of '*a* Rwanda', '*a* Srebrenica' – instances that are at once taken to be singularly terrible and yet also typical of a wider class of cases, the clear implication being that they are recurrent features of global politics. Thus humanitarian emergencies are seen here as both exceptional, in that they require extraordinary responses, *and* as repetitive phenomena, immanent to the processes of international politics.

The second point to note is that the doctrine necessitates significant reserves of concentrated political power outside that of the incumbent state: by definition, if the state is unable or unwilling to act, then external powers should act. The highest concentration of power is, of course, embodied in the five nuclear-armed members of the Security Council, whose role in maintaining international security is repeatedly affirmed throughout the various iterations of the doctrine of the responsibility to protect. Although there has been controversy over how far it is legitimate to confine enforcement of the doctrine within the UN system, even the 2001 ICISS report (which was willing to countenance unilateral 'protection interventions' outside the UN system) nonetheless disbarred the notion of intervention against a permanent member of the Security Council on the grounds of simple prudence: intervening against a nuclear-armed great power could unleash far greater human suffering.[35] Arguably, this logic could be extended to any nuclear-armed state, ruling out any kind of liberal or humanitarian intervention against India, Pakistan, Israel or North Korea. Perhaps one could also elaborate on the logic of the point: in order to ensure that there are states capable of intervening at all, it is important that there is a class of states exempt from possible intervention. Otherwise, were powerful states such as France, the US or the UK to be devastated by an intervention the same way Libya, Serbia, Iraq, Georgia and so on have been, we would end up in a situation in which no state was capable of maintaining the global humanitarian order. In short, for the doctrine to function, there need to be states that are exempt from it.

Although the doctrine does not necessitate intervention by the permanent five, with regional organisations or capable neighbouring states being acceptable substitutes, it is clear that there must be a backstop to the doctrine in order to provide some measure of firmness to the expectation of halting mass atrocity crimes, and that this backstop must be the great powers. In practice, this must encompass, most importantly of all, the P1 – the only state in the world capable of mounting global military operations simultaneously in multiple theatres, which must sanction intervention either implicitly or explicitly.

To be sure, documents of the responsibility-to-protect doctrine invariably list multiple actors with the potential duty to enforce the doctrine – but all this does is, paradoxically, reinforce the imperfect duties at the core of the doctrine – that is, the lack of any agent obliged to enact it.[36] There is no automaticity in the doctrine of the responsibility to protect. States are consistently willing to subscribe to that responsibility as long as they can preserve their room for manoeuvre and avoid any cast-iron commitments to intervene at specifically articulated junctures.[37] Importantly, therefore, an actual response to a mass atrocity crime remains at the discretion of the 'international community', which, in the end, will be the political will of major and powerful states (even if only to endorse intervention by a smaller power or to subsidise the activities of a regional body such as the African Union).

The commitments offered in the doctrine therefore extend a wide-ranging implicit guarantee of the global humanitarian order, but the concrete exercise of that guarantee is left to political discretion, which will need, at some level, to have the backing of the Security Council. What we have, then, is the potential discretionary exercise of military force within a potentially global space of application, in which this force is built into maintaining and guaranteeing the *form* of the humanitarian norm, while explicitly *not* committing to upholding the norm in every particular instance.

Here, then, we have an exceptionalist paradox derived from the need to prevent recurrent mass atrocities: we have the requirement for a political actor that, on the one hand, maintains a given normative order, while, on the other hand, also being exempted from it – it patrols the walls of this humanitarian order but does not enter through the gate, to paraphrase Robert Kagan. This actor is the UN Security Council, and especially its permanent five members. In the responsibility to protect, we have a normative order organised around limiting mass atrocities, which requires power that is not derived from or internal to the system of norms in question – effectively, a legally underived power. The recurrent possibility of humanitarian emergency, and the recurrent possibility of the failure of incumbent state authorities to prevent or halt mass atrocities, entail that the arbitrary, discretionary exercise of global power must be a 'permanent and immanent condition of normative order'.[38]

At the same time, enactment and enforcement of the doctrine remain at the discretion of that great power. This is a decisionistic model of humanitarian action – *decisionistic* because the normative order is maintained by the recurrent, discretionary exercise of political power. In this case, the recurrent transgression of sovereignty is seen to be a permanent, immanent feature of world order. Decisionism is not, properly speaking, a theory of the extreme at all, but rather normality – in which normality is defined through the exceptional. In Huysmans' words:

> Like normativist positions, decisionism seeks to incorporate normative exceptions into a legal order, but unlike normativism it makes arbitrary exercise of power, and thus exceptions, a normal phenomenon that is inherent in legally defined political orders.[39]

Huymsmans' explanation of this point is worth quoting at length, as he shows that decisionism is *not* an anti-normative politics akin to a vulgarised political realism, but rather:

> it asserts that the international rule of law can only operate under the watchful eye of the universal sovereign who guarantees the conditions of existence of the normative order, against enemies and against factual situations in which existing legal

procedures do not result in a decision. The universal sovereign guarantees that a decision will be made and that the essence of the legal form, the imperative to come to a decision, irrespective of its content, is continued. For decisionists, the exceptional exercise of political power by a universal sovereign is thus a normal, permanent, and necessary phenomenon in international relations.[40]

As we saw in chapter 2, the typical pluralist concern with intervention is that it represents a specific threat to the basis of the international political order and that it cuts at the normative restraints on war. This view is most pithily expressed by David Chandler:

> The term for the type of 'higher law' which justifies waging war, in spite of international law, is the law of the jungle, or a return to the pre-UN forms of 'anarchic' international society, in which the use of force was unregulated.[41]

Such a view is, however, to misconceive the claims embedded in the responsibility to protect, as if the likelihood of war is dependent on how tightly international law squeezes and binds the use of force. Instead, as Huysmans emphasises, decisionism is expressly *not* a political and theoretical critique of the international rule of law. Rather, decisionism sees exceptionalist responses as 'a permanent and inherent element of an effectively functioning normative "paradise"'.[42]

This decisionistic view of the global humanitarian order has repercussions for the role of sovereign states. Whereas in the domestic sphere, the sovereign is understood to have independence of the law in its very capacity to create law, in the international sphere the need for a power that guarantees the form and structure of international norms in the event of breakdown *and* that is external to the system of norms themselves can only entail a more ramified international hierarchy, with those capable of maintaining the global order accruing greater exemption and privilege within the international legal order. The tendency, then, of global humanitarianism, as embodied in the responsibility to protect, is to concentrate power and authority in a universal sovereign on the one hand, and to hollow out sovereignty as an attribute of all other states on the other. In particular, the doctrine scrubs out the space of sovereignty as autonomy – that space in which polities can develop, shape and articulate their political will independently of others – a capacity in which legal and normative barriers to the international use of force are vital. In responsibility-to-protect discourse, state sovereignty is repeatedly presented as the freedom of the state to repress its citizens with impunity rather than the capacity to generate political will independently of external influence.[43] Little wonder, as Jean Cohen argues, that we have seen a revival of a bundle theories of sovereignty that see it as a package of varied tools and capacities that can be stripped down or enlarged as needed – rather than as an expression of unified collective political will.[44]

With the corresponding tendency to elevate a single state as universal sovereign, force and power necessarily erode collective political agreement or institutionalised legal frameworks as the basis on which to secure normative order. Importantly, the new emphasis on force also reconfigures its place and role in international norms, endowing the international use of force with a new prominence. In the new humanitarian order, force is not being used to repress or deter inter-state wars as per the old vision of collective security, nor even to contain civil wars as per the post-Cold War model of UN activism. Rather, it is being wielded to enforce and uphold the simple shape of state authority itself. Under the terms of the responsibility to protect, the international use of force merely exercises the protection duties of the incumbent state when it is unable or unwilling to do so.

There is no escaping the fact that what such a global political order most closely resembles is a Schmittian global constitutionalism. We have a universal sovereign, and that sovereign is the power that upholds the framework of global humanitarian norms while not being bound by them, intervening on a discretionary basis when the existing normative order breaks down or fails, with extreme crises being an immanent feature of the normative order. In Schmitt's political theory, power allows for the imposition of a decision over existing institutionalised procedures, legal authorities and normative processes – the exception, when formal processes fail. The tendency of the responsibility to protect is to shift from questions of procedure or legitimacy of representation to questions of competence – who has the power to enforce a decision? Political power is justified not by reference to its representativeness but by reference to its effectiveness: in this, the responsibility to protect is eminently Schmittian.

This vision of universal sovereignty that is generated through upholding the global normative order also strongly resembles the neoconservative vision of international politics in which the US is the singular state capable of exercising the power necessary to maintain international normative frameworks. Importantly, the neoconservative vision is not opposed to a legally defined political order at the international level – but, rather, sees that exceptionalist power best embodied in US might, as 'a necessary and permanent condition of the international rule of law'.[45] The responsibility to protect legitimates the exceptionalism of universal sovereignty, complementing its other exceptionalist claims:

> The universal sovereign judges without being judged, disarms without disarming itself, controls the authority of the global institutions at the heart of the normative order (the UN) without being controlled by it, and imposes financial policies without imposing upon itself.[46]

This double standard is the common currency of neoconservative and postmodern visions of political order.[47] As a political theory of international order, the responsibility to protect is not a theory of crisis (in that it is limited to extreme situations) but rather humanitarian crisis is made into a permanent and general condition of political legal order, both within states and across them. Indeed, perhaps the only significant difference between the universal sovereignty embodied in the responsibility to protect and neoconservative political theory is scope and clarity: neo-conservative thought extends the scope of exceptionalism across the entirety of international normative order rather than being restricted to humanitarian norms alone.

The neoconservative project is beyond the scope of this book, but significant elements of existential exceptionalism are embedded in neoconservative thought and practice, and these produce similar effects of anti-diplomacy and sovereign suprema-cism (Figure 3.2 and see below). While the existential concerns of neoconservatism are buried more deeply than those of humanitar-ian liberalism and stretch back to a theory of modernity itself rather than merely a response to the horrors of the twentieth century, the neoconservatives have nonetheless cleaved tightly to humanitar-ian interventions as opportunities for exemplary demonstrations of the use of force in the maintenance of international order.[48]

In some respects, here the neoconservatives are more self-aware than humanitarian liberals for seeing the need for political confrontation and the friend–enemy dialectic as constitutive of *internal* political cohesion and sovereignty. Neoconservatives also have a more fully justified articulation of sovereign suprema-cism, where US exceptionalism is justified not as a result of the representation of the interests of US citizens, but as the supplier of global order through the exercise of state power.

For humanitarian liberals, sovereign supremacism is less the willed choice for generating political cohesion through confron-tation and more the by-product of the need for humanitarian enforcement – the need for existing power to actualise the new system of natural law embodied in human rights. The point is important to understand the paradox of humanitarian liberalism: despite the inverted revisionism that cuts against Charter law and subverts the functioning of the Security Council, humanitarian liberalism is not positioned as anti-normative per se. Humanitarian liberals do not oppose a world built around legal principles and

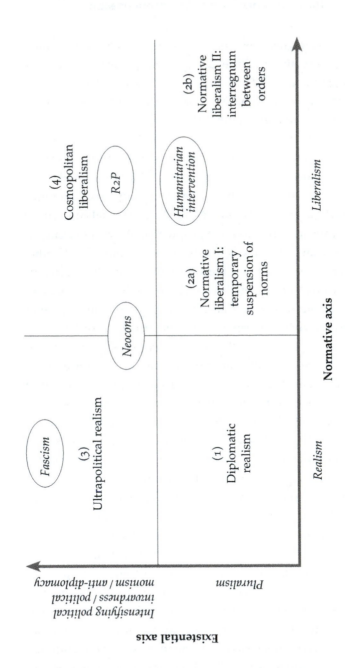

Figure 3.2: Locating cosmopolitan liberalism. Adapted from Huysmans, 'International politics of insecurity' (2006)

institutions. Quite the opposite: the era of human rights has seen the proliferation of international courts and a thickening of international criminal and humanitarian law – to say nothing of the dense network of NGOs and other civil society organisations built around the defence and promotion of human rights. All of this coexists, as we have seen, with the grave destabilisation of the international order and the sharpening of great-power antagonisms around the promulgation of intervention. While it is clear that humanitarian liberalism provided ideological ornamentation for the era of post-Cold War Western hegemony, this most basic realist insight cannot explain the specific forms of humanitarian liberalism, nor why it produces inverted revisionism.

Instead of seeing law as aggregating and formalising the political will and agreements of many states, humanitarian liberalism sees human rights law as necessarily higher than either state law or political will. Actualising this supranational human rights law in the states system requires significant political and military state power – hence the collapse of humanitarian liberalism into decisionistic sovereign supremacism, as mediated through the doctrine of the responsibility to protect.

If existential exceptionalism reveals deeper, more authentic forms of human identity *in extremis*, then this new political identity perforce must express itself against external limits and restraints. In international politics, according to Huysmans, this will mean cutting away at 'objectified frameworks, such as international law, multilateral security frameworks, and institutional frameworks based on cost–benefit calculations'.[49] Humanitarianism and liberal interventionism have consistently involved the attempt to thwart, outflank, undermine or collapse such objectified frameworks of international interaction. Most obviously, of course, intervention has necessitated undermining the cardinal rule of international order, that of non-intervention, without which, indeed, the very notion of international order as comprising multiple independent states is a nonsense.

However, claiming rights of intervention against those of sovereign states necessitated not only cutting against the practice of international law as enshrined in the UN Charter, but also subverting other existing practices and institutions. That this was deeply damaging and divisive is evident in the diplomatic controversy this caused, escalating at its worst into the UN 'constitutional crisis' over Iraq, in which the US and the UK ignored the prerogatives and authority of the UN Security Council, and for which the 1999 Kosovo War was the precursor. The confounding and disorganising effects of humanitarian politics have been elaborated in the repeat calls for the permanent five members of the Security Council to refrain from exercising their vetoes in situations of humanitarian emergency if their core interests are not at stake.[50] In other words, these are calls on countries whose vetoes are justified by the fact that they are global powers to refrain from casting their vetoes in situations of conflict that they are legally mandated, as global powers, to take responsibility for managing.

Against the imperative of humanitarian urgency, politics always fails: human suffering is cast against the sordidness of accommodating competing interests, against the lethargy of institutional processes and bureaucratic sclerosis, and against the sterility and remoteness of international law. Against humanitarian imperatives to relieve suffering, politics will always be found wanting. It is the United Nations and positive international law that have thus often borne the brunt of these moral criticisms, resulting in significant institutional reorganisation of peacekeeping following the early 1990s, and the warping of international law, with its relatively pluralist and egalitarian character being restructured around hegemonic and hierarchical paradigms of criminalisation and a new 'standard of civilisation'.[51]

Needless to say, bitter divisions at the UN are nothing new, nor is contempt for the organisation's putative incompetence and lassitude. Yet in the Cold War, UN gridlock was associated with a political conflict between the superpowers. Depending where one stood politically determined how one identified the nature of any particular political problem. In the immediate post-Cold War era, harmony tended to prevail on the Council. This was the precondition for the energetic expansion of the Council's remit over the 1990s, pushing its authority into new realms, such as the environment and civil wars. Yet this new global concert could not last and, indeed, it disintegrated in disputes over intervention, with clashes of growing intensity and bitterness over Kosovo, Iraq, Georgia, Libya, Syria and Ukraine. While the Council today is still not as deadlocked as it was in the Cold War, it has returned to an era of bitter, open recrimination and choreographed diplomacy by veto. The destructive effects of humanitarian norms have thus gone beyond the rivalries of the Cold War, however, inasmuch as it is politics itself that is seen to be problematic: governments in the developing world have been repeatedly cast as intrinsically corrupt and suspect in terms of delivering humanitarian resources to their populations, and any claims to be representative are seen to be illegitimate and partial, necessitating international oversight such as that embodied in the responsibility to protect.[52] Humanitarianism has helped to delegitimise politics as such, particularly in the developing world, casting the political sphere as elitist, corrupt, obstructionist, inhumane and inauthentic. The responsibility to protect has reinforced this tendency, with security trumping representation as the criterion of legitimacy (on which, see more in the next chapter).

Anti-diplomacy

This type of outlook and behaviour in which international diplomacy is subverted, in which the accommodation of interests is denounced, and the existence of separate interests and political pluralism itself is seen to be intrinsically illegitimate are so at odds with conventional expectations of international interaction that it seems a new category is appropriate. Jean Cohen talks of 'solipsistic sovereignty' in her 2012 book *Globalization and Sovereignty: Rethinking Legality, Legitimacy, and Constitutionalism*, but perhaps the most conceptually appropriate term is 'anti-diplomacy', inspired by Martin Wight's criticism of Wilsonian foreign policy in the inter-war period.[53] James Der Derian formalised the concept by contrasting it to diplomacy: 'the purpose of diplomacy is to *mediate* estranged relations; anti-diplomacy's aim is to transcend *all* estranged relations'.[54] As per Der Derian's conceptualisation, what defines and underpins these anti-diplomatic types of behaviour is the drive to suppress, if not eradicate, international political pluralism – the notion of a political order based on multiple power centres with divergent interests reflecting a multiplicity of political systems. Recognition of the political divergence of interests is derided in favour of the global projection of identity. Not unlike anti-diplomacy, inverted revisionism is the negation of the traditional category of revisionism – the theoretical expectation that emerging powers will seek actively to subvert and restructure international law, institutions and organisations to accommodate their interests.

Typical traits of anti-diplomacy for the humanitarian era include heavily moralised language that subverts and precludes negotiation, and the criminalisation of war that erodes sovereign impunity and may discourage and subvert the possibility of negotiated settlement and peace agreements. The incoherent shambles of the Western response to the civil war in Syria evinces this, as when the former British prime minister David Cameron argued on the one hand for negotiations with the government of Bashar al-Assad while also saying that Assad would have to face criminal charges for war crimes committed by his forces.[55] The moralising discourse of humanitarianism has delegitimised dissent and clashing interests – the very core of traditional diplomacy. The scale of the disorder and the magnitude of the unintended effects resulting from Western interventionism prompted Russian president Vladimir Putin to bait the Western powers in his speech to the seventieth anniversary session of the UN General Assembly on 21 September 2015: 'Instead of the triumph of democracy and progress, we got violence, poverty and social disaster — and nobody cares a bit about human rights [...] I cannot help asking those who have forced that situation: Do you realize what you have done?'[56]

Anti-diplomacy is not new: as suggested in Martin Wight's original criticisms of Woodrow Wilson, liberal international politics has a deep affinity with anti-diplomacy, as embodied in the Wilsonian notion that the world community would converge around common interest and homogenised, liberal democratic political systems. More recently, the Cold War was rife with anti-diplomatic behaviour – 'diplomacy by insult' and 'oratorical contest' as described by Hedley Bull.[57] One need only think of the anti-diplomatic grandstanding and manoeuvring seen on the UN Security Council, which has now returned in a humanitarian form. As a species of liberal politics, it is no surprise that the humanitarian politics of a cosmopolitan era should have anti-diplomatic traits. If anti-diplomacy is not new, then, following the logic of Huysmans' theory, humanitarian anti-diplomacy is the outward expression of a mode of politics focused on establishing deeper, more authentic and meaningful political identities rooted in opposition to extreme suffering and violence.

Political inwardness

Humanitarian intervention, international cosmopolitanism, the responsibility to protect are all known primarily for their suspicion and hostility to traditional conceptions of state sovereignty. It might come as a surprise therefore to note how the erosion of sovereign rights has corresponded with a renewed and reinvigorated claim to the political supremacy of state power – most noticeably in neoconservative justifications of force that combine humanitarian visions of intervention with the claims to US

exclusivity. In parallel, Russia has championed traditional interpretations of international law while claiming the same right of
intervention for itself as Western powers have enjoyed – right
down to cribbing the relevant *opinio juris* and UN resolutions.
Far from levelling the sovereign state or state power in general,
the age of humanitarian warfare has reduced the power rights of
some states while boosting that of others – unsurprisingly, mostly
those states with the power to enforce the new postmodern
natural law embodied in international human rights.

Yet this apparently unexpected result is consistent with what
would be predicted by humanitarian exceptionalism – existential
exceptionalism breeds the drive for a more authentic political
practice and identity manifested outwardly in an anti-diplomacy
of moral superiority, and in its disavowal of the most basic structures of political pluralism in the international order, denying
not only rights to non-interference in the internal affairs of other
states but also the legitimacy of competing interests *tout court*.
The result is not a global cosmopolitanism of inclusive new
supranational political structures. Instead we have seen the sovereignty of some states expanding to flatten out the sovereignty
and autonomy of other states, with the resultant hegemonic
polity circumscribed by no articulated frameworks, institutionalised or alternative poles of power, rights and interests. In this
model of sovereign power, the notion that sovereignty entails
equality between sovereigns is gone, in favour of specific sovereigns whose claims are not only more powerful in material terms
but also come with greater right.

Following the logic of Huysmans' framework, exceptionalism
and existentialism should correspond to a politics of inwardness
and authenticity – exceptional existential challenges being the
opportunity to disclose new identities. On the face of it, that
humanitarianism should be inwardly-oriented would seem a
strange claim – given that it is so strongly associated with charity,
compassion, external orientation to distant problems and the

suffering of others – 'saving strangers', as per the title of Nicholas Wheeler's classic study of humanitarian intervention.

Yet some of the most discerning analysts of intervention have been attuned to the fact that, for all the effusive spectacle of alleviating human suffering and gushing altruism associated with humanitarianism, it is an ostentatious disguise for a peculiar kind of identity politics. This observation was shared by analysts across the political spectrum and various theoretical traditions and, indeed, across both advocates and critics of humanitarian intervention. These most acute observers have long suspected that it was precisely the overly ostentatious character of humanitarian altruism that gave the clue to something else occurring. The French postmodernist thinker Jean Baudrillard, who criticised the prevarication over Western military intervention in the Bosnian civil war, held a unique perspective on the aid corridors protected by UN forces to supply the besieged Bosnian capital, Sarajevo:

> it is necessary to go and rebuild a reality for ourselves where the bleeding is. All these [humanitarian aid] 'corridors' we open up to send our supplies and our 'culture' are, in reality, corridors of distress through which we import their strength and the energy generated by their misfortune.[58]

The failed Canadian politician Michael Ignatieff, rector of Hungary's Central European University at the time of writing, has long suspected that such interventions ultimately had little to do with alleviating suffering in the countries concerned. With remarkably lucid cynicism, he observed:

> The Western need for noble victims and happy endings suggests that we are more interested in ourselves than we are in the places, like Bosnia, that we take up as causes. This may be the imperial kernel at the heart of the humanitarian enterprise. For what is empire but the desire to imprint our values, civilisation and achievements on the souls, bodies and institutions of another people? Imperialism is a narcissistic enterprise.[59]

Despite this insight into the ultimate lack of concern in the humanitarian enterprise, this did not stop Ignatieff from supporting liberal intervention, extending even to his support for the invasion of Iraq.

By way of contrast, David Chandler, a stringent critic of intervention, observed how domestic concerns and assertions frequently shadowed even scholarly and theoretical discussions of international human rights, and in particular concerns about the need to maintain social cohesion and morality through the defence of human rights abroad. Citing intellectuals such as Ignatieff as well as David Rieff and Mary Kaldor, Chandler observes that the

> human rights discourse of ethical politics, whether taken up by political engineering liberal academics and journalists or by pragmatic governments, has little to do with addressing real problems in the non-Western world and much to do with responses to the fragmentation of the political framework domestically.[60]

At the same time, discussions of effectiveness in humanitarian intervention were shadowed by frustration at the popular passivity, apathy and ultimate indifference towards intervention. Indeed, the intellectual supporters of humanitarianism openly touted their concerns as to whether democracy itself, with its predilection for materialist self-interest, was capable of rising to the demands of humanitarian altruism, in terms of the blood and treasure required to reshape the world.[61] The humanitarian authenticity that emerges through the extreme suffering and dislocation is a new type of global solidarity and connection. Responding to crisis and humanitarian emergency in turn constitute the identity of exceptionalist actors, as indicated in the commencement speech delivered by US president Barack Obama to West Point graduates in May 2014. In this speech, he outlined a globalised vision of traditional US exceptionalism:

> From Europe to Asia, we are the hub of alliances unrivalled in the history of nations.... And when a typhoon hits the Philippines, or girls are kidnapped in Nigeria, or masked men occupy a building in Ukraine – it is America that the world looks to for help. The United States is the one indispensable

nation. That has been true for the century passed, and will likely be true for the century to come.[62]

In many ways, the politics of humanitarian response is the prototypical form of exceptionalist politics in our era, and it was humanitarian emergency that pioneered the wider dystopian politics of risk, disaster and generalised emergency. As perceptively observed by International Relations theorist Zaki Laïdi, 'our societies claim that the urgency of problems forbids them from reflecting on a project, while in fact it is their total absence of perspective that makes them slaves of emergencies'.[63] The cumulative result of emergency politics has been a collapse of political perspectives and the prospects for deeper, systematic transformation.

The paradox of authenticity is that it can be demonstrated only by straining against existing political institutions, normative frameworks and structures that by default are rendered inauthentic and need to be cut away or restructured – hence the anti-diplomacy and inverted revisionism associated with the rise of humanitarian and liberal interventionism. In Huysmans' words, 'This political concept of inwardness defines the exception in the first instance on the basis of a break with ... the normal everydayness of politics, characterised by objectified forms of mediating relations with others rather than a collapse of norms'.[64] The need for Western / US power to maintain the humanitarian order complements the solipsistic nationalism of the US, as the indispensable nation whose security and freedom is intertwined and necessitates global protections. It complements the Western conceit that they are the states that must bear the burden of maintaining global norms and humanitarian order.

Conclusion

We have seen, then, that, at the core of the responsibility to protect, is an effort to norm the exception, and within this there is a decisionistic and existential rendering of humanitarian exceptionalism in which supreme humanitarian emergency is seen to be constitutive of an authentic political identity, and international order has to be held together by the recurrent transgression of international norms through the discretionary exercise of political power.

If we return to the question posed by Kofi Annan towards the start of the chapter – 'If humanitarian intervention is, indeed, an unacceptable assault on sovereignty, how should we respond to a Rwanda, to a Srebrenica, to gross and systematic violations of human rights that offend every precept of our common humanity?' – we can see that the question contains within it all the typical traits of exceptionalist politics. There is a putative crisis that is at once immediate yet abstract and indeterminate, torn out of any historical or political context. Framed as a question rather than an answer, we have the urgency and the use of the deceptively broad personal pronoun 'we'. This last feature in particular reveals how exceptionalist politics collapses all issues of the viability and legitimacy of political representation into the simple question of whether or not the exercise of power is effective and rapid – with the presumption being, of course, that the 'we' is always first and foremost 'we' in the West. The space for debate and the range of political options are drastically narrowed. These presumptions built into Annan's emergency hypothetical extend to those who feel the burden of supreme humanitarian emergency sufficiently strongly that they travel to resolve these problems themselves. Whether it is special forces, drones, NATO jets or jihadis flocking from London, Brussels and Paris to the Middle East, it is always the West and Westerners claiming the political right to resolve the world's suffering and conflicts.

The first step in critically responding to the politics of emergency is to refuse the insidious blackmail built into the emergency hypothetical: it is always possible, after all, to keep on modulating the assumptions around a hypothetical scenario to reach the point where everyone, regardless of political background and position – from the most zealous Marxist anti-imperialist through the most prudent political realist to the crustiest conservative isolationist – will eventually be forced to concede that, in a given scenario, *something must be done*. To refuse this blackmail, we have to shift registers and ask, how do claims of emergency function politically? As Jef Huysmans argues, we have to ask, how do claims of exceptionality 'structure stakes and positions in international struggle for legitimacy and authority'?[65] By doing so, we can develop the theoretical understanding and intellectual confidence to draw on a range of responses and to keep in sight a perspective that reaches beyond the militarised response to crisis as the highest form of political ethics.

In his attempt conceptually to map exceptionalism in international politics, Huysmans identified 'humanitarian exceptionalism' as 'the most difficult to explain' but nonetheless 'conceptually possible' and 'more importantly ... a particularly powerful strand in the Western debate about international politics after the end of the Cold War'.[66] Huysmans muses that a 'possible expression of this position' could, 'depending on the details', be a 'humanitarian intervention without the backing of the UN' that treats human rights instruments as a universal ethics and that imposes restrictive peacebuilding models on sovereign states.[67] Huysmans' efforts at conceptualising exceptionalism are focused on neoconservative political theory and its enactment in the war on terror, with its distortions of law and politics and concomitant hostility to international organisation and law. But, as we have seen, humanitarian exceptionalism is perhaps the most important variant of international exceptionalism, of which neoconservative and 'war on terror' exceptionalism remain a significant subset. In his theoretical sketch of the international politics of exceptionalism, Huysmans argues that this peculiar variant of liberal exceptionalism 'is the most difficult to explain' – because it asserts a normative order (human rights, cosmopolitan politics, international humanitarian and criminal law, etc.) at the same time as undermining the extant order through anti-diplomacy. Huysmans does not elaborate what humanitarian exceptionalism looks like, beyond observing that it involves treating law not as procedural frameworks to regulate decision-making and international interaction but, rather, as 'institutionalisations of universal substantive values' that must be imposed by 'representatives that claim a moral or civilizational high ground'.[68] What is described here is the cosmopolitan international order.

Humanitarian intervention established the context and precedent for the war on terror and its exceptionalist political imaginary, as well as its anti-diplomacy in relation to the UN and international law. As Cohen sums up the case:

> By undermining respect for sovereignty as a principle of legal and political autonomy, the ideological discourse that accompanied the enforcement model [of human rights] paved the way for present global security regime.[69]

The constitutional crisis of the UN in 2003 over intervention in Iraq was preceded by the constitutional crisis of the early 1990s, in which recurrent interventions helped to norm the exception. As we have seen, humanitarian intervention has proved a means for subverting sovereignty, and one manifestation of this is an international order in which hierarchy is more explicitly formalised and clustered around a postmodern natural law in the form of human rights.

Perversely, this has not resulted in the supersession of the sovereign state but a boost to state power, inflecting a distinctive new kind of sovereignty, less restrained by representative institutions and with undefined limits on its jurisdictional claims – the exceptionalist sovereign most clearly embodied in the US imperial state, theoretically articulated by neoconservative political theorists,[70] jealously and resentfully mimicked by the likes of Russia. The exceptionalist US state is so committed to maintaining the current international order and US leadership within it that it has ended up exacerbating relative US decline and undermining the credibility of US power.

US unilateralism has a long history, and indeed has long been a source of complaint for its allies, whether it be in the form of isolationist foreign policy in the inter-war period, the Nixon administration ending the convertibility of dollars into gold, through to the neo-isolationist impulses of the Trump administration. What we have tried to do in this chapter is to move beyond inveighing against unilateralism in security policies and to understand that 'unilateralism' covers different kinds of exceptionalist politics, which in turn generate different kinds of international order. From within the domain of international liberalism itself, the transformation wrought by exceptionalist politics is striking. In place of compressing the normative space for war through law and norms, it has expanded it. The result, in effect, is a universal, non-localised sovereignty: the humanitarian order can be maintained only by a global guarantee of power, the ultimate backstop of which is the P1. There is an overlapping, multilayered hierarchy of agencies, bodies and authorities potentially responsible for preserving the minimalistic humanitarian order, whose insufficiency and partiality eventually regress to the superpower. This means, in effect, that the integrity of a multiplicity of legal, normative orders is to be rooted ultimately in US power. The legitimacy of the universal sovereign derives from its capacity to prevent atrocities at the global level. The justification for power here is power itself.

Chapter 4

Failed states, failed empires and the new paternalism

In 2014 the people of Crimea voted to secede from Ukraine and join with Russia. For a vote held in haste and in a territory that had already been occupied by Russian special forces in any case, the Crimean secessionists demonstrated remarkable care in seeking to ground their efforts in international law: they cited as precedent the ruling of the International Court of Justice when it found that the secession of Kosovo from Serbia in 2008 did not breach international law. The 2008 Russian intervention in Georgia and subsequent recognition of that country's secessionist enclaves also cleaved tightly to the Kosovo precedent, which, unlike the secessions of Crimea, Abkhazia and South Ossetia, occurred with Western support. Kosovo, still denied membership of the United Nations at the time of writing due to Sino-Russian opposition on the Security Council, could now be held hostage to the fate of Ukraine, with Russia seeking Western recognition of its annexation of Crimea in return for allowing Kosovo entry to the United Nations.

How did it come to pass that the fate of a small new nation of two million in the Balkans became entwined with the territorial integrity of a country some distance to the east, of forty-five million? How did ethnic conflict in the Balkans become interdependent with ethnic conflict in the Caucasus? That the fates of these disparate peoples and states have been tied together reflects their origins in competing military interventions East and West, with the result that they have together ushered in an new era of territorial dismemberment, and a proliferation of statelets and protectorates under great-power patronage.

At the same time, the new protectorates expose the limits of empire in international affairs today. The reason why Kosovo was ushered to nominal independence under Western auspices was that the costs of holding down even this tiny, impoverished corner of Europe were too great, as a classified 2006 US cable made abundantly clear in the run-up to Kosovo's independence: 'the U.S. had troops on the ground and would not further delay a final status settlement and thus see U.S. and other NATO forces turn from liberators to increasingly unwelcome occupiers'.[1] The US inability to determine political outcomes in Iraq – let alone militarily subjugate the country – underscores the point: state-centred imperialism is unviable.

Fortunately for the great powers, they have managed to construct an alternative to formal empire that is much more viable, cost-effective and politically legitimate: neo-trusteeship, whereby formal legal independence is seen as compatible with international tutelage, supervision and even military occupa-tion – a more thorough-going subversion of self-determination than bullets and bombs could ever achieve. At the same time, neo-trusteeship is also more insidious than the old trusteeship, which at least had the merit of political transparency in denying independence outright and indefinitely suspending it to some remote future. It is a measure of Russia's relative weakness and international isolation that the country is forced to resort to such crude and overt displays of neo-imperial power over small populations and territories in the Caucasus. Neo-trusteeship, by contrast, is a political system that encompasses many millions of people. Indeed, in Africa it has grown to a continental scale, while enjoying thoroughly multilateral support, as described by one journalist:

> Driving round many African cities one is constantly struck by the blue and white of the UN flags and logos.... It is hard

to escape the conclusion that ... Africa is ... certainly being run at least as much from New York as it is from most of the continent's capitals.[2]

Yet even here, however, externally driven state-building projects totter on weak foundations as international elites fabricate institutions with no popular depth and legitimacy and hooked up to international life-support machinery, or alternatively they construct new rentier states, dependent on international aid rather than domestic tax revenue to function.[3] The game of fantasy nation-building that has absorbed so many in Washington, Brussels and New York was then darkly parodied in its grotesque and murderous though ultimately no less absurd form with Islamic State-building in Iraq and Syria.[4] After years of the domination of 'American empire studies' in the first decade of the twenty-first century, debate in International Relations seems to have jumped directly from scenarios of neo-conservative visions of 'full-spectrum dominance'[5] to a collapsing liberal international order and failed US leadership in a hop and a skip, leaping over the prior issue – the failure of imperialism. Part of the reason for this can be attributed to what I call the discourse of 'vulgar Leninism'.[6]

The rise and rise of vulgar Leninism

One of the ironic quirks of the post-Cold War era is the globalisation of vulgar Leninism as a default explanatory device for great-power politics in general, and interventions in particular. The old anti-Iraq war slogan 'No blood for oil!' captures the sentiment: Western military involvement in Central Asia and the Middle East is driven by efforts to gain control over natural resources and fossil fuel energy supplies – especially oil – in competition with other states. Here, one or perhaps two of Lenin's stylised characterisations of imperialism are taken for the entirety of an analysis of world politics.[7] The appeal of such a device is clear: it offers the reassurance of historical continuity with past political frameworks, a ready means of decoding complex patterns of politics, while resonating with contemporary cynicism regarding political institutions and grand rhetoric, larded with a moral suspicion of capitalism and its agents as well as propitiating green suspicions of ecological degradation and resource depletion. Given its provenance in the political thought of the Russian Revolution, it is remarkable what a tight and baleful grip vulgar Leninism has exerted on both the public and scholarly imagination.

Needless to say, this is not to deny that there is a political economy of intervention in terms of dynamics of the field deployments, military operations and state calculations about intervention, as well as the (big) business of intervention and reconstruction in terms of contracts for aid, deliveries, logistics, military and 'non-lethal' materiel and so on, as well as the restricted menu of market-dominated options offered to post-conflict societies. Acknowledging all of this should not be conflated with the idea that the overriding imperative of military force today is economic. Such notions reflect a fundamental confusion about the relationship between politics and economics.

Lenin's own account of the economic structure underpinning imperialist policies in his era was offered less as an 'explanation' of imperialist politics and more as a demonstration that overcoming imperialism was not a matter of changing governments but, rather, changing society (Lenin's opponents in the liberal Kerensky regime that replaced the tsar in 1917 committed themselves to the same war aims as those of the tsar). Moreover, Lenin's analysis of the politics of empire was focused less on international relations between the core and periphery, and more on rivalries *within* the core, using these as a prism through which to analyse class politics within imperialist states.[8] Far from merely collapsing liberal international policies into the decision-making of banks or multinational corporations, Lenin described international relations in terms of the degradation of classical nineteenth-century liberalism into racist nationalism, and militaristic and nationalistic expansionism.[9]

The point here is less to salvage Lenin's reputation as an international relations theorist than to show that, even by the standards of archetypal deterministic theories of force in core–periphery relations, it would be insufficient to discount politics simply by reference to economics. The differences between Lenin's era and ours should already put us on notice with regard to explanations-by-economy. The political economy of contemporary global capitalism is obviously beyond the scope of this book. All that needs to be said here is that whatever the significance of underlying economic structures for military power and interventionist strategies, inferring these structures from analysing military interventions cannot motivate the dismissal of the politics accompanying military intervention – not least the substitution of the discourse of human rights for national self-determination as the idiom of human emancipation.

Of the many problems associated with vulgar Leninism, there are two in particular that concern us here. The first is the flip side of this cynicism – political naïvety. In the first instance, and as already indicated in the introduction to the book, there is the problem of envisioning human rights merely as ideological buttresses for economic expansion. For such a cynical response to politics, vulgar Leninism evinces tremendous political naïvety in insulating humanitarian ethics from criticism and effectively turning human rights into a precious, fragile idealism. Perversely, the effect of dismissing the significance of human rights, international law and liberal ethics is to sanctify them, and de-implicate them in contemporary politics. If the problems of international politics are seen to be essentially external to politics as such – contamination by sinister economic imperatives – then the politics themselves are not subjected to critique, remaining ready to be pressed into service in the next humanitarian crusade. This is especially problematic when exceptionalist politics are present: as each new crisis is treated as if it were *sui generis*, then the politics of human rights remain ready to be weaponised once again. The question as to why human rights lend themselves so easily to being weaponised is never asked. The nature of exceptionalist frameworks is to generate exceptions – and even if every last round of military intervention had been nothing more than a vile war for oil, the next crisis will be an authentic humanitarian emergency, appropriate for the application of unadulterated humanitarian ethics. As we saw in the previous chapter, it is humanitarian exceptionalism itself that constitutes exceptions not as derogations from the ordinary functioning of international order, but as existential challenge to international order. As recent history suggests, the cost of avoiding a political critique of interventions is to be condemned to repeat them.

The second issue stemming from vulgar Leninism is that the focus on intricate realpolitik scheming and geopolitical stratagems and machinations has helped obscure what must be the single most important aspect of contemporary empire – its failure, most drastically and obviously in the Middle East. The long list of 'failed states' has provided licence for the exercise of Western force and imperial power, and the result can only be said to be 'failed empire'.

Empire on the couch

For all those who approbated American empire studies and vulgar Leninism, the crumbling of the post-war order in Afghanistan, Iraq and Libya and their descent into perpetual civil war – not to mention the fact that those conflicts were actively and willingly chosen in succession – exposes another problem to be addressed – imperial failure. It is obviously easier to rally the opposition to a successful nefarious scheme than that to a failing nefarious scheme. For if a nefarious project is failing, what is there to oppose? If it is its nefariousness that is problematic, then what threat does it pose, if it is failing? If it is the failure that is the problem, then is the nefariousness to be simply ignored?

Alert to the rapid crumbling of US and Western hopes in Afghanistan and Iraq, counterposed to the doyens of American empire studies were those who diagnosed the early and rapid failure of the occupation regimes as a basic failure of political will, casting the US as a 'reluctant imperialist', in the words of Sebastian Mallaby.[10] While International Relations scholars conceitedly debated how far they are mandated to provide 'advice to princes', this group embraced instead the role of imperial therapists, seeking to diagnose and psychoanalyse the existential maladies that supposedly gave rise to reluctant or disavowed empire – a process described, in the words of Niall Ferguson and, later, David Chandler, as 'empire in denial'.[11] If the discourse of vulgarised Leninism and American empire studies mixed crude economics and postmodern social theory, the discourse of these commentators was distinctly voluntaristic, borrowing the demotic language of self-help culture.

David Chandler in particular identified state-building as a form of imperial disavowal, tracking how discussions over intervention in the developing world shifted over time. From questions of intervention – whether that be aid and support delivered by non-governmental organisations or military interventions by NATO through to roll-out of policy by international advisers – the discussion switched to the issue of state-building. From discussing what to do to developing countries, the discussion became about how developing countries were to achieve transformation themselves through enhancing the infrastructure and machinery of state. The discourse of international ordering and management shifted from that of subjection to that of empowerment. The language of intervention became replete with terms such as 'capacity-building', 'local ownership' and 'bottom-up transformation'. Nonetheless, developing societies, particularly in Africa, were still being consistently reconfigured around international imperatives and this resulted in bizarre paradoxes: 'The more intervention there is, the more the target state is held to be responsible and accountable for the consequences of these practices', and states 'which resisted ... external assistance could, in the Orwellian language of international statebuilders, be accused of undermining their [own] sovereignty'.[12]

Chandler went further than exposing the shallowness and disingenuous character of international policy attached to development and conflict, arguing that it represented an unaccountable exercise of power. Chandler attributed this to a flight from power and responsibility, partly as a retrospective response to the destabilising consequences of degrading state authority, capacity and legitimacy through military intervention in the immediate aftermath of the Cold War. He also suggested that this new developmentalism represented a flight from the open expression of power and leadership, which was disavowed in favour of talking up the developing countries – thereby avoiding not only accountability for the exercise of power but also avoiding the need to express any vision of leadership. State-building was, in short, an intensely self-abnegating form of power. Chandler was certainly more alert to the form that power took in international affairs when compared with vulgar Leninist accounts of international politics. To be sure, tremendous resources were channelled into efforts to build strong, functioning institutions, coherent political bodies and state structures with representative legitimacy in countless post-conflict states.

Yet there were significant problems with the thesis. On the one hand, it did not extend far enough in its sweep and, on the other, it was internally contradictory. In the first case, international state-building allowed not only Western states and their state-builders to avoid accountability for their policies, but it has also empowered domestic elites within targeted states in much the same way. The extent of outside control over policy has allowed those domestic elites to disavow their own power and need to exercise authority and leadership by reference to their own lack of control.

Empire in denial could also therefore be inverted. Much of the force of the Chandler thesis comes from the contrast not so much with concrete historical episodes of empire but rather with what we might call an 'imperial imaginary' populated by the stock concepts and ideas of vulgar Leninism – of rapacious empire, overt domination and authoritarian subjugation. Yet the contrast is a forced one: the range and sophistication of political and institutional forms through which imperial power was exercised are greater than the monolithic and centralised connotations of the word 'empire'. Indeed, for much of the twentieth century the European imperial powers were forced to disavow empire through a wide range of claims and forms – international mandates, trusteeship, protectorates, even outright assimilation to the metropole – as a way of denying that colonies existed, as with the Portuguese empire or the fact that Algeria was annexed to metropolitan France. The heyday of the open celebration of imperial civilisation as the zenith of progress and political achievement was long since past and it would be inaccurate to collapse all forms of historic imperialism into one abiding, mostly nineteenth-century image.

Moreover, state-building and nation-building have a longer pedigree than the post-Cold War era, going back to the permutations of American developmentalism over the course of the Cold War – President Kennedy's Alliance for Progress, for instance, or the Nixon administration's efforts to devolve the military struggle against Asian communism to the South Vietnamese state. Indeed, at one level it is difficult to see any plausible alternative to the 'empire in denial' as a generic form of post-colonial Western power in the developing world: for what can an empire be, politically speaking, in a post-colonial world founded around the legal independence of states and the UN Charter system? The thesis of empire in denial ends up simply re-describing a world of independent nation-states in which open empire through military conquest is simply so illegitimate and non-functional as to be politically impossible. Pushed to its logical conclusion, the thesis begins to crumble under the weight of its own contradictions: on the one hand, Chandler wishes to suggest the exercise of imperial authority is confused and prevaricating, while on the other he imputes to imperial power the stratagem of explicit deception and political evasion by resort to more sophisticated forms of imperial camouflage ... all of which is to say that empire in denial does not escape the conceptual redundancy of imperial theorising in which every re-description becomes yet another more refined and intricate 'latest stage' of imperialism.

As should be abundantly clear, at least since the destruction of the Gaddafi regime in Libya, the issue for theorists and scholars of International Relations is not to construct highest-and-latest-stages-of-imperialism arguments but to deal with the issue of imperial failure – the failure to create viable, lasting institutions of political order, whether at the national or regional level. Critique of empire has usually had two cutting edges: attacking the chaotic and destructive character of empire resulting from imperial rivalries; and its oppressive character, in which peoples and societies are subordinated by and then ruled from an imperial centre. The last kind of criticism, at least, was predicated on the effective imposition of political order. The issue for critics of empire is the character and process of imposition, and the character of the ensuing political order.

The question now is, what happens when that imposition fails? Alert to the unintended consequences and distorting effects implicit in intervention, a varied group of thinkers were willing to embrace a laissez-faire attitude to questions of international order, pulling back the various prongs of liberal intervention in favour of accepting and adapting to the spontaneous and indigenous processes of state-building in the periphery.

Dynamics of state-building

After such a long period of degrading state capacity and sub-verting state authority in the developing world through repeat military interventions, it was inevitable that a backlash would develop regarding the importance of centralised institutions and authorities to deliver the liberal social and political trans-formation envisaged in intervention. Hence the new era of 'state-building' with the focus shifted to upgrading institutional infrastructure in the developing world, rather than rolling it back in favour of the market, or, indeed, bombing it into rubble.[13] Yet state-building also carried with it a strong counterclaim to liberal interventionism and its impact on international order. A varied group of scholars and analysts argued that human rights and pro-democracy interventions would subvert the process of state formation, leading to greater human suffering in the long run, because these states would be barred from developing the institutional infrastructure required to maintain public order.[14] Others argued that peace-making efforts would artificially freeze conflicts, fail to provide decisive resolution and block sustainable, long-run social development.[15] Others still maintained that it was only by letting conflicts burn themselves out that a durable politi-cal order could be secured in the long run, its durability to be proved and consolidated through struggle and contestation.

Such hard-headed analyses should not be lightly dismissed in light of what we have seen in Libya, Iraq and Afghanistan, and how paltry, limited and compromised outcomes have been in those new trust territories which have at least been spared the chaos of perpetual civil war. It is not difficult to show how even the most brutal and authoritarian state-building in Ba'athist Iraq achieved more effective measures of human welfare and develop-mentalist indicators than post-Saddam Iraq.[16]

Nonetheless, to accept internally driven state-building as immediately preferable to externally driven or imposed state-building is still problematic, for a number of reasons. First, ideas of internally driven state-building are heavily predicated on the assumption of state fragility and artificiality in the developing world – hence the fear that a Western intervention could send an unstable state spinning off into an irrevocable trajectory of state failure. Yet these conditions are themselves often exaggerated. After all, all states and nations are artificial – that is, human artefacts – so drawing up a ready-made spectrum of greater or lesser artificiality in a way that could yield predictions or understanding is in no way obvious or straightforward, if, indeed, at all meaningful.[17]

The second assumption underpinning these claims is that of inhabiting a separate timeline – namely, the idea that these countries exist on a different timeline, in which they must replicate every step and stage of the historic process of state formation in early modern Europe, blow by bloody blow. These countries do not exist in a different temporal dimension, separate from the rest of the world. We can certainly accept insights from the historic process of state formation and modernisation in the global core without needing to assume historical or developmental synchronicity. Nor would it make sense to assume that there is some magical point at which all these timelines converge and in which all developmental trajectories are unified and homogenised. Social development is always complex, multilayered and uneven. Nor can these developing states simply be carved out of the world as if their conflicts could be neatly cleaved from the global economy or the interests of neighbouring states and regional powers.

In all these cases, the underlying assumption is that politics is essentially the formation of institutions for extraction and order-building. It is an image of politics that is the mirror image of that of the liberal peacebuilders and state-builders – except in this image the relevant institutions are generated indigenously rather than externally imposed and regulated from New York or Brussels. What is missing in both images is the explicitly political dimension concerning ideas of rule, rights, representation and self-determination. The debate, to that extent, is about effectiveness rather than right, and how far external interventions may or may not knock developmental trajectories off course. What this misses is the political value of self-determination independently of effectiveness in generating outcomes – that is, the value of self-determination for clarifying the exercise of power and institutionalising participation in a common, joint process of social choice and decision-making. These principles need defending and instantiating independently of the success of long-term state-building processes; nor can they be instrumentalised for the sake of state-building.

If empire is mostly disparaged, so too is the ideal of sovereign statehood. While some neo-imperialists have made the case for systematising intervention and nation-building in a new mandates system and formalising new forms of trusteeship, it is cosmopolitan theorists who have who set themselves more firmly against the state as such, for they envisage military interventions to defend human rights less as a way of maintaining international order and more as stepping stones to a future political system built around global law that prioritises the rights of individuals rather than states. Yet even this most explicitly anti-state political theory did not envisage a world empire or a world state as its desirable end-point; instead, there was a longing for a soft-focus, politically plural and polycentric idyll of fuzzy borders and shimmering networks of global NGOs, in which state sovereignty is blurred rather than rubbed out. In short, what is needed is an account of state sovereignty fixed around the value of self-determination.

If Iraq and the new protectorates exhibit the failure of cosmopolitanism at its most imperial, that is not to say that failed imperial nation-building projects are the only remnants of cosmopolitan dystopia. For what is striking in places such as Libya or Iraq is the absence of any strong force militating for sovereign self-determination and national self-assertion.

Perhaps this exacerbates the problems of our era, in the inability to establish viable, legitimate institutions of state-level political order. The dialectic between empire and sovereignty that has shaped so much of international politics in the modern era has ebbed away, with the state of the cosmopolitan era not one built around autonomy and independence, but responsibility and interdependence. In other words, it is not just a question of the effectiveness of institutions and policies, but the ideal of statehood that underpins them, too. The disparagement of empire has not led to the elevation of state sovereignty. This has consequences not only for the state's external relations but also its internal political structures – consequences that can be best explored through the responsibility to protect.

The reigning international consensus on state authority today, the doctrine of the responsibility to protect, resoundingly reaffirms the state as the building block of international order. In 2005, the Outcome Document of the UN Millennium summit was unanimously endorsed by all member-states of the world body – almost every state in the world – in the presence of what was the greatest gathering of world leaders in history. Contained within the document's hundreds of provisions were two in particular that committed all signatories to the 'responsibility to protect' people on their territory from the most heinous crimes under international law. Having emerged as an effort to solidify the gains of humanitarian intervention while conciliating sceptical developing countries, the fact that the document won such global support was seen as a crucial marker of international progress. In particular, the fact that even powerful authoritarian regimes such as China were forced to give ground before the globalisation of human rights was seen to be a boon for the doctrine. Others argued that the acceptance of the proposals exposed how empty they were, too innocuous and inoffensive to genuinely threaten abusive regimes.

Here, I want to advance a different possibility – namely, that the global acceptance of the Outcome Document revealed instead the deep complementarity between state power and the responsibility to protect doctrine. This is the argument developed in the remainder of this chapter. The purpose of the doctrine (as discussed in chapter 3) was, in Alex Bellamy's words, to help us avoid the choice of 'sending in the Marines or doing nothing', by helping to ensure that such crises never emerged in the first place through states observing responsibilities to their own populations.[18] This has implications for how we understand state power. Here, building on Bellamy's claim, I will try to treat the responsibility to protect not as a theory of intervention or international politics, but rather as a model of state power and authority – to treat it, in other words, as a serious political theory. According to this doctrine, endorsed by the UN and its member states, it is only in certain extreme circumstances (involving terrible crimes and great human suffering) that state authority may be legally and legitimately limited by outside powers. What I argue is that the responsibility to protect represents a paternalistic model of state power and political authority – one in which political representation is eliminated by security, embodying the most conservative understanding of political responsibility – responsibility for rather than responsibility to people.

To be sure, liberal theory has always been about justifying state power by reference to protection from disorder. Yet, as we shall see below, the responsibility to protect exceeds even the most authoritarian justifications for Leviathan, dissolving the dialectic of reciprocity and representation embedded in contractarian thinking in favour of a circular theory of power in which state power is justified by reference only to itself. The idea of steering a society towards a particular goal or collective transformation dissolves in favour of protection from the most extreme violence. It is a resolutely exceptionalist justification of political power. Thus far, too much analysis of the doctrine of the responsibility to protect is effectively scriptural – that is to say, focused on the specific words in UN Security Council resolutions, reports of the secretary-general and so on – interpreting shifts in emphasis, divining the intent behind specific phrases, tracking the evolution of terms. The approach offered below is more conceptual.

From Hammarskjöld to Hobbes: international authority and the responsibility to protect

As we have seen, the doctrine of the responsibility to protect is frequently seen as applying primarily to relations between states. It was the work of Anne Orford that represented a crucial shift in terms of the debate on the responsibility to protect.[19] With her work, the debate on the doctrine shifted from discussion of appropriate triggers for intervention, or about the degree of consensus over the doctrine at the international level or about the degree to which the tenets of the doctrine have evolved since the publication of the original report in 2001, and so on. Instead, Orford took the doctrine as a theory of state power. This was logical, as the whole rationale for the responsibility to protect was to shift the focus onto the practice and behaviour of states towards their populations, and to get away from focusing purely on state-to-state interaction.

Yet despite this shift, no one had taken the state-centric focus of the responsibility to protect seriously – that is to say, in the standard terms of political justification, authorisation and power. Orford not only did this but, moreover, drew attention to the authoritarian implications of the politics of protection, noting the possibility that it could displace principles of representation. She also rooted the discussion of protection in those thinkers whose understanding of state authority is most clearly allied to the focus on security and protection – Thomas Hobbes and Carl Schmitt. She usefully traces the evolution of the politics and law of international administration and executive authority, noting in particular how the UN had had to innovate forms of de facto rule in the wake of decolonisation. In this way, Orford identified in concrete detail and specificity the development of genuinely transnational forms of authority and rule that were not straightforwardly reducible to interactions between states, nor were these new legal and political structures simply neo-colonial efforts or great-power machination. Further, she gave due regard to the genuinely novel developments of transnational authorities embodied in the new discourse and institutions of international governance.

Nonetheless, as we shall see, Orford's thesis remains highly ambivalent. On the one hand, while Orford is alert to the authoritarian implications of the new international politics of protection, in other respects she deems the responsibility to protect a welcome development. Rooting the responsibility to protect in transnational administrative and executive law pioneered by the likes of UN secretary-general Dag Hammarskjöld makes her receptive to the devolution of power and authority in the responsibility-to-protect doctrine to the state level. Indeed, she welcomes this as a recapture by the state of unrooted and unviable transnational law, thereby undercutting a functionalist vision of international law that has no roots in state power. She thus sees the responsibility to protect as belonging to the long tradition of dissolving trans- and supranational, imperialistic structures of political authority, such as the Holy Roman Empire and the medieval papacy. In this case, the responsibility to protect may help to prevent the UN functioning as a kind of secular global church as its Christological humanitarian authority is decentred and dispersed among states by devolving responsibilities back to national capitals.[20] Indeed, Orford especially welcomes the focus on the effectiveness of state protection, as she sees this as militating for a pluralistic and devolved state system.

Despite all this, Orford remains critical of the doctrine – she recognises that the doctrine still significantly fails to resolve system versus state-level conflicts in authority (that is to say, disputes between the UN and states in terms of determining when a breach of the doctrine has occurred, and who is entitled to rectify that breach). She also bemoans the fact that the doctrine bears the functionalist imprint and phoney neutrality of apolitical and administrative law, as indicated in the unsuppressed contradictions over different authorities in the doctrine.[21] Thus, all told, Orford welcomes the responsibility to protect as an end to the crusading, utopian dimension of human rights. The pivot back to concrete institutions, devolved and plural political authorities and states gets away from the abstract, Christological dimensions of international human rights.

There are a number of problems with this scenario, however, particularly in how Orford sees these various issues as intersecting. For a start, the devolution of human rights protection to states under the terms of the responsibility to protect is more ambivalent than Orford makes out. As noted by Jean Cohen, the effect is to produce a world in which states are effectively rendered as 'administrative units in a decentralized, "multileveled" global governance structure that accords "autonomy" provisionally'.[22] Orford sees these issues as intersecting. She invokes the politics of protection in Schmitt and Hobbes and links it to the Hammarskjöld era of the UN by common reference to revolutionary periods: the English revolution and European wars of religion in the case of Hobbes, the German revolution and twenty years' crisis in the case of Schmitt, and the Third World global revolution in the case of Hammarskjöld. The politics of protection seems to track revolutionary disruptions of pre-existing authority.

Yet with the comparison across seventeenth- and early twentieth-century European revolutions already stretched taut when extended to post-war Afro-Asian revolutions, it surely cannot stretch further, to cover the era of the responsibility to protect, in the decisively non-revolutionary era of the early twenty-first century. If the locus and structure of political authority are contested today, it is not down to the deep divisions in civil wars at the core of the international system, nor the strength and fervour of oppositional revolutionary challenges to established authority. Whatever motivates the shift to cosmopolitan liberalism, it is not the result of a revolutionary challenge either in the West or the Third World. The rise of the responsibility to protect is consistent with the era of inverted revisionism, and the confusion over final authority with the decisionism of universal sovereignty.[23] Focused on distinctively international conceptions of authority, Orford does not venture far enough in considering the internal ramifications of the politics of protection embodied in the responsibility to protect. As we shall see below, tilting the balance back to the state and away from international structures risks crushing those beneath the state, when it is loaded with greater political significance in the balance with international governance. Hobbes and Schmitt are useful thinkers in this context, not so much for reasons of historical resonance and contextual congruence as their efforts systematically to map out the logic and structure of political authority predicated on protection and security. The reframing of sovereign authority in the doctrine intertwines domestic and international conceptions in intricate ways that require careful untangling.

The paternalist legitimation of state power: the responsibility to protect as a theory of the state

The responsibility-to-protect doctrine is usually seen as an artefact of international affairs: its political domain is international councils not national parliaments, its concerns are conflicts and crises of global import – mass atrocities, massive refugee flows. Its agents and institutions are at the international level: foreign ministers, UN agencies, the Security Council, advisers to the secretary-general, international peacekeepers, perhaps even NATO forces. Its key documents and texts are UN resolutions, publications and reports by international, not national organisations and commissions. Its scholars and students are International

Relations theorists, analysts and international lawyers. All this begs the question of why treat the doctrine as a theory of state, why shift the focus from the international to the national level?

Part of the answer is, of course, that the national, domestic focus is already there in the doctrine: it is about how states behave with respect to people under their authority and on their territory and how this links into international responsibilities and oversight. Indeed, perhaps the most succinct way to define the theory is that it is about conceptualising that moment at which domestic authority gives way to international authority: the whole premise of the doctrine is about the transition between two adjoining political realms. Yet the theory of the responsibility to protect has not been properly adapted to fit its object.

Taking up Orford's challenge, therefore, to conceive of the responsibility to protect as a capacious doctrine, what happens when we consider political structures *within* states rather than merely political relations *between* states. Specifically: how does the responsibility to protect re-articulate the legitimation of state power as such? Part of the new consensus around the responsibility to protect rests on the agreement that it is states that bear the duty to protect people on their territories from mass atrocity, conceived of in its widest sense.[24] On the face of it, this would seem to be one of those commonplaces that accompany attempts at cohering diplomatic consensus – so banal that it barely merits comment. In the ICISS report, for instance, the insistence on states as bearers of the duty to protect was clearly offered as a means of quelling fears of human rights imperialism among developing countries.[25] Evidently seeking to avoid anything as controversial as questioning the legitimacy of internal political arrangements, the framers of the doctrine have settled on a formula acceptable to any state. The idea that states are required to provide certain fundaments of social and political order is, after all, a basic tenet of modern government as such. To the extent that the doctrine clearly privileges extant authorities and incumbent states in any particular territory (assuming that they are functioning to some degree), it is a conservative prescription for international stability, whose appeal to incumbent states and regimes is evident.

However, it would be a mistake to classify these ideas as merely empty diplomatic phrases. The conception of state legitimacy in the doctrine is based on the ability of states *effectively* to provide a particular set of *internationally sanctioned* security requirements. The emphasis that the doctrine places on security can be seen in the fact that states are viewed as dispensable providers of security, and can be substituted by the international community should they fail in their role. Indeed, while the ICISS report refers to states as the primary providers of the 'responsibility to protect', former UN secretary-general Kofi Annan went as far as to claim that the 'primary *raison d'être* and duty' of every state is to protect its population.[26]

If the legitimacy of statehood is to be judged on the provision of certain internationally sanctioned types of security, this can only have the effect of relativising states as institutionalised expressions of collective political will. In this vision, the rights of state sovereignty flow not from the will of the people, but downwards from the international community. This is the only way in which we can logically interpret the claim that states can be primary duty bearers but, at the same time, that it can be legitimate for their rights to be rescinded by the international community. Therefore, it is not merely that the doctrine does not distinguish between authoritarian and democratic states, but that it rewrites the very idea of representative government in such a way that favours state power in place of people power. More than revamping international norms governing the use of force, the responsibility to protect recasts the rationale for sovereignty. The norms governing the use of force change as a secondary effect of this prior recalibration of sovereign responsibilities – intervention is no longer seen as intervention, but simply as the fulfilment of pre-ordained international duties.[27]

Judging by the UN General Assembly debate in 2009 on the responsibility to protect, the majority of states are keen to avoid issuing licences for external intervention in states' internal affairs, while the great powers are keen to avoid the responsibility to protect limiting their freedom of manoeuvre.[28] Perhaps some developing countries even see the responsibility to protect as fostering a language under whose rubric resource transfer could be affected, which would help strengthen their institutional machinery and security apparatus, the better to help maintain their domestic 'responsibility to protect'. They will squabble with the West over where the boundaries can be set. But what underlies this consensus of overlapping interests is a 'paternalist legitimation of state power through the inflation of security into the supreme objective of politics'.[29] If the state can be held accountable by external powers for the duties it owes its people, then the only logical interpretation is that the state is in the position of having responsibility for its people rather than to its people.

As we saw above, Cohen describes this process as the reduction of states to vectors of the international community, 'administrative units in a decentralized, "multileveled" global governance structure that accords "autonomy" provisionally'.[30] This is consistent with the logic of exceptionalism – the blurring of the distinction between constitutive and constituted political power.[31] The politics of emergency frames legitimacy around questions of efficacious action rather than legitimate representation. Exceptionalism invokes a politics of fear that collapses the dialectic of mediated representation into one where the efficiency of power and protection is privileged over all else. Yet sovereignty cannot be decentred without loosening the bonds of internal political representation that restrain state power.

It is difficult to underestimate just how significant this shift is, as it goes beyond even the most Hobbesian understanding of the legitimation of state power.[32] In Hobbes's framework, questions of both origin and form are immaterial.[33] That is to say, whether the authority of the sovereign originates in conquest or consent is irrelevant – the historical process through which sovereign authority was constituted is not important from the viewpoint of the current authority.[34] Likewise, the specific form of government – whether monarchical or republican – had no bearing on the legitimacy of sovereign authority. In this, the responsibility to protect is close to the Hobbesian conception: the origins of existing states, whether revolutionary, counter-imperial, pre-modern, and so on, is irrelevant. Whether the government be single-party, liberal democracy, hybrid democracy, totalitarian is also irrelevant. In all the cases, the rationale is the same: disputes over originary legitimacy or disputes over the legitimacy of the internal configuration of government are licences for conflict, turmoil and instability. Hence the logic of Hobbes's relentless focus on security: the only criterion for legitimate sovereignty in general terms is the effectiveness of the sovereign's provision of security.

Effective security is likewise the overriding focus of the responsibility to protect, too – the doctrine dismissing as immaterial whether the sovereign is incapable or unwilling to provide such security or the Leviathan itself is predatory – in which case it fails to provide security and loses the title to sovereignty. Thus there is remarkable symmetry between the two doctrines of sovereignty. Protection is the supreme end of the state, and all other possible ends – say representation, implementation and transmission of political will – are all relegated, seen either as irrelevant or as political prostheses, expendable at best. We could even go as far as to say that 'R2P' is Hobbesian in its overriding emphasis on politics and state authority being grounded in the provision of security: all politics is the politics of security, and security is the foundation of everything else. In both cases, the emphasis on security is justified by reference to the depiction of a state of nature prior to sovereign security: a quasi-fictional inference in Hobbes, a heavily stylised, decontextualised and allusive invocation of the worst moments of the twentieth century underpinning the theory of the responsibility to protect: the Holocaust, Rwanda, Srebrenica....

Where the two doctrines diverge is in claims that can be made against the sovereign and by whom. To be sure, there is no right of resistance or rebellion in either doctrine: Hobbes notoriously ruled out the possibility of democratic overthrow.[35] The absence of any right to resistance means, of course, that there is no conception of the possibility of subjects holding sovereignty to account. Hobbes discerns circumstances in which the compact of sovereignty dissolves: 'The Obligation of Subjects to the Soveraign, is understood to last as long, and no longer, than the power lasteth, by which he is able to protect them.'[36] The responsibility to protect goes further still, however, in limiting the rights of its subjects. Although the doctrine of the responsibility to protect at least implicitly countenances the possibility of revolt against an incumbent state, it would be wrong to see this as any kind of 'right'. Revolt, civil war, insurgency register in the doctrine only inasmuch as they are evidence of the insufficiency or failure of Leviathan; the rights and wrongs of any particular rebellion or insurrection are irrelevant to the judgement of sovereign failure. Rebellion is a failure of security, not the consummation to a popular insurrection, nor the riposte to oppression and injustice; the only relevant facts are the presence or absence of state protection. In neither doctrine, then, does the potential for force enter the scales of political accountability. Yet, whereas Hobbes justifies political obedience as a return for sovereign protection, no such obedience is built into the structure of the responsibility to protect. This absence of a right to resistance is crucial, as we shall shortly see.

Another point where the responsibility to protect and Hobbes depart is the rights accorded to the subjects under the sovereign: while Hobbes's subjects renounce natural rights upon entry into society under the authority of the sovereign, preserving at best some vestigial right of self-preservation, the subjects of the responsible sovereign retain their human rights and particularly those associated with individual security and bodily integrity. Yet if the subjects of the responsible sovereign retain their human rights, they cannot enforce them because they have no rights of revolt or resistance. To be sure, a popular rebellion and civil war may signal the inability of a sovereign to provide effective protection, and thus at most could be seen as a way of drawing the attention of the international community to the problem. Yet the consummation of the responsibility to protect is not revolution (in the sense of the domestic overthrow of an oppressive regime) but the *restoration* of effective protection by another sovereign or alliance of sovereigns. The only accountability in the doctrine is thus between sovereigns, not between sovereigns and peoples. The structure of political obligation in the responsibility to protect is thus entirely one-sided – all obligations are held by states, and not even political obedience is expected in the doctrine. Yet if this seems appealing (inasmuch as the human rights subject is emancipated from political burdens of protection, which are overseen in turn by the great powers), it comes with costs.

Consider what happens in the case of sovereign failure. For Hobbes, obligations of obedience and political loyalty dissolve where the sovereign fails. The individual is freed of any obedience to the sovereign. It is different with humanitarian subjects. Not only are they free of obligation to the sovereign, but they also, in principle, benefit from a concatenation of protection, with a diffuse structure of duties of protection overlapping with those of their incumbent sovereign. Under the terms of the responsibility to protect, sovereign failure nullifies territorial exclusivity, nullifies the right to non-intervention, and, by default, protection obligations shift to the international community, that is, to other sovereigns.

Unbundling the ties that bind subjects to the sovereign may appear emancipatory. In fact, it is a demotion: there is no promise of security, as the responsibility of the sovereign is ultimately discretionary (no outside state is obliged to exercise the responsibility to protect). So, not only do the claims of the humanitarian subjects on their incumbent sovereign diminish, but these are not compensated for by any other stronger claims against external, super or universal sovereigns – making all such promises enunciated in the United Nations ultimately chimerical. The only political self-assertion left to subjects in this paradigm is that of histrionic rebellion: a violence that will draw the attention of other sovereigns to assert *their* control over that of the incumbent sovereign.

With a panoply of protections but no obligations, the humanitarian subjects have no agency, for their consent is meaningless. While there may be no quasi-mythical 'state of nature' origin stories built into the conceptual structure of responsible sovereignty, this reflects less the lucidity of the doctrine and more the fact that it has no contractual structure or expectation of reciprocity. Humanitarian subjects freed of obligations to the sovereign are also freed of agency. To be sure, Hobbesian assent and obligation are extracted, once and for all, in a single act of political acclaim, and then relegated to some indeterminate, quasi-mythical past. Yet this moment is also an act of political creativity, a collective agreement that generates the sovereign, this 'mortal god'. Humanitarian subjects have no formal rights over which power may intervene in their favour to protect them against incumbent state authority. Without any agency or political creativity or contractual structure of reciprocal expectation, there is no integration between subjects and sovereign. Under the terms of the responsibility to protect there remains merely in Hobbesian terms a multitude – a disconnected, unintegrated morass of individuals with no political force or power. In his theory, Hobbes tightly bound subjects to the sovereign, and this binding provides the logical basis for further development – that is to say, the potential for accountability and, ultimately, democracy. The responsibility to protect dissolves these ties, consigning its subjects to powerlessness.

The purpose of this comparison is to show that, even by the standards of the most centralising, authoritarian and rigid of the supposedly contractarian political theorists, the responsibility to protect can be found wanting. As a political vision for social order, it is in many ways as dark as, if not darker than, that of Hobbes: rooted in a grim disorder of mass murder and abuse, there is no political transformation onto a higher plane as with Hobbes's social contract. With protections offered that may or may not fail, the solution is to shunt hapless victims from the oversight of one state to another. Each protection regime is substitutable for the other, there being no other criterion of political loyalty – such as authentic or effective representation, accountability or transparency. Sovereigns hold each other to account only for their maintenance of order. Thus, the highest possible goal of responsible sovereignty would be to have the universal sovereign, the US, as a patron or ally.

The disorder and insecurity envisioned in the responsibility to protect are not exactly a state of nature, however, for they are not pro-social nor pre-state; it is not a war of all against all. Indeed, the state is always implicated in the security threat, whether by its omission to provide security or commission of actions that victimise its subjects. This lack of a fundamental distinction between a state of nature and society is important in the implications of the theory. We saw in earlier chapters how the responsibility to protect can be seen as an attempt to norm the exception, to build the extreme into the functioning of ordinary political order, and we explored some of these consequences of this normalisation at the international level. Now we can see the results of that for domestic political order – logically speaking, norming the exception can result only in the displacement of other political concerns: incorporation of the responsibility to protect warps every premise of sovereignty as contractual and thus ultimately as responsible government – responsibility for, but not responsibility to. As a non-contractarian theory of sovereignty, the status of the sovereign's subjects is inevitably reduced to that of ward. The potential to transform this situation politically, through a collective act of will or through the creation of new collectively binding political institutions, is eviscerated: only protection remains, by whoever is able or willing to provide it.

It could be objected that it is ultimately an unfair exercise to compare diplomatic pronouncements or the stilted language of diplomatic compromise and consensus embodied in reports by the secretary-general and UN resolutions against the detailed and systematic schemes of some of the greatest political thinkers of the past. But this would be a mistake. Not only have many important political thinkers been intimately involved in shaping the new paradigms of sovereignty as well as in shaping the parameters of debate in their own times, but it would also be a mistake to imagine that the thinkers of the past were not responding to the immediate and practical problems of their own day. In the European context, at least, this included the great wars of religion, the clash over secular versus religious sources of authority, order and control versus revolution, and extending claims of authority, justifying war and conflict. To consider the doctrine of the responsibility to protect in this way is thus consistent with a new strain of scholarship seeking to contextualise the responsibility to protect in a historic, centuries-long process of evolving debates about the needs and ends of political authority in changing circumstances and contexts.[37]

Conclusion

Political theorist James Martel famously offered up a clever, radical re-interpretation of Hobbes as a self-subverting ironist, a radical democrat who, far from esteeming the Leviathan with panegyric, actually invites the reader to sly revolt.[38] No one could ever (mis)interpret 'R2P' in such a way. Although there has been some debate about how far the increased proclivity to intervention encourages and exacerbates opportunistic revolts against states in the interest of inviting outside intervention in their favour,[39] no one could think that the provisions of R2P offer a covert manifesto for popular revolt and radical subversion. The hinge of the entire architecture of the responsibility to protect is the great veto-wielding powers of the UN Security Council. Any injunction to revolt against them is inconceivable in the terms of the doctrine, as it would collapse the doctrine into international anarchy, political self-help and security autarchy. Any number of sovereigns could lose their title under the terms of the responsibility to protect as long as the super-sovereigns of the Security Council retained their power to police infringements of other sovereigns' responsibilities. Obviously, without any subversion of the status of super-sovereigns in the theory, there could be no way to conceive of the doctrine as containing within it a prescription for radical overthrow or restructuring of power relations and global hierarchy. As no political transformation is possible, all that can be hoped for is security.

It could be reasonably countered that diplomacy is awash with solemn proclamations and platitudinous phrases. Why treat the responsibility-to-protect doctrine any more seriously than this? This takes us back to the very beginning of the book. If politics is more than just scheming and machinations and material interests, then we should take it very seriously indeed. All states in the world have agreed to be bound by this doctrine, and there are many people who intend to hold states to those promises – promises whose fulfilment will only strengthen the paternalistic vision of state power. The fact that the US and China agree on a specific model of state authority and political power should at least give us pause, if not arouse our concern and consternation.

The premise of this book is that the decay of the liberal world order is internal; it is eroding from within. The sabotage of the principle of non-interference, and with it self-determination and non-aggression, come from the Western states most closely identified with that order. An analogous point could be made about the shift away from the paradigm of 'sovereignty as control' to 'sovereignty as responsibility': it embodies a more promiscuous but nonetheless tighter vision of social control. A morass of vulnerable humanity is placed under a transnational regime of interlocking political structures that alternately protect or prey on them but that never serve them. While there are widespread fears of the threat posed to liberal democracy by populism, xenophobia, renewed nationalism and authoritarianism, less attention has been paid to the ways in which liberal prescriptions have undermined the tenets of representative government. If the classical ideal of the social contract gives space for the pursuit of social and political goods once security has been achieved, the responsibility-to-protect doctrine cleaves ever more tightly to protection from disorder. It embodies a decayed liberalism, where the justification for state power has sunk beneath classical theories of collective order and representation. It shows the logic of human rights taken to their authoritarian conclusion.

Conclusion: waiting for the Americans

John Wyndham's 1951 science fiction novel *The Day of the Triffids* begins after the majority of people in the country have been left blind as a result of mysterious, apparently malfunctioning space weaponry exploding in the night sky. The blind masses are thus vulnerable not only to the generalised chaos but also to the venomous, marauding triffids, another mysterious Cold War technology – in this case, gigantic, carnivorous and possibly self-aware plants genetically engineered to be exploited for their oils. The sinister triffids take Darwinian advantage of the general disorder to supplant humanity as the dominant species on the planet.

In one particularly memorable scene, the protagonist, who has only by chance avoided being struck blind, stumbles across various fragmented, small bands of survivors who, despite being fortunate enough still to be sighted, are consumed with lethargy. These despondent bands make no effort to agglomerate into larger groups for the purposes of self-help and survival. The reason why they do not do so is that they are waiting for the Americans to arrive, as the Americans 'were bound to find a way'. The protagonist of Wyndham's novel is fascinated by 'this Micawber fixation on American fairy godmothers' and its imperviousness to reason in the face of cataclysm. Wyndham's protagonist is particularly fascinated by one of these survivors, an upper-class young woman, 'quite the least troubled person I had encountered since the catastrophe took place'. Her apathy reflects not only her social background, with 'no real surprise over whatever life might hand her next', but also her 'utterly un-shakeable conviction that nothing serious could have happened to America, and that it was only a matter of holding out for a while until the Americans arrived to put everything in order'.[1] The lethargy in the face of the apocalypse rests on the fantasy of American rescue: 'Our suggestions that any surviving Americans would be likely to have their hands more than full at home was received as so much wet blanketry. The Americans, they assured us, would never have allowed such a thing to happen in their own country.'[2] Needless to say, the triffids over-run the country, eliminate most of the small bands of survivors and, we are left to assume, take control of the world itself.

Wyndham's book is notable in many ways, and is still remark-ably affecting and immediate even today, when contemporary culture is saturated with catastrophism and apocalypse, many of whose themes and tropes themselves stem from the influence of Wyndham. One thing absent in today's public culture of catastro-phism and of which Wyndham made a great deal in his novel, however, is the specific role of the US in the imagined apocalypse. The device of apocalypse throws into sharp relief the elements of a global, generalised system of dependence on US rescue, all the more striking for the fact that Wyndham portrays this in the era of the High Cold War, long before the era of unipolarity and post-Cold War cosmopolitanism. The ardent belief in 'American fairy godmothers' is the counterpoint to the fatalistic lethargy and fragmentation that immobilises the fictional inhabitants of Wyndham's apocalyptic wasteland.

I raise Wyndham's novel here because it helps illuminate certain aspects of the liberalism of fear – not least how deeply embedded it is in contemporary culture but that it also stretches back to the Cold War era, if not before. The historic proximity and immanence of catastrophe means that the only political hope rests in avoiding the worst, in being pulled back from the precipice. Wyndham's re-imagining of a Cold War-era state of nature dramatises in extreme form a basic truth about the powerful imaginative grip of the 'American fairy godmother' and its debilitating consequences. Of course, the fear of disorder is deeply rooted in the liberal imagination, with the need for security being constitutive not only of state power and authority but, in the last instance, of society itself. Yet what Wyndham's fable suggests is that the liberalism of fear – the prospect of civilisational collapse and regression into primitive barbarism – not only motivates the construction of sovereign power but may even *disable* it, as with Wyndham's fragmented bands of survivors, morally paralysed by the prospect of American rescue. If the counterpart of the state of nature in classical contractarian liberalism is the sovereign state, perhaps the counterpart of the post-sovereign state of nature in the liberalism of fear is not a sovereign but a global super-sovereign.

John Wyndham's Cold War-era fable pushes us to reflect on how much of political life is implicitly or explicitly predicated on the ultimately illusory promise of outside support. Wyndham takes this notion to its logical extreme, where social order outside America is inconceivable without the power of the American state. If the liberalism of fear is deeply rooted in the catastrophic nadir of the mid-twentieth century, so too is the 'Micawber fixation on American fairy godmothers', which stretches back to the shattered promises of Wilsonian liberalism in the inter-war period. The spread and deepening of the liberalism of fear coincides with the precipitous US ascent to global supremacy. After all, consider how much of modern political life has been organised around and vested in the superabundance and munificence of American wealth and power reaching back to the First World War – 'a power unlike any other', in the words of historian Adam Tooze: 'a novel kind of "super-state", exercising a veto over the financial and security concerns of the other major states of the world'.[3]

On the one hand, America's globalised vision of super-sovereignty has taken the form of destroying self-determination in the Third World with multi-pronged assaults on what were once leading states of that group – Indonesia, Yugoslavia, Iraq, Libya – alongside overseeing triumphant NATO and EU expansion eastwards, in the lands of the old Warsaw Pact. The assault on actually existing self-determination in the old Third World also corresponded with the devaluation of the idea of self-determination, which was exploded into its constituent functions, to be annexed by various transnational governance structures in peacebuilding and nation-building exercises, while retaining the shell of formal, legal independence. The panoply of liberal intervention and its associated structures, techniques, instruments, devices and regimes has served to substitute interdependence for independence, and has undermined the appeal and legitimacy of one of the core political ideals of the modern age – that of the value and dignity of self-rule and autonomy.

On the other hand, the erosion of this ideal goes further still, as suggested in Wyndham's novel. The globalisation of humanitarianism and liberal intervention has also entrenched a political infantilism, implicit in the politics of humanitarian rescue – the belief, as with Wyndham's hapless survivors, that someone, somewhere is able and willing to take charge of your situation – in global politics, the 'American fairy godmother'. It is redundant to recount the many times when people in desperate circumstances – whether Kurds, Rwandans, Bosnians, Tamils, Kosovars, Chechens, Somalis, Darfuris, Congolese, Afghans, Liberians, Iraqis, Libyans, Yazidis – have betrayed themselves by vesting their hopes in the promise of outside support, which, if it arrives at all, is inevitably belated, lacking, insufficient, problematic, conditional, self-interested, limited, ambivalent. The era of humanitarian intervention and the responsibility to protect helped to globalise the liberalism of fear, reorganising various civil wars, secessionist movements, revolutionary upsurges and insurgent movements around the prospect of support from a liberal international community ultimately centred on US power and exceptionalism.

This belief in US exceptionalism is not, however, restricted to its wards – it has contributed to shaping the orientation of US politics in very distinctive ways. A global constitutionalism that is effectively Schmittian in conception, in which the US is a super-sovereign at once inside and outside the global order, has facilitated the extraordinary political conceit that international order can be held together with will alone, given the overwhelming character of US power. This conceit, problematic enough in the context of domestic politics circumscribed by the sovereign state, is catastrophic on the global scale by virtue of the fact that international order is thus seen as nothing but rules and institutions that the US can choose whether or not to uphold and/or abide by. Paradoxically, this double view of international order, by which the US can see from both inside and outside, contributes to the view that the entirety of the international order is wholly visible and malleable.

Thus, in a global order in which there is no strong competitive necessity driving the imposition of monopolistic and unitary empires, in which there are strong (albeit contested and crumbling) norms against the territorial adjustment of borders, annexations and conquest, the political articulation of intervention must be cast as rule-breaking – that is to say, an exception to the routine of political and legal interaction among nominally independent states. Debates about when it is right to break rules can be extraordinarily difficult and indirect – it is little surprise that they breed such strong suspicions of bad faith on both sides. After all, everyone can think of circumstances in which the rules – however functional, practical, just, right and venerable – should or must be broken in order to preserve some higher good. If rule-breaking is an inevitable part of politics, this is not to say that all forms of rule-breaking are the same: there are different ways of breaking and justifying the breaking of rules, which in turn refract political options in different ways. The stakes are made dramatically higher if rule-breaking is cast as meeting an existential challenge, as the pattern has been with much liberal and especially humanitarian intervention. In this book I have sought to show how cosmopolitanism emerged from liberal internationalism as part of an existential exceptionalism. I have also tried to show that there are dangerous implications to a politics where authority and power derive from extreme human distress and deprivation, where the predominant form of collective human identification is suffering and victimisation, and where the most we aim for is protection from (only) the most extreme forms of cruelty and depravity – a world in which always insufficient security continually erodes and subverts the practice of autonomy.

International order is, of course, more than simply rules and institutions: this is the foundational premise of modern international relations as a discipline, and some schools of thought, at least – such as the English School, realism, political economy – view institutions, rules, laws, norms as rooted in and expressive of an underlying structure – a distribution of power, patterns and arrangements of units that produce effects independent of the will of any particular actor. The Schmittian global constitutionalism adopted by the US with its exceptionalist vision has prompted imperial overreach, in which there is nothing that is not beyond the reach or concern of US power, as most memorably expressed by one US official after the fall of Baghdad, and commonly attributed to former Republican Party strategist Karl Rove:

> That's not the way the world really works anymore.... We're an empire now, and when we act, we create our own reality. And while you're studying that reality – judiciously, as you will – we'll act again, creating other new realities, which you can study too, and that's how things will sort out. We're history's actors ... and you, all of you, will be left to just study what we do.[4]

Here, US exceptionalism was not merely a statement of imperial hubris after a military victory nor the shop-worn presidential rhetoric of the 'city on the hill', but an explicit rejection of any notion of political modernity, inasmuch as it was a rejection of the notion that international order encompasses spontaneous dynamics beyond the control of any single state, even a super-state or super-sovereign. The modernist vision was the classical notion of international order as a systematic pattern of behaviour with its effects autonomously produced through the interaction of its constituent units. The most obvious manifestation of such order on the international plane was, of course, the balance of power, precisely that manifestation of international order that has been noticeable by its absence since the end of the Cold War. The risks here are not merely the 'blowback' of unintended consequences when interventions fail, but correctly identifying changes in the legitimation and practice of power, ensuring political account-ability for the use of force, and exercising democratic control over executive power. Thus, what is at stake here are not just relations between the global North and South – important as these are – but also identifying the retroactive effects of intervention on political structures in Western states.

The conventional critique of humanitarian intervention is usually a variation on a similar theme: it is a tale of idealism debased by political scheming, of noble intentions overwhelmed by unintended consequences, of humane aspirations subverted by sinister elites and rigid bureaucracies. The structure of the story is typically the search for the 'real' reason for intervention that sabotaged the noble ideal: geopolitical gambits and rivalries, cynical foreign adventurism as a diversion from domestic troubles, neo-colonial manoeuvres, competition over spheres of influence, a struggle for natural resources – diamonds, coltan and rubber in Africa, oil in the Middle East and oil pipelines wherever there are no natural resources. However the story begins and wherever it happens to take place, the denouement is always the same: human rights and international ethics are contaminated by ulterior motives. Political analysis collapses into an unchanging narrative of cynicism and greed.

The problem with such stories is not that they are too critical, but that they are not critical enough; not that they are too political, but that they are ultimately apolitical. In such 'critiques', politics is only ever power politics, and critique only ever the exposure of hidden machinations. Perversely, the ethical systems in question remain unscathed; their status as noble ideals remains intact if not reinforced, ready for use again in the next crusade for human rights and democracy. Thus, as we have seen, the core of human rights has thus far been preserved from critique. What is cast as deep and cutting criticism of human rights is often nothing more than glancing blows, in which cynical criticism that sees human rights as nothing more than a cover for oil wars is married to an idealistic, even naïve reaffirmation of these very same ideals. This pattern is visible even in the most supposedly stringent and stinging criticisms of human rights and humanitarian intervention, such as that from Noam Chomsky, who castigated what he called 'military humanism' and whose very name became an adjective to exemplify a certain kind of radical left critique of human rights. Yet even this supposedly ultra-radical critic has argued that human rights can be redeemed, arguing that human rights still serve useful purposes for civil society groups in the global South.[5]

The critique presented in this book has sought to break with these critical conventions in a number of respects. First, it is not a tale of ethics being undermined by politics but the ethics themselves that are identified as the problem; not the cynical subversion of human rights, but the framing of problems of political order as problems of humanitarian suffering. Further, on the international plane, the critique presented here is not an account of empire run amok. Instead of offering the study of ever more exquisitely refined and elevated stages of imperialism, or describing ethereal new structures of global power, or seeking therapeutically to coax would-be empires out of their delusions, what must be studied and explained instead are the imperial failure resulting from recurrent warfare and the emergent structures of political authority resulting from the incessant use of force. To do all this, I argued that we needed to place the study of intervention on a new footing, by thinking beyond causes and motivations, to rethink the relationship between intervention and political order in the framework of exceptionalism.

The conclusion reached is that it is the human rights themselves that are the problem – and not their manipulation. There is no longer any avoiding the issue – that it is human rights that are the ideology of state paternalism and permanent war. They give expression to the liberalism of fear and have normalised crisis as the permanent condition of international order, in which extreme visions of human suffering have come to define political organisation and identity. What is needed is not a more finely poised balance between ethical aspirations and political realities, but a re-posing of fundamental and ultimately political questions regarding the nature of rights and the structure of political authority and representation.

Notes

Notes to preface and acknowledgements

1 See Yanis Varoufakis, *The global minotaur: America, Europe and the future of the global economy* (London: Zed Books, 2015), *passim*; and Emmanuel Todd, *After the empire: the breakdown of the American order* (New York: Columbia University Press, 2003), *passim*. See also Slavoj Žižek, *Like a thief in broad daylight: power in the era of post-humanity* (London: Penguin, 2018), p. 92.

2 John J. Mearsheimer, *The great delusion: liberal dreams and international realities* (New Haven: Yale University Press, 2018); and Stephen M. Walt, *The hell of good intentions: America's foreign policy elite and the decline of US primacy* (New York: Farrar, Straus & Giroux, 2018).

Notes to introduction

1 Islamic State initially called itself and was known as the Islamic State of Iraq and the Levant (ISIS per the Arabic acronym, or ISIL in its English version). Later, after further military victories, they called themselves Islamic State. In this book, for the sake of consistency and convenience, I simply use Islamic State, abbreviated to ISIS to be consistent with reporting on the group.

2 Five Pillars, 'Abu Bakr al-Baghdadi urges Muslims to make hijrah to the "Islamic state"', at https://5pillarsuk.com/2014/07/02/abu-bakr-al-baghdadi-urges-muslims-to-make-hijrah-to-the-islamic-state (accessed 28 May 2019).

3 See further Scott Shane, 'From Minneapolis to ISIS: an American's path to jihad', *New York Times*, 21 March 2015.

4 See Ben Taub, 'Journey to jihad', *New Yorker*, 1 June 2015; Yasmin Alibhai Brown, 'How to treat returning jihadis', *New European*, 25 March 2018.

5 Michael Muhammad Knight, 'I was nearly an American jihadi and I understand why young men are joining Isis – we are raised to love violence', *Independent*, 4 September 2014. Knight's piece is

self-evidently tendentious and self-exculpatory, but nonetheless important and insightful.

6 Jürgen Habermas, *The postnational constellation: political essays*, trans. Max Pensky (Cambridge: MIT Press, 2001).

7 Slavoj Žižek, 'NATO, the left hand of God', *Nettime*, 29 June 1999, available at https://www.lacan.com/zizek-nato.htm (accessed 13 July 2018).

8 Jürgen Habermas, 'Bestiality and humanity: a war on the border between legality and morality', *Constellations* 6.3 (1999), p. 270.

9 Habermas, 'Bestiality and humanity', p. 264.

10 Patrick Hayden, *Cosmopolitan global politics* (Farnham: Ashgate, 2005), p. 92. See further David Held, *Cosmopolitanism: ideals and realities* (Cambridge: Polity, 2010), pp. 196–198; see also Richard Beardsworth, *Cosmopolitanism and international relations theory* (Cambridge: Polity, 2011). Whereas the most intensive scholarly and theoretical debates in cosmopolitanism have been regarding obligations, rights and justice – such as the merits of wealth transfer from global North to global South – I do not engage these discussions in this book.

11 Perry Anderson, 'Arms and rights: Rawls, Habermas and Bobbio in an age of war', *New Left Review* 31 (January–February 2005), p. 5. See further Costas Douzinas, *Human rights and empire: the political philosophy of cosmopolitanism* (Abingdon: Routledge, 2007); Habermas, *Postnational constellation, passim*.

12 John Rawls, *The law of peoples, with 'The idea of public reason revisited'* (Cambridge: Harvard University Press, 2001), p. 6.

13 Samuel Moyn, *The last utopia: human rights in history* (Cambridge: Harvard University Press, 2012). The subsequent discussion in this introduction draws mostly on the arguments in Moyn's book.

14 See Moyn, *The last utopia, passim*; Patrick William Kelly, *Sovereign emergencies: Latin America and the making of global human rights politics* (Cambridge: Cambridge University Press, 2018).

15 On this strain of liberalism see ch. 6 in Nicholas Rennger, *The anti-Pelagian imagination in political theory and international relations: dealing in darkness* (Abingdon: Routledge, 2017). Rennger refers to this strain of liberalism as 'dystopic liberalism'. Although I have drawn on Rennger's work, given the argument developed in this book, for the sake of avoiding confusion I have avoided reproducing his labels. See also ch. 4 in David Chandler, *From Kosovo to Kabul: human rights and international intervention* (London: Pluto Press, 2002).

16 As Rennger shows, Raymond Aron was even suspicious of the 1941 Atlantic Charter, fearing that it overreached the purview of traditional liberalism in promising freedom from fear. Rennger, *The anti-Pelagian imagination*.

17 See Moyn, *The last utopia, passim*. See also Kirsten Sellars on the origins of human rights in the foreign policy of the Carter administration.

Kirsten Sellars, *The rise and rise of human rights* (Stroud: Sutton Publishing, 2002).

18 On matters of definition and distinction with regard to humanitarian intervention and the responsibility to protect and so on, see below.

19 Powell, cited in Sarah Kenyon Lischer, 'Military intervention and the "humanitarian force multiplier"', *Global Governance* 13 (2007), p. 99. Powell was referring specifically to the US intervention in Afghanistan in 2001.

20 Habermas, 'Bestiality and humanity', p. 268.

21 This debate is taken up in greater detail in chapter 2.

22 See Gregory H. Fox, *Humanitarian occupation* (Cambridge: Cambridge University Press, 2008).

23 In addition to Moyn, see, *inter alia*: Chandler, *From Kosovo to Kabul*; Douzinas, *Human rights and empire*; Alain Badiou, *Ethics: An essay on the understanding of evil* (London: Verso, 2013); and Stephen Hopgood, *The endtimes of human rights* (Ithaca: Cornell University Press, 2013).

24 For concepts and definitions of exceptionalism, see chapter 3.

25 Regarding how the justification given for the intervention in Afghanistan evolved from counter-terrorism to humanitarianism, see Simon Chesterman, 'Humanitarian intervention and Afghanistan', in Jennifer M. Welsh, ed., *Humanitarian intervention and international relations* (Oxford: Oxford University Press, 2003).

26 See, *inter alia*, Lawrence Freedman, 'The age of liberal wars', *Review of International Studies* 31.SI (2005), pp. 93–107.

27 See Philip Cunliffe, *Legions of peace: UN peacekeepers from the global South* (London: Hurst, 2013), *passim*.

28 See for example Gareth Evans, Ramesh Thakur and Robert Pape, 'Correspondence: humanitarian intervention and the responsibility to protect', *International Security* 37.4 (2013), pp. 199–214.

29 On Iraq, see Richard B. Miller, 'Justifications of the Iraq war examined', *Ethics and International Affairs* 22.1 (2008), pp. 43–67. For an overview of the debate on Georgia, see Roy Allison, 'The Russian case for intervention in Georgia: international law, norms and political calculation', *European Security* 18.2 (2009), pp. 173–200.

30 See 'Conclusion' in Nicolas J. Wheeler, *Saving strangers: humanitarian intervention in international society* (Oxford: Oxford University Press, 2002).

31 See Wheeler, *Saving strangers*, pp. 305–306, and, more generally, Nicholas J. Wheeler, 'The humanitarian responsibilities of sovereignty: explaining the development of a new norm of military intervention for humanitarian purposes in international society', in Welsh, ed., *Humanitarian intervention*. On the question of selectivity in intervention, see further Martin Binder, 'Humanitarian crises and the international politics of selectivity', *Human Rights Review* 10.3 (2009), pp. 327–348.

32 On non-Western interventions, see further below.
33 I owe this characterisation to John Macmillan.
34 See further Martha Finnemore, *The purpose of intervention: changing beliefs about the use of force* (Ithaca: Cornell University Press, 2003), p. 6.
35 Finnemore, *The purpose of intervention, passim.*

Notes to chapter 1

1 See, for example, Azar Gat, 'The return of authoritarian great powers', *Foreign Affairs* 86 (2007), pp. 59–69.
2 White House, *National Security Strategy of the United States of America,* December 2017, available at https://www.whitehouse.gov/wp-content/uploads/2017/12/NSS-Final-12-18-2017-0905.pdf (accessed 20 October 2019), pp. 25, 46.
3 Richard Haass, 'International order for 4 centuries has been based on non-interference in the internal affairs of others and respect for sovereignty. Russia has violated this norm by seizing Crimea and by interfering in the 2016 US election. We must deal w Putin's Russia as the rogue state it is.' Tweet @RichardHaas, 14 July 2018, 21:26.
4 See Sarah Begley, 'Read the full text of Samantha Power's scathing attack on Russia', *Time,* 17 January 2017, available at https://time.com/4637117/samantha-power-united-nations-russia-speech-transcript (accessed 9 August 2018).
5 Will Dunham, 'Kerry condemns Russia's "incredible act of aggression" in Ukraine', Reuters, 2 March 2014, available at https://www.reuters.com/article/2014/03/02/us-ukraine-crisis-usa-kerry-idUSBREA210DG20140302 (accessed 9 August 2018).
6 This section draws on Roland Dannreuther, 'Understanding Russia's return to the Middle East', *International Politics,* May 2018, pp. 1–17.
7 Viatcheslav Morozov, 'Subaltern empire? Toward a postcolonial approach to Russian foreign policy', *Problems of Post-Communism* 60.6 (2013), pp. 16–28.
8 See, for example, Zheng Bijian, 'China's "peaceful rise" to great-power status', *Foreign Affairs* 84 (2005), p. 18.
9 Kathrin Hille, 'China commits combat troops to Mali', *Financial Times,* 27 June 2013.
10 Logan Pauley, 'China takes the lead in UN peacekeeping', *The Diplomat,* 17 April 2018, available at https://thediplomat.com/2018/04/china-takes-the-lead-in-un-peacekeeping (accessed 20 August 2018).
11 See UN Security Council Report, *The Veto,* October 2015, available at https://www.securitycouncilreport.org/research-reports/the-veto.php (accessed 20 August 2018).
12 See Adam Tooze, *Crashed: how a decade of financial crises changed the world* (London: Allen Lane, 2018), especially ch. 5.

13 A point made forcefully by G. J. Ikenberry, 'The end of liberal inter-national order?', *International Affairs* 94.1 (2019), pp. 7–23.
14 On China's 'Westphalianism', see Barry Buzan, 'China in international society: is "peaceful rise" possible?', *Chinese Journal of International Politics* 3.1 (2010), pp. 5–36.
15 The classic statement of this view would be Stephen Krasner, *Sovereignty: organised hypocrisy* (Princeton: Princeton University Press, 1999).
16 See Morozov, 'Subaltern empire?'; and Daniel Drezner, 'Why China will be able to sell itself as the last liberal great power', *Washington Post*, 24 January 2017.
17 Quentin Peel, 'Russia's reversal: where next for humanitarian inter-vention', *Financial Times*, 22 August 2008.
18 Christian A. Nielsen, 'The Kosovo precedent and the rhetorical deployment of former Yugoslav analogies in the cases of Abkhazia and South Ossetia', *Southeast European and Black Sea Studies* 9.1–2 (2009), pp. 171–189.
19 Morozov, 'Subaltern empire?', p. 22.
20 See Tooze, *Crashed*, ch. 5; and Richard Sakwa, *Russia against the rest: the post-Cold War crisis of world order* (Cambridge: Cambridge University Press, 2017), *passim*.
21 Ishaan Tharoor, 'Russia stays in the driver's seat in Syria', *Washington Post*, 10 July 2018.
22 Morozov, 'Subaltern empire?', p. 25.
23 Sakwa, *Russia against the rest*, *passim*.
24 On UN peacekeeping and Western control over UN operations, see Philip Cunliffe, *Legions of peace: UN peacekeepers from the global South* (London: Hurst, 2013).
25 This argument is developed in more detail in Cunliffe, *Legions of peace*, chs 4 and 5.
26 See for instance, Alex J. Bellamy, 'Responsibility to protect or Trojan horse? The crisis in Darfur and humanitarian intervention after Iraq', *Ethics and International Affairs* 91. 2 (2005), pp. 31–54.
27 For example James Traub, 'The end of American intervention', *New York Times*, 18 February 2012, available at https://www.nytimes.com/2012/02/19/opinion/sunday/the-end-of-american-intervention.html (accessed 15 November 2018).
28 These Cold War-era interventions constitute important case studies for Nicholas J. Wheeler's classic study *Saving strangers: humanitarian intervention in international society* (Oxford: Oxford University Press, 2000).
29 Some estimates of casualties in the Bangladesh liberation war are over twice the highest estimates of casualties in Rwanda. In this case too, India confronted a regime, in the form of Yahya Khan's Pakistan, that had firm US support.

30 See Mark Mazower, *Governing the world: the history of an idea* (New York: Allen Lane, 2012), ch. 13 and *passim*.

31 See further Peter Dombrowski and Rodger A. Payne, 'The emerging consensus for preventive war', *Survival* 48.2 (2006), pp. 115–136; and Jack Donnelly, 'Human rights: a new standard of civilization?', *International Affairs* 74.1 (1998), pp. 1–23.

32 See further Perry Anderson, 'Arms and rights: Rawls, Habermas and Bobbio in an age of war', *New Left Review*, 31 (January–February 2005).

33 The exemplar of this approach would be Stephen Krasner, *Sovereignty: organized hypocrisy* (Princeton: Princeton University Press, 1999).

34 See for example, Daniel Philpott, 'Sovereignty: an introduction and brief history', *Journal of International Affairs* 48.2 (1995), pp. 353–368; and especially Georg Sørensen, 'Sovereignty: change and continuity in a fundamental institution', *Political Studies* 47.3 (1999), pp. 590–604.

35 Carl Schmitt, 'Ethic of state and pluralistic state', in Chantal Mouffe, ed., *The Challenge of Carl Schmitt* (London: Verso, 1999), p. 202.

36 John G. Mearsheimer says that the 'total mismanagement of the relationship with Russia ever since the downfall of communism' has been more catastrophic in foreign policy terms than the invasion of Iraq. Cited in Sakwa, *Russia against the rest*, p. 169.

37 Barry Buzan, *People, states and fear: an agenda for international security studies in the post-Cold War era*, 2nd edition (London: Harvester Wheatsheaf, 1991), p. 304.

38 For a contrary view, see Ian Hurd, 'Breaking and making norms: American revisionism and crises of legitimacy', *International Politics* 44.2–3 (2007), pp. 194–213.

39 E. H. Carr, *The twenty years' crisis, 1919–1939: reissued with a new preface from Michael Cox* (Basingstoke: Palgrave Macmillan, 2016).

40 The following discussion all draws from Buzan, *People, states and fear*, pp. 303–324.

41 On the peculiar dynamics of disavowal in ethical foreign policy, see David Chandler, 'Rhetoric without responsibility: the attraction of "ethical" foreign policy', *British Journal of Politics and International Relations* 5.3 (2003), pp. 295–316.

42 Buzan, *People, states and fear*, p. 307. Emphasis added.

43 For this debate, see Payam Akhavan, 'Are international criminal tribunals a disincentive to peace? Reconciling judicial romanticism with political realism', *Human Rights Quarterly* 31.3 (2009), pp. 624–654.

44 Marie-Joëlle Zahar, 'The (in)efficiency of mediation in contemporary conflict: a question of design?', Annual John Burton Lecture, delivered at University of Kent, 12 November 2018.

45 See Alan J. Kuperman, 'The moral hazard of humanitarian intervention: lessons from the Balkans', *International Studies Quarterly* 52.1 (2008), pp. 49–80.

46 See, *inter alia*, James Carden, 'Why does the US continue to arm

terrorists in Syria?', *The Nation*, 2 March 2017; Theodore McLaughlin, 'Why has the Syrian civil war lasted so long?', *Washington Post*, 27 July 2018.

47 See Cunliffe, *Legions of peace*, chs 1 and 2; see also Roland Paris, *At war's end: building peace after civil conflict* (Cambridge: Cambridge University Press, 2004), *passim*.

48 See, respectively, Frank Füredi, *The new ideology of imperialism: renewing the moral imperative* (London: Pluto Press, 1994); Mohammed Ayoob, 'Humanitarian intervention and international society', *Global Governance* 7.3 (2001), pp. 225–230; David Chandler, *From Kosovo to Kabul and beyond: human rights and international intervention*, 2nd edition (London: Pluto Press, 2006); Richard Kareem Al-Qaq, *Managing world order: United Nations peace operations and the security agenda* (London: I. B. Tauris, 2009); Tariq Ali, ed., *Masters of the universe? NATO's Balkan crusade* (London: Verso, 2000).

49 Thomas E. Doyle, 'When liberal peoples turn into outlaw states: John Rawls' Law of Peoples and liberal nuclearism', *Journal of International Political Theory* 11.2 (2015), pp. 257–273.

50 See Nuno P. Monteiro, 'Unrest assured: why unipolarity is not peaceful', *International Security* 36.3 (2011/2012), pp. 9–40.

51 Hedley Bull, 'The great irresponsibles? The United States, the Soviet Union, and world order', *International Journal* 35.3 (1980), pp. 437–447.

52 Bull, 'The great irresponsibles?', p. 447.

53 Dannreuther, 'Understanding Russia's return to the Middle East', *passim*.

54 For this kind of argument see Monteiro, 'Unrest assured'.

55 This is the core argument of Simon Chesterman, *Just war or just peace? Humanitarian intervention and international law* (Oxford: Oxford University Press, 2002). See, further, Chandler, *From Kosovo to Kabul and beyond*, ch. 6.

56 A theme taken from the title of Olivier Roy, *The politics of chaos in the Middle East* (London: Hurst, 2008).

57 See, for example, W. J. Hennigan, Brian Bennett and Nabih Bulos, 'In Syria, militias armed by the Pentagon fight those armed by the C.I.A.', *Los Angeles Times*, 27 March 2016. G. K. Chesterton's Edwardian absurdist fable of a nineteenth-century anarchist terror cell that consists of nothing but secret police infiltrators unaware of each other illustrates by way of analogy the bizarre global construct of contemporary jihadism that has been so heavily backed by Western states during the Cold War and since. G. K. Chesterton, *The man who was Thursday* (London: Penguin, 2012).

58 See, *inter alia*, David E. Sanger, 'Rebel arms flow is said to benefit jihadists in Syria', *New York Times*, 14 October 2012; Mark Mazetti, Adam Goldman and Michael S. Schmidt, 'Behind the sudden death of a $1 billion secret C.I.A. war in Syria', *New York Times*, 2 August

2017; Patrick Cockburn, 'Thanks to UK and US intervention, al-Qaeda now has a mini-state in Yemen. It's Iraq and Isis all over again', *The Independent*, 15 April 2016, available at https://www.independent.co.uk/voices/thanks-to-uk-and-us-intervention-al-qaeda-now-has-a-mini-state-in-yemen-its-iraq-and-isis-all-over-a6986086.html (accessed 23 August 2018); Maggie Michaels, Trish Wilson and Lee Keath, '"Unite with the devil": Yemen war binds US, allies, al-Qaida', Associated Press, 7 August 2018, at https://www.apnews.com/9bf91c535f274925a2be802 93e121446 (accessed 11 March 2019).

59 Malfrid Braut-Heghammer, 'Why North Korea succeeded in getting nuclear weapons – where Libya and Iraq didn't', *Washington Post*, 2 January 2018, available at https://www.washingtonpost.com/news/monkey-cage/wp/2018/01/02/why-north-korea-succeeded-at-getting-nuclear-weapons-when-iraq-and-libya-failed/?utm_term=.728f21a8a02b (accessed 23 August 2018); Wyn Bowen and Matthew Moran, 'What North Korea learned from Libya's decision to give up nuclear weapons', *The Conversation*, 11 May 2018, available at https://theconversation.com/what-north-korea-learned-from-libyas-decision-to-give-up-nuclear-weapons-95674 (accessed 23 August 2018).

60 See, further, David Zounmenou, 'The National Movement for the Liberation of Azawad factor in the Mali crisis', *African Security Review* 22.3 (2013), pp. 164–174.

61 Rajapaksa, quoted in Christopher Caldwell, 'Communiste et Rastignac'. *Review of Le Monde selon K*, by Pierre Péan, *London Review of Books* 31.13 (2009), pp. 7–10.

62 See International Coalition for the Responsibility to Protect, 'Crisis in Sri Lanka',, at https://www.responsibilitytoprotect.org/index.php/crises/crisis-in-sri-lanka#response (accessed 24 August 2018); see also Alex J. Bellamy, *Responsibility to protect: a defense* (Oxford: Oxford University Press, 2014).

63 This is indeed the core of an entire research agenda. See, for example, Amitav Acharya, 'How ideas spread: whose norms matter? Norm localization and institutional change in Asian regionalism', *International Organization* 58.2 (2004), pp. 239–275.

64 Acharya, 'How ideas spread', *passim*; and on the 'good norm bias' see Regina Heller and Martin Kahl. 'Tracing and understanding "bad" norm dynamics in counterterrorism: the current debates in IR research', *Critical Studies in Terrorism* 6.3 (2013), pp. 414–428.

65 Wheeler, *Saving strangers*, pp. 305–306, and, more generally, Nicholas J. Wheeler, 'The humanitarian responsibilities of sovereignty: explaining the development of a new norm of military intervention for humanitarian purposes in international society', in Jennifer Welsh, ed., *Humanitarian intervention and international relations* (Oxford: Oxford University Press, 2004).

66 For a critique of this norm-based theory of sovereignty, see Jeremy

Moses, *Sovereignty and responsibility: power, norms and intervention in international relations* (Basingstoke: Palgrave, 2014), ch. 3.

67 The logical integration of non-interference with sovereignty has been challenged by some, a position that will be taken up in later chapters. See Luke Glanville, *Sovereignty and the responsibility to protect: a new history* (Chicago: University of Chicago Press, 2013). Suffice to say here that if, as Glanville alleges, non-intervention is an innovation and artefact of the UN Charter rather than intrinsic to the norm of sovereignty, it does not invalidate the points about inverted revisionism being a form of revisionism which is self-inflicted, as these institutions are still the products of the liberal world order.

Notes to chapter 2

1 See Tara Golshan, 'John McCain's shocking concession on the Iraq War: it was a "mistake"', *Vox*, 25 May 2018, available at https://www.vox.com/2018/5/25/17394466/john-mccain-memoir-iraq-war-mistake (accessed 5 July 2018).

2 BBC News, 'President Obama: Libya aftermath "worst mistake" of presidency', 11 April 2016, at https://www.bbc.co.uk/news/world-us-canada-36013703 (accessed 5 July 2018).

3 Gordon Lubold and Dion Nissenbaum, 'Trump bowed to Pentagon restraint on Syria strikes', *Wall Street Journal*, 16 April 2018.

4 Joel Gehrke, 'Theresa May: Syria strike "not about regime change"', *Washington Examiner*, 13 April 2018, available at https://www.washingtonexaminer.com/policy/defense-national-security/theresa-may-syria-strike-not-about-regime-change (accessed 5 July 2018).

5 See, for example, France Diplomatie, 'G5 Sahel Joint Force and the Sahel Alliance',, at https://www.diplomatie.gouv.fr/en/french-foreign-policy/defence-security/crisis-and-conflicts/g5-sahel-joint-force-and-the-sahel-alliance (accessed 30 August 2018).

6 Ian Traynor, 'EU to launch military operations against migrant-smugglers in Libya', *Guardian*, 20 April 2015.

7 There is, to be sure, a complex knot of criticisms of humanitarian intervention and the humanitarian era in war and foreign policy – criticisms from the viewpoint of theories of international order and strategic failure. This range of criticisms is discussed across chapters 2 and 4. Here I only want to sketch out the limits of conventional criticisms of humanitarianism in foreign policy in order to raise the question of what counts as criticism as such.

8 See, for example, Kenneth Roth, 'Was the Iraq War a humanitarian intervention?', *Journal of Military Ethics* 5.2 (2006), pp. 84–92; Ramesh Thakur 'Iraq and the responsibility to protect', *Behind the Headlines* 62 (2004), pp. 1–16.

9 Ian McEwan, *Saturday* (London: Vintage, 2005), p. 72.

10 The discussion in this section draws on: the classical pluralism of Hedley Bull, especially his two essays 'Society and anarchy in international relations' and 'The Grotian concept of international society' in Herbert Butterfield and Martin Wight, eds, *Diplomatic investigations: essays in the theory of international politics* (London: George Allen & Unwin, 1966); William Bain, 'The political theory of trusteeship and the twilight of international equality', *International Relations* 17.1 (2003), pp. 59–77; and, especially, Robert Jackson, *The global covenant: human conduct in a world of states* (London: Oxford University Press, 2000) and *Sovereignty: the evolution of an idea* (Cambridge: Polity, 2007). See also Hedley Bull. 'International law and international order', *International Organization* 26.3 (1972), pp. 583–588.

11 See Hedley Bull and Adam Watson (eds), *The expansion of international society* (Oxford: Clarendon Press, 1984).

12 This is the core argument of Steven Pinker's book *The better angels of our nature: why violence has declined* (London: Allen Lane, 2011).

13 See, for example, Tim Murithi, 'The responsibility to protect as enshrined in Article 4 of the Constitutive Act of the African Union', *African Security Review* 16.3 (2007), pp. 14–24.

14 I base this on Cornelia Navari's work. See Cornelia Navari, 'Modelling the relation of fundamental institutions and international organizations', in Tonny Brems Knudsen and Cornelia Navari, eds, *International organization in the anarchical society: the institutional structure of world order* (Basingstoke: Palgrave Macmillan, 2018).

15 'Charterism' is an outlook largely compounded from the constituent elements of other theories and outlooks that will be addressed further below. These strands are drawn from: Simon Chesterman, *Just war or just peace? Humanitarian intervention and international law* (Oxford: Oxford University Press, 2002) and, *inter alia*, Simon Chesterman, 'Legality versus legitimacy: humanitarian intervention, the Security Council, and the rule of law', *Security Dialogue* 33.3 (2002), pp. 293–307, as well as David Chandler, *From Kosovo to Kabul and beyond: human rights and international intervention*, 2nd edition (London, Pluto Press, 2006). One analyst whose work would straddle the outlook of both pluralism and Charterism would be Mohammed Ayoob in his piece 'Third World perspectives on humanitarian intervention and international administration', *Global Governance* 10 (2004), pp. 99–118.

16 On this point see Jennifer Welsh, 'Taking consequences seriously: objections to humanitarian intervention', in Jennifer Welsh, ed., *Humanitarian intervention and international relations* (Oxford: Oxford University Press, 2003), p. 55.

17 See Independent International Commission on Kosovo (IICK), *The Kosovo report: international response and lessons learned* (Oxford: Oxford University Press, 2001).

18 See the discussion in chs 2–5, and especially ch. 3, in Kirsten Sellars, *The rise and rise of human rights* (London: Sutton, 2002).

19 See Robert Hilderbrand, *Dumbarton Oaks: the origins of the United Nations and the search for postwar security* (Durham: University of North Carolina Press, 1990), p. 15.

20 The story is recounted in Chesterman, *Just war or just peace?*

21 On this point, see Mark Mazower, *No enchanted palace: the end of empire and the ideological origins of the United Nations* (Princeton: Princeton University Press, 2009).

22 It forms a component of Pinker's argument in *The better angels of our nature.*

23 This specific example is recounted in Rodric Braithwaite, *Afghantsy: the Russians in Afghanistan 1978–89* (London: Profile Books, 2011), p. 105.

24 The sections draws on the thought of Stephen M. Walt, 'Top 10 warning signs of "liberal imperialism"', *Foreign Policy*, 23 May 2013, available at https://foreignpolicy.com/2013/05/20/top-10-warning-signs-of-liberal-imperialism (accessed 5 September 2018), *inter alia*; Henry Kissinger, 'New world disorder', *Newsweek*, 31 May 1999; Patrick Porter, 'Iraq: a liberal war after all. A critique of Dan Deudney and John Ikenberry', *International Politics* 55.1 (2017), pp. 334–348; John J. Mearsheimer, 'Why the Ukraine crisis is the West's fault: the liberal delusions that provoked Putin', *Foreign Affairs* 93.5 (2014), pp. 77–89; Jeremy Moses, 'Peace without perfection: the intersections of realist and pacifist thought', *Cooperation and Conflict* 53.1 (2017), pp. 42–60; Andrew J. Bacevich, *Washington rules: America's path to permanent war* (New York: Metropolitan Books, 2011).

25 See Nuno P. Monteiro, *Theory of unipolar politics* (Cambridge: Cambridge University Press, 2013).

26 On 'strategic traditionalism', see C. Dale Walton, 'The case for strategic traditionalism: war, national interest and liberal peacebuilding', *International Peacekeeping* 16.5 (2009), pp. 717–734.

27 John J. Mearsheimer, *The great delusion: liberal dreams and international realities* (New Haven: Yale University Press, 2018), p. 139.

28 See especially Stephen M. Walt, *The hell of good intentions: America's foreign policy elite and the decline of US primacy* (New York: Farrar, Straus & Giroux, 2018), ch. 5.

29 Although Lebow's discussion is framed around a study of Thucydides, Carl von Clausewitz and Hans J. Morgenthau, it is also clear that Lebow sees US unilateralism with respect to Iraq in 2003 as a proximate inspiration for his book. Richard Ned Lebow, *The tragic vision of politics: ethics, interests and orders* (Cambridge: Cambridge University Press, 2003), p. 13. See, further, Toni Erskine and Richard Ned Lebow, eds, *Tragedy and international relations* (Basingstoke: Palgrave Macmillan, 2012).

30 Lebow, *The tragic vision of politics*, fn 13, pp. 18–19.

31 Lebow, *The tragic vision of politics*, p. 116.

32 Roland Paris, 'The "responsibility to protect" and the structural problems of preventive humanitarian intervention', *International Peacekeeping* 21.5 (2014), p. 572. This part of the discussion draws on Paris's arguments in this paper.

33 See Nicholas J. Wheeler, 'Legitimating humanitarian intervention: principles and procedures', *Melbourne Journal of International Law* 2.2 (2001), pp. 554–560. See also David Luban, 'Just war and human rights', *Philosophy and Public Affairs* 9.2 (1980), pp. 160–181.

34 Nicholas J. Wheeler, *Saving strangers: humanitarian intervention in international society* (Oxford: Oxford University Press, 2000), p. 39.

35 See further Morris Morley and Chris McGillion, '"Disobedient" generals and the politics of redemocratization: the Clinton administration and Haiti', *Political Science Quarterly* 112.3 (1997), pp. 363–384.

36 See, for example, Michael Mandelbaum, 'The failure of intervention', *Foreign Affairs* 78.5 (1999), pp. 2–8.

37 See Hew Strachan, 'The lost meaning of strategy', *Survival* 47.3 (2005), pp. 33–54.

38 See, for example, Hans J. Morgenthau, 'Vietnam: another Korea?', in *The restoration of American politics* (Chicago: University of Chicago Press, 1962).

39 On Cold War nostalgia in strategic studies, see Patrick Porter, 'Twilight struggle: the Cold War was neither stable nor simple', 3 August 2015, at War on the Rocks, https://warontherocks.com/2015/08/twilight-struggle-the-cold-war-was-not-stable-or-simple (accessed 6 September 2018).

40 On the Khrushchev threat, see Geoffrey Roberts, *The Soviet Union in world politics: coexistence, revolution and Cold War, 1945–1991* (London: Routledge, 1999), p. 59.

41 On this point, see Andrew J. Bacevich, *The new American militarism: how Americans are seduced by war* (New York: Oxford University Press, 2005), especially ch. 1.

42 This section draws on: Jean Cohen, *Globalization and sovereignty: rethinking legality, legitimacy, and constitutionalism* (Cambridge: Cambridge University Press, 2012); Simon Chesterman, *Just war or just peace?*; Welsh, 'Taking consequences seriously'; and Jef Huysmans, 'International politics of exception: competing visions of international political order between law and politics', *Alternatives* 31.2 (2006), pp. 135–165. Huysmans' work in particular is dealt with in more detail in the next chapter.

43 See Chesterman, *Just war or just peace?*, ch. 4.

44 Chesterman makes this case in ch. 6 of *Just war or just peace?*

45 Welsh, 'Taking consequences seriously', pp. 54–57.

46 Cohen, *Globalization and sovereignty*, p. 459.

47 Cohen, *Globalization and sovereignty*, p. 459.
48 Cohen, *Globalization and sovereignty*, p. 460.
49 Cohen, *Globalization and sovereignty*, p. 478.
50 Jean Cohen, 'Whose sovereignty? Empire versus international law', *Ethics and International Affairs* 18.3 (2004), pp. 1–24.
51 Cohen, *Globalization and sovereignty*, pp. 471–472.
52 Cohen, *Globalization and sovereignty*, p. 472.
53 Cohen, *Globalization and sovereignty*, p. 474.
54 John Rawls, *The law of peoples, with 'The idea of public reason revisited'* (Cambridge: Harvard University Press, 2001), p. 36.
55 On this last, overlooked episode of regime change, see Philip Cunliffe, *Legions of peace: UN peacekeepers from the global South* (London: Hurst, 2013), pp. 57–59.

Notes to chapter 3

1 The Watson Institute estimates the combined number of deaths in Iraq, Pakistan and Afghanistan alone since 2001 is in the realm of half a million. Casualties in the Syrian civil war, ongoing at the time of writing, are also estimated at half a million dead. In addition there are the casualties from humanitarian intervention, peacekeeping and nation-building efforts in Somalia, Bosnia-Herzegovina, Sierra Leone, Kosovo, Haiti, East Timor, the Democratic Republic of Congo and Côte d'Ivoire. See Tom O'Connor, 'U.S. has spent six trillion dollars on wars that killed half a million people since 9/11, report says', *Newsweek*, 14 November 2018, available at https://www.newsweek.com/us-spent-six-trillion-wars-killed-half-million-1215588 (accessed 16 November 2018).
2 United Nations, *We the peoples: the role of the United Nations in the twenty-first century* (New York: General Assembly, 2000), p. 35, available at https://undocs.org/A/54/2000 (accessed 21 November 2018).
3 Ian Zuckerman, 'One law for war and peace? Judicial review and emergency powers between the norm and the exception', *Constellations: Journal of Democratic and Critical Theory* 13.4 (2006), p. 523.
4 Nicholas J. Wheeler, *Saving strangers: humanitarian intervention in international society* (Oxford: Oxford University Press 2000), p. 34.
5 Zuckerman, 'One law for war and peace?', p. 523. On humanitarian intervention as exceptionalist, see, *inter alia*, Alex J. Bellamy, 'Ethics and intervention: the "humanitarian exception" and the problem of abuse in the case of Iraq', *Journal of Peace Research* 41.2 (2004), pp. 131–147.
6 Zuckerman, 'One law for war and peace?', p. 523.
7 Michael Walzer, *Just and unjust wars*, 3rd edition (New York: Basic Books, 2000), ch. 16.

8 For example Walzer, ibid.

9 John Stuart Mill, 'A few words on non-intervention', in Gertrude Himmelfarb, ed., *Essays on Politics and Culture* (New York: Doubleday, 1963).

10 Martin Wight is arguably the archetypal exponent of such a view: see Martin Wight, 'Why is there no international theory?', *International Relations* 2.1 (1960), pp. 35–48.

11 On the political project of 'domestication', see Hidemi Suganami, *The domestic analogy and world order proposals* (Cambridge: Cambridge University Press, 1989).

12 Jef Huysmans, 'International politics of exception: competing visions of international political order between law and politics', *Alternatives* 31.2 (2006). p. 140. For a counter-point see Ronnie Hjorth, 'The poverty of exceptionalism in international theory', *Journal of International Political Theory* 10.2 (2014), pp. 169–187.

13 See *Guardian*, 'George Bush's speech to the UN general assembly', 12 September 2002, available at https://www.theguardian.com/world/2002/sep/12/iraq.usa3 (accessed 9 October 2018).

14 This is an example developed by Slavoj Žižek, 'Are we at war? Do we have an enemy?', *London Review of Books* 24.10 (2002), pp. 3–6.

15 See, further, Nicholas Vinocur, 'New French anti-terror law to replace 2-year state of emergency', *Politico*, 31 October 2017, available at https://www.politico.eu/article/new-french-anti-terror-law-to-replace-2-year-state-of-emergency (accessed 9 October 2018).

16 Of course, it is possible to deny *any* normative validity to the patterns of international politics at all, and to claim that the only relevant factors are natural-like laws and systemic processes that induce certain types of recurrent state behaviour. Such a position would be consistent with a structural realist perspective that simply discounts the relevance of norms and values for international order. Even this, though, does not nullify the problem of exceptionalism – it simply displaces it, from violation of human-constructed rules to the violation of human-constraining systemic laws (laws that 'punish' such deviation through the structural constraints exerted on state behaviour that will restore normal functioning). As the argument in this book is predicated on the notion that normative concerns *do* matter in international politics, we need not consider this countervailing argument here. On this specific point, see Jef Huysmans, 'International politics of exception', pp. 154–156.

17 See ch. 2 in Wheeler, *Saving strangers*.

18 Jef Huysmans, 'International politics of insecurity: normativity, inwardness and the exception', *Security Dialogue* 37.1 (2006), p. 21.

19 Huysmans, 'International politics of insecurity', p. 22.

20 Huysmans, 'International politics of insecurity', p. 26.

21 Huysmans, 'International politics of insecurity', p. 26.

22 On natural law, see further Martti Koskenniemi, 'Miserable comforters: international relations as new natural law', *European Journal of International Relations* 15.3 (2009), pp. 395–422.

23 See, for instance, Robert W. Murray et al., eds, *Into the eleventh hour: R2P, Syria and humanitarianism in crisis* (Bristol: E-International Relations, 2014), available at openresearch-repository.anu.edu.au/ bitstream/1885/27292/2/01_Evans_The_Consequences_of_2014.pdf (accessed 19 November 2018).

24 Ramesh Thakur, *The United Nations, peace and security: from collective security to the responsibility to protect* (Cambridge: Cambridge University Press, 2006), pp. 250–251.

25 International Commission on Intervention and State Sovereignty, *The responsibility to protect: report of the International Commission on Intervention and State Sovereignty* (Ottawa: International Development Research Centre, 2001), p. 6.

26 Francis M. Deng et al., *Sovereignty as responsibility: conflict management in Africa* (Washington, DC: Brookings Institution Press, 1996).

27 See, for example, Thomas Weiss, 'The sunset of humanitarian intervention? The responsibility to protect in a unipolar era', *Security Dialogue* 35.2 (2004), pp. 135–153.

28 On these respective points, see, for instance: Jennifer M. Welsh and Maria Banda, 'International law and the responsibility to protect: clarifying or expanding states' responsibilities?', *Global Responsibility to Protect* 2, no. 3 (2010): 213–223; Carsten Stahn, 'Responsibility to protect: political rhetoric or emerging legal norm?', *American Journal of International Law* 101.1 (2007), pp. 99–120; Louise Arbour, 'The responsibility to protect as a duty of care in international law and practice', *Review of International Studies* 31.3 (2008), pp. 445–458.

29 On the issue of pillars, see, for instance, David Chandler, 'R2P or not R2P? More statebuilding, less responsibility', *Global Responsibility to Protect* 2.1 (2010), pp. 161–166. On the doctrine and peacekeeping, see Hitoshi Nasu, 'Operationalizing the responsibility to protect in the context of civilian protection by UN Peacekeepers', *International Peacekeeping* 18.4 (2011), pp. 364–378.

30 Ramesh Thakur, 'The responsibility to protect at 15', *International Affairs* 92.2 (2016), p. 418.

31 Tony Blair, *A journey: my political life* (London: Hutchinson, 2010), p. 250.

32 Mary Kaldor, *Human security: reflections on globalization and intervention* (Cambridge: Polity, 2007).

33 See, for instance, Hjorth, 'The poverty of exceptionalism in international theory', p. 181; Stahn, 'Responsibility to protect'.

34 See for instance, Cristina G. Badescu and Linnea Bergholm. 'The responsibility to protect and the conflict in Darfur: the big let-down', *Security Dialogue* 40.3 (2009), pp. 287–309.

35 International Commission on Intervention and State Sovereignty, *The responsibility to protect*, ch. 4.

36 For more on the problems of imperfect duties in the doctrine, see Philip Cunliffe, 'Dangerous duties: power, paternalism and the responsibility to protect', *Review of International Studies* 36.SI (2010), pp. 79–96.

37 On this point, see Alex J. Bellamy, 'Responsibility to protect or Trojan horse? The crisis in Darfur and humanitarian intervention after Iraq', *Ethics and International Affairs* 19.2 (2005), pp. 31–54.

38 Huysmans, 'International politics of exception', p. 148.

39 Huysmans, 'International politics of exception', p. 46. On decisionism in international politics, see, further, Steven C. Roach, 'Decisionism and humanitarian intervention: reinterpreting Carl Schmitt and the global political order', *Alternatives* 30.4 (2005), pp. 443–460.

40 Huysmans, 'International politics of exception', p. 150.

41 David Chandler, *From Kosovo to Kabul and beyond: human rights and international intervention*, 2nd edition (London: Pluto Press, 2006), p. 90.

42 Huysmans, 'International politics of exception', pp. 147–148.

43 A point made by Louis Henkin, 'Kosovo and the law of "humanitarian intervention"', *American Journal of International Law* 93.4 (1999), pp. 824–828.

44 Jean L. Cohen, *Globalization and sovereignty: rethinking legality, legitimacy, and constitutionalism* (Cambridge: Cambridge University Press, 2012), p. 215.

45 Huysmans, 'International politics of exception', p. 147.

46 Huysmans, 'International politics of exception', p. 147.

47 On this latter point, see Robert Cooper, *The breaking of nations: order and chaos in the twenty-first century* (London: Atlantic Books, 2003).

48 The following brief section draws on Huysmans, 'International politics of exception', as well as Jean-Francois Drolet, *American neoconservatism: the politics and culture of a reactionary idealism* (London: Hurst, 2011).

49 Huysmans, 'International politics of exception', p. 21.

50 See, *inter alia*, Ariela Blätter and Paul D. Williams, 'The responsibility not to veto', *Global Responsibility to Protect* 3.3 (2011), pp. 301–322.

51 See Gerry Simpson, *Great powers and outlaw states: unequal sovereigns in the international legal order* (Cambridge: Cambridge University Press, 2004).

52 On this general point, on how humanitarianism undermined the representative claims of governments in the developing world, see Mark Duffield, *Global governance and the new wars: the merging of development and security* (London: Zed Books, 2001).

53 Robert Jackson, 'Martin Wight's thought on diplomacy', *Diplomacy and Statecraft* 13.4 (2002), p. 16.

54 James Der Derian, *On Diplomacy: A Genealogy of Western Estrangement* (Oxford: Oxford University Press, 1987), p. 135, original emphasis.

55 BBC News, 'David Cameron to call for new Syria peace drive at UN', 27 September 2015, at https://www.bbc.co.uk/news/uk-34372286 (accessed 22 November 2018).

56 Vladimir Putin, cited in Everett Rosenfeld, 'Putin: do you realise what you have done?', CNBC, 28 September 2015, at https://www.cnbc.com/2015/09/28/putin-do-you-realize-what-you-have-done.html (accessed 18 October 2018).

57 See Ian Hall, 'Diplomacy, anti-diplomacy and international society', in Richard Little and John Williams, eds, *The anarchical society in a globalised world* (Basingstoke: Palgrave, 2006), p. 144; cf. David Chandler, 'The security–development nexus and the rise of "anti-foreign policy"', *Journal of International Relations and Development* 10.4 (2007), pp. 362–386.

58 Jean Baudrillard, 'No pity for Sarajevo', in *Screened out*, trans. Chris Turner (London: Verso, 2002), p. 47.

59 Michael Ignatieff, *Empire lite: nation-building in Bosnia, Kosovo, Afghanistan* (London: Vintage, 2003), p. 42. An essay in the same book, 'The humanitarian as imperialist', takes Bernard Kouchner as an exemplar of the imperialist narcissist.

60 David Chandler, *From Kosovo to Kabul and beyond: human rights and international intervention*, 2nd edition (London: Pluto Press, 2006), p. 223.

61 Chandler, *Kosovo to Kabul and beyond*, pp. 222–224.

62 BBC News, 'Obama West Point speech in full with analysis', 29 May 2014, at https://www.bbc.co.uk/news/world-us-canada-27606537 (accessed 22 November 2018).

63 Zaki Laïdi, *A world without meaning: the crisis of meaning in international politics* (London: Routledge, 1998), p. 11.

64 Huysmans, 'International politics of exception', p. 22.

65 Huysmans, 'International politics of exception', p. 12.

66 Huysmans, 'International politics of exception', p. 26.

67 Huysmans, 'International politics of exception', p. 26.

68 Huysmans, 'International politics of exception', p. 26.

69 Jean L. Cohen, 'A global state of emergency or the further constitutionalization of international law: a pluralist approach', *Constellations* 15.4 (2008), p. 460.

70 Drolet, *American neoconservatism*.

Notes to chapter 4

1 Public Library of US Diplomacy, 'A/S Fried's November 15 meeting with DFM Titov on Kosovo', 21 November 2006, at https://search.

wikileaks.org/plusd/cables/o6MOSCOW12549_a.html (accessed 15 November 2018).

2   Martin Plaut, 'The UN's all pervasive role in Africa', 18 July 2007, at http://news.bbc.co.uk/1/hi/world/africa/6903196.stm (accessed 15 November 2018).

3   See, for example, Erlend Grøner Krogstad, 'Local ownership as dependence management: inviting the coloniser back', *Journal of Intervention and Statebuilding* 8.2–3 (2014), pp. 105–125.

4   See, for instance, Ghaith Abdul-Ahad, 'Bureaucracy of evil: how Islamic State ran a city', *Guardian*, 29 January 2018.

5   See, further, James Heartfield, 'Zombie anti-imperialists versus the "Empire"', Spiked Online, 1 September 2004, at https://spiked-online.com/newsite/article/2236#.W-lM7uKnwyU (accessed 12 November 2018).

6   On the influence of 'American empire studies', former Clinton administration official James Rubin observed that the policy of the first Bush administration 'appears to have spawned a brand new field of academic inquiry, what might be called American Empire studies'. James Rubin, 'Base motives', *Guardian*, 8 May 2004.

7   See V. I. Lenin, *Imperialism: the highest stage of capitalism. A popular outline* (London: Pluto Press/Junius, 1996), p. 90.

8   See Lenin, *Imperialism*, chs 9 and 10.

9   Lenin, *Imperialism*, chs 9 and 10.

10 Sebastian Mallaby, 'The reluctant imperialist: terrorism, failed states and the case for American empire', *Foreign Affairs* 81.2 (2002), pp. 2–7.

11 Niall Ferguson, 'An empire in denial: the limits of US imperialism', *Harvard International Review* 25.3 (2003), p. 64; David Chandler, *Empire in denial: the politics of state-building* (London: Pluto Press, 2006).

12 Chandler, *Empire in denial*, p. 36.

13 Francis Fukuyama, *State building: order and governance in the 21st century* (London: Profile Books, 2004).

14 For an excellent review of these kinds of arguments, see Roland Paris, 'Saving liberal peacebuilding', *Review of International Studies* 36.2 (2010), pp. 337–365. See also Mohammed Ayoob, *The third world security predicament: state making, regional conflict, and the international system* (Boulder, CO: L. Rienner, 1995).

15 The classic statement of this view is Edward Luttwak, 'Give war a chance', *Foreign Affairs* 78.4 (1999), pp. 36–44.

16 See, for example, Toby Dodge, *Iraq: from war to a new authoritarianism* (Abingdon: Routledge, 2013).

17 For an example of this view, see Mohammed Ayoob, 'Humanitarian intervention and state sovereignty', *International Journal of Human Rights* 6.1 (2002), pp. 81–102; and Mohammed Ayoob, 'Humanitarian intervention and international society', *Global Governance* 7.3 (2001), pp. 225–230.

18 The quote is adapted from Lee Feinstein, cited in Alex J. Bellamy,

Responsibility to protect: the global effort to end mass atrocities (Cambridge: Polity, 2009), p. 132.

19 Anne Orford, *International authority and the responsibility to protect* (Cambridge: Cambridge University Press, 2011).

20 Orford, *International authority*, ch. 5 and passim.

21 Orford, *International authority*, pp. 186–187.

22 Jean L. Cohen, 'Sovereign equality versus imperial right: the battle over the "new world order"', *Constellations: A Journal of Critical and Democratic Theory* 13.4 (2006), p. 489.

23 For a parallel argument regarding the decisionistic theory of sovereignty at the core of the responsibility to protect doctrine, see Jeremy Moses, *Sovereignty and responsibility: power, norms and intervention in international relations* (Basingstoke: Palgrave, 2014), especially ch. 2. Moses' argument does not account for the tendency to generate a universal sovereignty under the terms of the responsibility to protect, and sees decisionism as essential to sovereignty *tout court*.

24 See the resources available through the Global Centre for the Responsibility to Protect, at https://www.globalr2p.org/about_r2p (accessed 15 November 2018).

25 International Commission on Intervention and State Sovereignty, *The responsibility to protect: report of the International Commission on Intervention and State Sovereignty* (Ottawa: International Development Research Centre, 2001), pp. 44–45.

26 Kofi Annan, *In larger freedom: towards development, security and human rights for all. Report of the secretary-general* (UN Doc A/59/2005) (New York: United Nations Publications, 2005): §135.

27 James Pattison, 'Legitimacy and humanitarian intervention: who should intervene?', *International Journal of Human Rights* 12.3 (2008), pp. 395–413. Pattison seems either incognisant or unconcerned by just how extraordinary this recalibration of sovereign responsibilities is from the viewpoint of self-determination and representative government.

28 See United Nations, 'Statement at the opening of the thematic dialogue of the General Assembly on the responsibility to protect', General Assembly, 23 July 2009, available at www.un.org/ga/president/63/statements/openingr2p230709.shtml (accessed 10 March 2010).

29 Ian Zuckerman, 'One law for war and peace? Judicial review and emergency powers between norm and exception', *Constellations: A Journal of Critical and Democratic Theory* 13.4 (2006), p. 539.

30 Cohen, 'Sovereign equality versus imperial right', p. 489.

31 Jef Huysmans, 'The jargon of exception – on Schmitt, Agamben and the absence of political society', *International Political Sociology* 2.2 (2008): 170.

32 On Hobbes and sovereignty, see Moses, *Sovereignty and responsibility*, especially ch. 1.

33 Thomas Hobbes, *Leviathan*, ed. C. B. Macpherson (London: Penguin, 1968), ch. 19.
34 See, further, Orford, *International authority and the responsibility to protect*, p. 114.
35 Hobbes, *Leviathan*, ch. 25.
36 Hobbes, *Leviathan*, p. 272 and ch. 21, *passim*.
37 See, for example, Luke Glanville, *Sovereignty and the responsibility to protect: a new history* (Chicago, IL: University of Chicago Press, 2013).
38 James Martel, *Subverting the Leviathan: reading Thomas Hobbes as a radical democrat* (New York: Columbia University Press, 2007).
39 See, for instance, Alan J. Kuperman, 'The moral hazard of humanitarian intervention: lessons from the Balkans', *International Studies Quarterly* 52.1 (2008): 49–80.

Notes to conclusion

1 John Wyndham, *The day of the triffids* (London: Penguin, 2001), p. 107.
2 Wyndham, *The day of the triffids*, p. 111.
3 Adam Tooze, *The deluge: The Great War, America and the remaking of the global order, 1916–1931* (London: Penguin, 2015), p. 6.
4 In the quotation, Rove also sweeps aside the 'enlightenment principles and empiricism' of his interlocutor. Attributed to Rove, cited in Ron Susskind, 'Faith, certainty and the presidency of George W. Bush', *New York Times*, 17 October 2004.
5 See Noam Chomsky, 'The skeleton in the closet: the responsibility to protect in history', in Philip Cunliffe, ed., *Critical perspectives on the responsibility to protect: interrogating theory and practice* (Abingdon: Routledge, 2011).

Bibliography

Abbott, Kenneth W., and Duncan Snidal. 'Hard and soft law in international governance'. *International Organization* 54.3 (2000): 421–456.

Abdul-Ahad, Ghaith. 'Bureaucracy of evil: how Islamic State ran a city'. *Guardian*, 29 January 2018.

Acharya, Amitav. 'How ideas spread: whose norms matter? Norm localization and institutional change in Asian regionalism'. *International Organization* 58.2 (2004): 239–275.

Akhavan, Payam. 'Are international criminal tribunals a disincentive to peace? Reconciling judicial romanticism with political realism'. *Human Rights Quarterly* 31.3 (2009): 624–654.

Akhavan, Payam. 'Beyond impunity: can international criminal justice prevent future atrocities?' *American Journal of International Law* 95.1 (2001): 7–31.

Ali, Tariq, ed. *Masters of the universe? NATO's Balkan crusade*. Verso, 2000.

Allison, Roy. 'The Russian case for military intervention in Georgia: international law, norms and political calculation'. *European Security* 18.2 (2009): 173–200.

Al-Qaq, Richard. *Managing world order: United Nations peace operations and the security agenda*. I. B. Tauris, 2009.

Anderson, Perry. 'Arms and rights: Rawls, Habermas and Bobbio in an age of war'. *New Left Review* 31 (January–February 2005): 5.

Annan, Kofi. *In larger freedom: towards development, security and human rights for all. Report of the secretary-general* (UN Doc A/59/2005). United Nations Publications, 2005.

Arbour, Louise. 'The responsibility to protect as a duty of care in international law and practice'. *Review of International Studies* 34.3 (2008): 445–458.

Ayoob, Mohammed. 'Humanitarian intervention and international society'. *Global Governance* 7.3 (2001): 225–230.

Ayoob, Mohammed. 'Humanitarian intervention and state sovereignty'. *International Journal of Human Rights* 6.1 (2002): 81–102.

Ayoob, Mohammed. *The third world security predicament: state making, regional conflict, and the international system*. L. Rienner, 1995.

Ayoob, Mohammed. 'Third World perspectives on humanitarian intervention and international administration'. *Global Governance* 10 (2004): 99–118.

Bibliography

Bacevich, Andrew J. *America's war for the Greater Middle East: a military history*. Random House, 2016.

Bacevich, Andrew J. *The new American militarism: how Americans are seduced by war*. Oxford University Press, 2005.

Bacevich, Andrew J. *Washington rules: America's path to permanent war*. Metropolitan Books, 2011.

Badescu, Cristina G., and Linnea Bergholm. 'The responsibility to protect and the conflict in Darfur: the big let-down'. *Security Dialogue* 40.3 (2009): 287–309.

Badiou, Alain. *Ethics: An essay on the understanding of evil*. Trans. Peter Hallward. Verso, 2013.

Bain, William. 'The political theory of trusteeship and the twilight of international equality'. *International Relations* 17.1 (2003): 59–77.

Barber, Rebecca. 'The responsibility to protect the survivors of natural disaster: Cyclone Nargis, a case study'. *Journal of Conflict and Security Law* 14.1 (2009): 3–34.

Barry, Buzan. *People, states and fear: an agenda for international security studies in the post-Cold War era*. Pearson-Longman, 1991.

Baudrillard, Jean. 'No pity for Sarajevo'. In *Screened out*, trans. Chris Turner. Verso, 2002.

BBC News. 'David Cameron to call for new Syria peace drive at UN'. 27 September 2015. At https://www.bbc.co.uk/news/uk-34372286 (accessed 22 November 2018).

BBC News. 'Obama West Point speech in full with analysis'. 29 May 2014. At https://www.bbc.co.uk/news/world-us-canada-27606537 (accessed 22 November 2018).

BBC News. 'President Obama: Libya aftermath "worst mistake" of presidency'. 11 April 2016. At https://www.bbc.co.uk/news/world-us-canada-36013703 (accessed 5 July 2018).

Beardsworth, Richard. *Cosmopolitanism and international relations theory*. Polity, 2011.

Begley, Sarah. 'Read the full text of Samantha Power's scathing attack on Russia', *Time*, 17 January 2017. Available at https://time.com/4637117/samantha-power-united-nations-russia-speech-transcript (accessed 9 August 2018).

Bellamy, Alex J. 'Ethics and intervention: the "humanitarian exception" and the problem of abuse in the case of Iraq'. *Journal of Peace Research* 41.2 (2004): 131–147.

Bellamy, Alex J. 'Humanitarian responsibilities and interventionist claims in international society'. *Review of International Studies* 29.3 (2003): 321–340.

Bellamy, Alex J. *Responsibility to protect: a defense*. Oxford University Press, 2014.

Bellamy, Alex J. 'Responsibility to protect or Trojan horse? The crisis in Darfur and humanitarian intervention after Iraq'. *Ethics and International Affairs* 19.2 (2005): 31–54.

Bibliography

Bellamy, Alex J. *Responsibility to protect: the global effort to end mass atrocities*. Polity, 2009.

Bellamy, Alex J. 'The responsibility to protect and the problem of military intervention'. *International Affairs* 84.4 (2008): 615–639.

Bellamy, Alex J. 'Whither the responsibility to protect? Humanitarian intervention and the 2005 World Summit'. *Ethics and International Affairs* 20.2 (2006): 143–169.

Bellamy, Alex J., and Paul D. Williams. 'The new politics of protection? Côte d'Ivoire, Libya and the responsibility to protect'. *International Affairs* 87.4 (2011): 825–850.

Bijian, Zheng. 'China's "peaceful rise" to great-power status'. *Foreign Affairs* 84 (2005): 18.

Binder, Martin. 'Humanitarian crises and the international politics of selectivity'. *Human Rights Review* 10.3 (2009): 327–348.

Blair, Tony. *A journey: my political life*. Hutchinson, 2010.

Blätter, Ariela, and Paul D. Williams. 'The responsibility not to veto'. *Global Responsibility to Protect* 3.3 (2011): 301–322.

Bowen, Wyn, and Matthew Moran. 'What North Korea learned from Libya's decision to give up nuclear weapons'. *The Conversation*, 11 May 2018. Available at https://theconversation.com/what-north-korea-learned-from-libyas-decision-to-give-up-nuclear-weapons-95674 (accessed 23 August 2018).

Braithwaite, Rodric. *Afgantsy: the Russians in Afghanistan 1979–89*. Profile Books, 2011.

Braut-Heghammer, Malfrid. 'Why North Korea succeeded in getting nuclear weapons – where Libya and Iraq didn't'. *Washington Post*, 2 January 2018. Available at https://www.washingtonpost.com/news/monkey-cage/wp/2018/01/02/why-north-korea-succeeded-at-getting-nuclear-weapons-when-iraq-and-libya-failed/?utm_term=.728f21a8a02b (accessed 23 August 2018).

Brown, Yasmin Alibhai. 'How to treat returning jihadis', *New European*, 25 March 2018.

Buchanan, Allen, and Robert O. Keohane. 'The preventive use of force: a cosmopolitan institutional proposal'. *Ethics and International Affairs* 18.1 (2004): 1–22.

Bull, Hedley. 'International law and international order'. *International Organization* 26.3 (1972): 583–588.

Bull, Hedley. 'Society and anarchy in international relations', in Herbert Butterfield and Martin Wight, eds, *Diplomatic investigations: essays in the theory of international politics*. George Allen & Unwin, 1966.

Bull, Hedley. 'The great irresponsibles? The United States, the Soviet Union, and world order'. *International Journal* 35.3 (1980): 437–447.

Bull, Hedley. 'The Grotian concept of international society', in Herbert Butterfield and Martin Wight, eds, *Diplomatic investigations: essays in the theory of international politics*. George Allen & Unwin, 1966.

Bibliography

Bull, Hedley. 'The universality of human rights'. *Millennium* 8.2 (1979): 155–159.

Bull, Hedley, and Adam Watson, eds. *The expansion of international society*. Clarendon Press, 1984.

Butterfield, Herbert, and Martin Wight, eds. *Diplomatic investigations: essays in the theory of international politics*. George Allen & Unwin, 1966.

Buzan, Barry. 'China in international society: is "peaceful rise" possible?' *Chinese Journal of International Politics* 3.1 (2010): 5–36.

Buzan, Barry. *People, states and fear: an agenda for international security studies in the post-Cold War era*, 2nd edition. Harvester Wheatsheaf, 1991.

Caldwell, Christopher. 'Communiste et Rastignac'. *Review of Le Monde selon K*, by Pierre Péan. *London Review of Books* 31.13 (2009): 7–10.

Carden, James. 'Why does the US continue to arm terrorists in Syria?', *The Nation*, 2 March 2017.

Carr, E. H. *The twenty years' crisis, 1919–1939: reissued with a new preface from Michael Cox*. Palgrave Macmillan, 2016.

Chandler, David. *Empire in denial: the politics of state-building*. Pluto Press, 2006.

Chandler, David. *From Kosovo to Kabul and beyond: human rights and international intervention*, 2nd edition. Pluto Press, 2006.

Chandler, David. *From Kosovo to Kabul: human rights and international intervention*. Pluto Press, 2002.

Chandler, David. 'R2P or not R2P? More statebuilding, less responsibility'. *Global Responsibility to Protect* 2.1 (2010): 161–166.

Chandler, David. 'Rhetoric without responsibility: the attraction of "ethical" foreign policy'. *British Journal of Politics and International Relations* 5.3 (2003): 295–316.

Chandler, David. 'The responsibility to protect? Imposing the "liberal peace"'. *International Peacekeeping* 11.1 (2004): 59–81.

Chandler, David. 'The security–development nexus and the rise of "anti-foreign policy"'. *Journal of International relations and Development* 10.4 (2007): 362–386.

Chesterman, Simon. 'Humanitarian intervention and Afghanistan', in Jennifer M. Welsh, ed., *Humanitarian intervention and international relations*. Oxford University Press, 2003.

Chesterman, Simon. *Just war or just peace? Humanitarian intervention and international law*. Oxford University Press, 2002.

Chesterman, Simon. 'Legality versus legitimacy: humanitarian intervention, the Security Council, and the rule of law'. *Security Dialogue* 33.3 (2002): 293–307.

Chesterton, G. K. *The man who was Thursday*. Penguin, 2012.

Chimni, B. S. 'Forum replies: a new humanitarian council for humanitarian interventions?' *International Journal of Human Rights* 6.1 (2002): 103–112.

Bibliography

Chinkin, Christine M. 'The challenge of soft law: development and change in international law'. *International and Comparative Law Quarterly* 38.4 (1989): 850–866.

Chomsky, Noam. 'The skeleton in the closet: the responsibility to protect in history', in Philip Cunliffe, ed., *Critical perspectives on the responsibility to protect: interrogating theory and practice*. Routledge, 2011.

Cockburn, Patrick. 'Thanks to UK and US intervention, al-Qaeda now has a mini-state in Yemen. It's Iraq and Isis all over again'. *The Independent*, 15 April 2016. Available at https://www.independent.co.uk/voices/thanks-to-uk-and-us-intervention-al-qaeda-now-has-a-mini-state-in-yemen-its-iraq-and-isis-all-over-a6986086.html (accessed 23 August 2018).

Cohen, Jean L. 'A global state of emergency or the further constitutionalization of international law: a pluralist approach'. *Constellations* 15.4 (2008): 456–484.

Cohen, Jean L. *Globalization and sovereignty: rethinking legality, legitimacy, and constitutionalism*. Cambridge University Press, 2012.

Cohen, Jean L. 'Rethinking human rights, democracy, and sovereignty in the age of globalization'. *Political Theory* 36.4 (2008): 578–606.

Cohen, Jean L. 'Sovereign equality versus imperial right: the battle over the "new world order"'. *Constellations: A Journal of Critical and Democratic Theory* 13.4 (2006): 489.

Cohen, Jean L. 'Whose sovereignty? Empire versus international law'. *Ethics and International Affairs* 18.3 (2004): 1–24.

Cooper, Robert. *The breaking of nations: order and chaos in the twenty-first century*. Atlantic Books, 2003.

Cunliffe, Philip, ed. *Critical perspectives on the responsibility to protect: interrogating theory and practice*. Taylor & Francis, 2011.

Cunliffe, Philip. 'Dangerous duties: power, paternalism and the responsibility to protect'. *Review of International Studies* 36.SI (2010): 79–96.

Cunliffe, Philip. *Legions of peace: UN peacekeepers from the global South*. Hurst, 2013.

Dannreuther, Roland. 'Understanding Russia's return to the Middle East'. *International Politics*, May 2018: 1–17.

Deng, Francis M., Sadikiel Kimaro, Terrence Lyons, Donald Rothchild and I. William Zartman. *Sovereignty as responsibility: conflict management in Africa*. Brookings Institution Press, 2010.

Der Derian, James. 'Anti-diplomacy, intelligence theory and surveillance practice'. *Intelligence and National Security* 8.3 (1993): 29–51.

Der Derian, James. *On diplomacy: a genealogy of Western estrangement*. Oxford University Press, 1987.

Dodge, Toby. *Iraq: from war to a new authoritarianism*. Routledge, 2013.

Dombrowski, Peter, and Rodger A. Payne. 'The emerging consensus for preventive war'. *Survival* 48.2 (2006): 115–136.

Donnelly, Jack. 'Human rights: a new standard of civilization?' *International Affairs* 74.1 (1998): 1–23.

Bibliography

Douzinas, Costas. *Human rights and empire: the political philosophy of cosmopolitanism*. Routledge-Cavendish, 2007.

Doyle, Michael W. 'The new interventionism'. *Metaphilosophy* 32.1–2 (2001): 212–235.

Doyle, Thomas E. 'When liberal peoples turn into outlaw states: John Rawls' Law of Peoples and liberal nuclearism'. *Journal of International Political Theory* 11.2 (2015): 257–273.

Drezner, Daniel. 'Why China will be able to sell itself as the last liberal great power'. *Washington Post*, 24 January 2017.

Drolet, Jean-François. *American neoconservatism: the politics and culture of a reactionary idealism*. Hurst, 2011.

Duffield, Mark. *Global governance and the new wars: the merging of development and security*. Zed Books, 2001.

Dunham, Will. 'Kerry condemns Russia's "incredible act of aggression" in Ukraine'. Reuters. 2 March 2014. Available at https://www.reuters.com/article/2014/03/02/us-ukraine-crisis-usa-kerry-idUSBREA210DG20140302 (accessed 9 August 2018).

Erskine, Toni, and Richard Ned Lebow, eds. *Tragedy and international relations*. Palgrave Macmillan, 2012.

Etzioni, Amitai. 'Sovereignty as responsibility'. *Orbis* 50.1 (2006): 71–85.

Evans, Gareth, Ramesh Thakur and Robert Pape. 'Correspondence: humanitarian intervention and the responsibility to protect'. *International Security* 37.4 (2013): 199–214.

Farer, Tom J., et al. 'Roundtable: humanitarian intervention after 9/11'. *International relations* 19.2 (2005): 211–250.

Ferguson, Niall. 'An empire in denial: the limits of US imperialism'. *Harvard International Review* 25.3 (2003): 64.

Finnemore, Martha. *The purpose of intervention: changing beliefs about the use of force*. Cornell University Press, 2003.

Five Pillars. 'Abu Bakr al-Baghdadi urges Muslims to make hijrah to the "Islamic state"'. At https://5pillarsuk.com/2014/07/02/abu-bakr-al-baghdadi-urges-muslims-to-make-hijrah-to-the-islamic-state (accessed 28 May 2019).

Fox, Gregory H. *Humanitarian occupation*. Cambridge University Press, 2008.

France Diplomatie. 'G5 Sahel Joint Force and the Sahel Alliance'. At https://www.diplomatie.gouv.fr/en/french-foreign-policy/defence-security/crisis-and-conflicts/g5-sahel-joint-force-and-the-sahel-alliance (accessed 30 August 2018).

Freedman, Lawrence. 'The age of liberal wars'. *Review of International Studies* 31.S1 (2005): 93–107.

Fukuyama, Francis. *State building: governance and world order in the 21st century*. Profile Books, 2004.

Füredi, Frank. *The new ideology of imperialism: renewing the moral imperative*. Pluto Press, 1994.

Bibliography

Gat, Azar. 'The return of authoritarian great powers'. *Foreign Affairs* 86 (2007): 59–69.

Gehrke, Joel Gehrke. 'Theresa May: Syria strike "not about regime change"'. *Washington Examiner*, 13 April 2018. Available at https://www.washingtonexaminer.com/policy/defense-national-security/theresa-may-syria-strike-not-about-regime-change (accessed 5 July 2018).

Glanville, Luke. 'Norms, interests and humanitarian intervention'. *Global Change, Peace and Security* 18.3 (2006): 153–171.

Glanville, Luke. *Sovereignty and the responsibility to protect: a new history.* University of Chicago Press, 2013.

Global Centre for the Responsibility to Protect. At https://www.globalr2p.org/about_r2p (accessed 15 November 2018).

Golshan, Tara. 'John McCain's shocking concession on the Iraq War: it was a "mistake"', *Vox*, 25 May 2018. Available at https://www.vox.com/2018/5/25/17394466/john-mccain-memoir-iraq-war-mistake (accessed 5 July 2018).

Greaves, Wilfrid. 'The intervention imperative: contradictions between liberalism, democracy, and humanitarian intervention'. *Innovations: Journal Politics* 8 (2008): 59–72.

Griffin, James. 'Discrepancies between the best philosophical account of human rights and the international law of human rights'. *Proceedings of the Aristotelian Society* 101.1 (2001): 1–28.

Grøner Krogstad, Erlend. 'Local ownership as dependence management: inviting the coloniser back'. *Journal of Intervention and Statebuilding* 8.2–3 (2014): 105–125.

Guardian, 'George Bush's speech to the UN General Assembly', 12 September 2002. Available at https://www.theguardian.com/world/2002/sep/12/iraq.usa3 (accessed 9 October 2018).

Haass, Richard. Tweet @RichardHaas, 14 July 2018, 21:26.

Habermas, Jürgen. 'Bestiality and humanity: a war on the border between legality and morality'. *Constellations* 6.3 (1999): 263–272.

Habermas, Jürgen. *The postnational constellation: political essays*, trans. Max Pensky. MIT Press, 2001.

Hall, Ian. 'Diplomacy, anti-diplomacy and international society'. In Richard Little and John Williams, eds, *The anarchical society in a globalized world*, 141–161. Palgrave Macmillan, 2006.

Harris, Ian. 'Order and justice in "The anarchical society"'. *International Affairs* 69.4 (1993): 725–741.

Hayden, Patrick. *Cosmopolitan global politics*. Ashgate, 2005.

Heartfield, James. 'Zombie anti-imperialists versus the "empire"'. Spiked Online, 1 September 2004. At https://spiked-online.com/newsite/article/2236#.W-lM7uKnwyU (accessed 12 November 2018).

Hehir, Aidan. 'The permanence of inconsistency.' *International Security* 38.1 (2013): 137–159.

Held, David. *Cosmopolitanism: ideals and realities*. Polity, 2010.

Heller, Regina, and Martin Kahl. 'Tracing and understanding "bad" norm dynamics in counterterrorism: the current debates in IR research'. *Critical Studies on Terrorism* 6.3 (2013): 414–428.

Henkin, Louis. 'Kosovo and the law of "humanitarian intervention"'. *American Journal of International Law* 93.4 (1999): 824–828.

Hennigan, W. J., Brian Bennett and Nabih Bulos. 'In Syria, militias armed by the Pentagon fight those armed by the C.I.A.' *Los Angeles Times*, 27 March 2016.

Hilderbrand, Robert C. *Dumbarton Oaks: the origins of the United Nations and the search for postwar security*. University of North Carolina Press, 2001.

Hille, Kathrin. 'China commits combat troops to Mali', *Financial Times*, 27 June 2013.

Hillgenberg, Hartmut. 'A fresh look at soft law'. *European Journal of International Law* 10.3 (1999): 499–515.

Hjorth, Ronnie. 'The poverty of exceptionalism in international theory'. *Journal of International Political Theory* 10.2 (2014): 169–187.

Hobbes, Thomas. *Leviathan*, ed. C. B. Macpherson. Penguin, 1968.

Hopgood, Stephen. *The endtimes of human rights*. Cornell University Press, 2013.

Humphreys, Stephen. 'Legalizing lawlessness: on Giorgio Agamben's state of exception'. *European Journal of International Law* 17.3 (2006): 677–687.

Hurd, Ian. 'Breaking and making norms: American revisionism and crises of legitimacy'. *International Politics* 44.2–3 (2007): 194–213.

Huysmans, Jef. 'International politics of exception: competing visions of international political order between law and politics'. *Alternatives* 31.2 (2006): 135–165.

Huysmans, Jef. 'International politics of insecurity: normativity, inwardness and the exception'. *Security Dialogue* 37.1 (2006): 11–29.

Huysmans, Jef. 'Minding exceptions: the politics of insecurity and liberal democracy'. *Contemporary Political Theory* 3.3 (2004): 321–341.

Huysmans, Jef. 'The jargon of exception – On Schmitt, Agamben and the Absence of political society'. *International Political Sociology* 2.2 (2008): 165–183.

Ignatieff, Michael. *Empire lite: nation building in Bosnia, Kosovo, Afghanistan.* Vintage, 2003.

Ikenberry, G. John. 'The end of liberal international order?' *International Affairs* 94.1 (2018): 7–23.

Independent International Commission on Kosovo (IICK). *The Kosovo report: international response and lessons learned*. Oxford University Press, 2001.

International Coalition for the Responsibility to Protect, 'Crisis in Sri Lanka'. At https://www.responsibilitytoprotect.org/index.php/crises/crisis-in-sri-lanka#response (accessed 24 August 2018).

Bibliography

International Commission on Intervention and State Sovereignty. *The responsibility to protect: report of the International Commission on Intervention and State Sovereignty.* International Development Research Centre, 2001.

Jackson, Robert. 'Martin Wight's thought on diplomacy'. *Diplomacy and Statecraft* 13.4 (2002): 1–28.

Jackson, Robert. 'Sovereignty in world politics: a glance at the conceptual and historical landscape'. *Political Studies* 47.3 (1999): 431–456.

Jackson, Robert. *Sovereignty: the evolution of an idea.* Polity, 2007.

Jackson, Robert. *The global covenant: human conduct in a world of states.* Oxford University Press, 2000.

Jacques, Rancière. 'Who is the subject of the rights of man?' *South Atlantic Quarterly* 103.2–3 (2004): 297–310.

James, Alan. 'The practice of sovereign statehood in contemporary international society'. *Political Studies* 47.3 (1999): 457–473.

Kaldor, Mary. *Human security: reflections on globalization and intervention.* Polity, 2007.

Kelly, Patrick William. *Sovereign emergencies: Latin America and the making of global human rights politics.* Cambridge University Press, 2018.

Kingsbury, Benedict. 'Sovereignty and inequality'. *European Journal of International Law* 9.4 (1998): 599–625.

Kirsch, Adam. 'Beware of pity. Hannah Arendt and the power of the impersonal'. *New Yorker,* 12 January 2009.

Kissinger, Henry. 'New world disorder'. *Newsweek,* 31 May 1999.

Knight, Michael Muhammad. 'I was nearly an American jihadi and I understand why young men are joining Isis – we are raised to love violence', *Independent,* 4 September 2014.

Knudsen, Tonny Brems, and Cornelia Navari, eds. *International organization in the anarchical society: the institutional structure of world order.* Palgrave Macmillan, 2018.

Koskenniemi, Martti. 'Miserable comforters: international relations as new natural law'. *European Journal of International Relations* 15.3 (2009): 395–422.

Krasner, Stephen. *Sovereignty: organised hypocrisy.* Princeton University Press, 1999.

Kuperman, Alan J. 'The moral hazard of humanitarian intervention: lessons from the Balkans'. *International Studies Quarterly* 52.1 (2008): 49–80.

Laïdi, Zaki. *A world without meaning: the crisis of meaning in international politics.* Trans. June Burnham and Jenny Coulon. Routledge, 1998.

Lebow, Richard Ned. *The tragic vision of politics: ethics, interests and orders.* Cambridge University Press, 2003.

Lenin, Vladimir Ilich. *Imperialism: the highest stage of capitalism. A popular outline.* Pluto Press/Junius, 1996.

Lischer, Sarah Kenyan. 'Military intervention and the "humanitarian force multiplier"'. *Global Governance* 13 (2007): 99.

Bibliography

Little, Richard, and John Williams, eds. *The anarchical society in a globalized world*. Palgrave Macmillan, 2006.

Luban, David. 'Just war and human rights'. *Philosophy and Public Affairs* 9.2 (1980): 160–181.

Lubold, Gordon, and Dion Nissenbaum. 'Trump bowed to Pentagon restraint on Syria strikes'. *Wall Street Journal*, 16 April 2018.

Luck, Edward C. 'R2P at ten: a new mindset for a new era'. *Global Governance* 21 (2015): 499–504.

Luttwak, Edward. 'Give war a chance'. *Foreign Affairs* 78.4 (1999): 36–44.

Makinda, Samuel M. 'The global covenant as an evolving institution'. *International Journal of Human Rights* 6.1 (2002): 113–126.

Mallaby, Sebastian. 'The reluctant imperialist: terrorism, failed states, and the case for American empire'. *Foreign Affairs* 81.2 (2002): 2–7.

Mandelbaum, Michael. 'The failure of intervention'. *Foreign Affairs* 78.5 (1999): 2–8.

Martel, James. *Subverting the Leviathan: reading Thomas Hobbes as a radical democrat*. Columbia University Press, 2007.

Mayall, James. 'Non-intervention, self-determination and the "new world order"'. *International Affairs* 67.3 (1991): 421–429.

Mazetti, Mark, Adam Goldman and Michael S. Schmidt. 'Behind the sudden death of a $1 billion secret C.I.A. war in Syria'. *New York Times*, 2 August 2017.

Mazower, Mark. *Governing the world: the history of an idea*. Allen Lane, 2012.

Mazower, Mark. *No enchanted palace: the end of empire and the ideological origins of the United Nations*. Princeton University Press, 2009.

McEwan, Ian. *Saturday*. Vintage, 2005.

McLaughlin, Theodore. 'Why has the Syrian civil war lasted so long?' *Washington Post*, 27 July 2018.

Mearsheimer, John J. *The great delusion: liberal dreams and international realities*. Yale University Press, 2018.

Mearsheimer, John J. 'Why the Ukraine crisis is the West's fault: the liberal delusions that provoked Putin'. *Foreign Affairs* 93.5 (2014): 77–89.

Michaels, Maggie, Trish Wilson and Lee Keath. '"Unite with the devil": Yemen war binds US, allies, al-Qaida'. Associated Press, 7 August 2018. At https://www.apnews.com/9bf91c535f274925a2be80293e121446 (accessed 11 March 2019).

Mill, John Stuart, 'A few words on non-intervention'. In Gertrude Himmelfarb, ed., *Essays on politics and culture*. Doubleday, 1963.

Miller, Richard B. 'Justifications of the Iraq war examined'. *Ethics and International Affairs* 22.1 (2008): 43–67.

Monteiro, Nuno P. *Theory of unipolar politics*. Cambridge University Press, 2013.

Monteiro, Nuno P. 'Unrest assured: why unipolarity is not peaceful'. *International Security* 36.3 (2011/2012): 9–40.

Morgenthau, Hans J. 'Vietnam: another Korea?' In *The restoration of American politics*. University of Chicago Press, 1962.

Morley, Morris, and Chris McGillion. '"Disobedient" generals and the politics of redemocratization: the Clinton administration and Haiti'. *Political Science Quarterly* 112.3 (1997): 363–385.

Morozov, Viatcheslav. 'Subaltern empire? Toward a postcolonial approach to Russian foreign policy'. *Problems of Post-Communism* 60.6 (2013): 16–28.

Moses, Jeremy. 'Peace without perfection: the intersections of realist and pacifist thought'. *Cooperation and Conflict* 53.1 (2017): 42–60.

Moses, Jeremy. *Sovereignty and responsibility: power, norms and intervention in international relations*. Palgrave, 2014.

Mouffe, Chantal, ed. *The challenge of Carl Schmitt*. Verso, 1999.

Moyn, Samuel. *The last utopia: human rights in history*. Harvard University Press, 2012.

Murithi, Tim. 'The responsibility to protect as enshrined in Article 4 of the Constitutive Act of the African Union'. *African Security Studies* 16.3 (2007): 14–24.

Murray, Robert W., et al., eds. *Into the eleventh hour: R2P, Syria and humanitarianism in crisis*. E-International Relations, 2014. Available at openresearch-repository.anu.edu.au/bitstream/1885/27292/2/01_Evans_ The_Consequences_of_2014.pdf (accessed 19 November 2018).

Nasu, Hitoshi. 'Operationalizing the responsibility to protect in the context of civilian protection by UN peacekeepers'. *International Peacekeeping* 18.4 (2011): 364–378.

Navari, Cornelia. 'Modelling the relation of fundamental institutions and international organizations'. In Tonny Brems Knudsen and Cornelia Navari, eds, *International organization in the anarchical society: the institutional structure of world order*. Palgrave Macmillan, 2018.

Nielsen, Christian Axboe. 'The Kosovo precedent and the rhetorical deployment of former Yugoslav analogies in the cases of Abkhazia and South Ossetia'. *Southeast European and Black Sea Studies* 9.1–2 (2009): 171–189.

O'Connor, Tom. 'U.S. has spent six trillion dollars on wars that killed half a million people since 9/11, report says', *Newsweek* 14 November 2018. Available at https://www.newsweek.com/us-spent-six-trillion-wars-killed-half-million-1215588?utm_medium=Social&utm_campaign =NewsweekFacebookSF&utm_source=Facebook&fbclid=IwAR2 C2hB99ft4O5Rv59JWJf964HL84K1Fo1xP11wW6bKosrFv24XFQvuYLdY (accessed 16 November 2018).

Orford, Anne. *International authority and the responsibility to protect*. Cambridge University Press, 2011.

Owens, Patricia. 'Accidents don't just happen: the liberal politics of high-technology "humanitarian" war'. *Millennium* 32.3 (2003): 595–616.

Owens, Patricia. 'Theorizing military intervention'. *International Affairs* 80.2 (2004): 355–365.

Bibliography

Owens, Patricia. 'Xenophilia, gender, and sentimental humanitarianism'. *Alternatives* 29.3 (2004): 285–304.

Paris, Roland. *At war's end: building peace after civil conflict*. Cambridge University Press, 2004.

Paris, Roland. 'Saving liberal peacebuilding'. *Review of International Studies* 36.2 (2010): 337–365.

Paris, Roland. 'The "responsibility to protect"' and the structural problems of preventive humanitarian intervention'. *International Peacekeeping* 21.5 (2014): 569–603.

Pattison, James. 'Legitimacy and humanitarian intervention: who should intervene?' *International Journal of Human Rights* 12.3 (2008): 395–413.

Pauley, Logan. 'China takes the lead in UN peacekeeping', *The Diplomat*, 17 April 2018. Available at https://thediplomat.com/2018/04/china-takes-the-lead-in-un-peacekeeping (accessed 20 August 2018).

Peel, Quentin. 'Russia's reversal: where next for humanitarian intervention'. *Financial Times*, 22 August 2008.

Philpott, Daniel. 'Sovereignty: an introduction and brief history'. *Journal of International Affairs* (1995): 353–368.

Pinker, Steven. *The better angels of our nature: why violence has declined*. Allen Lane, 2011.

Plaut, Martin. 'The UN's all pervasive role in Africa', 18 July 2007. At http://news.bbc.co.uk/1/hi/world/africa/6903196.stm (accessed 15 November 2018).

Porter, Patrick. 'Iraq: a liberal war after all. A critique of Dan Deudney and John Ikenberry'. *International Politics* 55.1 (2017): 334–348.

Porter, Patrick, 'Twilight struggle: the Cold War was neither stable nor simple', 3 August 2015. At War on the Rocks, https://warontherocks.com/2015/08/twilight-struggle-the-cold-war-was-not-stable-or-simple (accessed 6 September 2018).

Public Library of US Diplomacy. 'A/S Fried's November 15 meeting with DFM Titov on Kosovo', 21 November 2006. At https://search.wikileaks.org/plusd/cables/06MOSCOW12549_a.html (accessed 15 November 2018).

Rawls, John. *The law of peoples, with 'The idea of public reason revisited'*. Harvard University Press, 2001.

Rengger, Nicholas. *The anti-Pelagian imagination in political theory and international relations: dealing in darkness*. Routledge, 2017.

Reus-Smit, Christian. 'Human rights and the social construction of sovereignty'. *Review of International Studies* 27.4 (2001): 519–538.

Reus-Smit, Christian. 'Liberal hierarchy and the licence to use force'. *Review of International Studies* 31.S1 (2005): 71–92.

Roach, Steven C. 'Decisionism and humanitarian intervention: reinterpreting Carl Schmitt and the global political order'. *Alternatives* 30.4 (2005): 443–460.

Roberts, Geoffrey. *The Soviet Union in world politics: coexistence, revolution and Cold War, 1945–1991*. Routledge, 1999.

Rosenfeld, Everett. 'Putin: do you realise what you have done?' CNBC, 28 September 2015. At https://www.cnbc.com/2015/09/28/putin-do-you-realize-what-you-have-done.html (accessed 18 October 2018).

Roth, Kenneth. 'Was the Iraq war a humanitarian intervention?' *Journal of Military Ethics* 5.2 (2006): 84–92.

Roy, Olivier. *The politics of chaos in the Middle East*. Hurst, 2008.

Rubin, James. 'Base motives', *Guardian*, 8 May 2004.

Sakwa, Richard. *Russia against the rest: the post-Cold War crisis of world order*. Cambridge University Press, 2017.

Sakwa, Richard. 'The cold peace: Russo-Western relations as a mimetic cold war'. *Cambridge Review of International Affairs* 26.1 (2013): 203–224.

Sanger, David E. 'Rebel arms flow is said to benefit jihadists in Syria'. *New York Times*, 14 October 2012.

Schmitt, Carl. 'Ethic of state and pluralistic state', in Chantal Mouffe, ed., *The challenge of Carl Schmitt*. Verso, 1999.

Sellars, Kirsten. *The rise and rise of human rights*. Sutton, 2002.

Shane, Scott. 'From Minneapolis to ISIS: an American's path to jihad', *New York Times*, 21 March 2015.

Simpson, Gerry. *Great powers and outlaw states: unequal sovereigns in the international legal order*. Cambridge University Press, 2004.

Slomp, Gabriella. 'Carl Schmitt's five arguments against the idea of just war'. *Cambridge Review of International Affairs* 19.3 (2006): 435–447.

Sørensen, Georg. 'Sovereignty: change and continuity in a fundamental institution'. *Political Studies* 47.3 (1999): 590–604.

Stahn, Carsten. 'Responsibility to protect: political rhetoric or emerging legal norm?' *American Journal of International Law* 101.1 (2007): 99–120.

Strachan, Hew. 'The lost meaning of strategy'. *Survival* 47.3 (2005): 33–54.

Suganami, Hidemi. *The domestic analogy and world order proposals*. Cambridge University Press, 1989.

Susskind, Ron 'Faith, certainty and the presidency of George W. Bush', *New York Times*, 17 October 2004.

Taub, Ben. 'Journey to jihad', *New Yorker*, 1 June 2015.

Thakur, Ramesh. 'Iraq and the responsibility to protect'. *Behind the Headlines* 62 (2004): 1–16.

Thakur, Ramesh. 'Outlook. Intervention, sovereignty and the responsibility to protect: experiences from ICISS'. *Security Dialogue* 33.3 (2002): 323–340.

Thakur, Ramesh. 'The responsibility to protect at 15'. *International Affairs* 92.2 (2016): 415–434.

Thakur, Ramesh. *The United Nations, peace and security: from collective security to the responsibility to protect*. Cambridge University Press, 2006.

Tharoor, Ishaan. 'Russia stays in the driver's seat in Syria'. *Washington Post*, 10 July 2018.

Bibliography

Todd, Emmanuel. *After the empire: the breakdown of the American order.* Columbia University Press, 2003.

Tondini, Matteo. 'From neo-colonialism to a "light-footprint approach": restoring justice systems'. *International Peacekeeping* 15.2 (2008): 237–251.

Tooze, Adam. *Crashed: how a decade of financial crises changed the world.* Allen Lane, 2018.

Tooze, Adam. *The deluge: the Great War, America and the remaking of the global order, 1916–1931.* Penguin, 2015.

Traub, James. 'The end of American intervention'. *New York Times,* 18 February 2012. Available at https://www.nytimes.com/2012/02/19/opinion/sunday/the-end-of-american-intervention.html (accessed 15 November 2018).

Traynor, Ian. 'EU to launch military operations against migrant-smugglers in Libya'. *Guardian,* 20 April 2015.

UN Security Council. *The Veto.* Security Council Report, October 2015. Available at https://www.securitycouncilreport.org/research-reports/the-veto.php (accessed 20 August 2018).

United Nations. 'Statement at the opening of the thematic dialogue of the General Assembly on the responsibility to protect', General Assembly, 23 July 2009. Available at https://www.un.org/ga/president/63/statements/openingr2p230709.shtml (accessed 10 March 2010).

United Nations. *We the peoples: the role of the United Nations in the twenty-first century.* General Assembly, 2000. Available at https://undocs.org/A/54/2000 (accessed 21 November 2018).

Varoufakis, Yanis. *The global minotaur: America, Europe and the future of the global economy.* Zed Books, 2015.

Vinocur, Nicholas. 'New French anti-terror law to replace 2-year state of emergency'. *Politico,* 31 October 2017. Available at https://www.politico.eu/article/new-french-anti-terror-law-to-replace-2-year-state-of-emergency (accessed 9 October 2018).

Walker, Rob B. J. 'Lines of insecurity: international, imperial, exceptional'. *Security Dialogue* 37.1 (2006): 65–82.

Walt, Stephen M. *The hell of good intentions: America's foreign policy elite and the decline of US primacy.* Farrar, Straus & Giroux, 2018.

Walt, Stephen M. 'Top 10 warning signs of "liberal imperialism"'. *Foreign Policy,* 23 May 2013. Available at https://foreignpolicy.com/2013/05/20/top-10-warning-signs-of-liberal-imperialism (accessed 5 September 2018).

Walton, C. Dale. 'The case for strategic traditionalism: war, national interest and liberal peacebuilding'. *International Peacekeeping* 16.5 (2009): 717–734.

Walzer, Michael. *Just and unjust wars,* 3rd edition. Basic Books, 2000.

Warner, Daniel. 'The responsibility to protect and irresponsible, cynical engagement'. *Millennium* 32.1 (2003): 109–121.

Weber, Patricia. 'Too political or not political enough? A Foucauldian reading of the responsibility to protect'. *International Journal of Human Rights* 13.4 (2009): 581–590.

Weiss, Thomas G. 'The sunset of humanitarian intervention? The responsibility to protect in a unipolar era'. *Security Dialogue* 35.2 (2004): 135–153.

Weiss, Thomas G., et al. *The responsibility to protect: report of the International Commission on Intervention and State Sovereignty.* IDRC, 2001.

Welsh, Jennifer M. 'From right to responsibility: humanitarian intervention and international society'. *Global Governance* 8 (2002): 503–521.

Welsh, Jennifer M., ed. *Humanitarian intervention and international relations.* Oxford University Press, 2003.

Welsh, Jennifer M. 'Taking consequences seriously', in Jennifer M. Welsh, ed., *Humanitarian intervention and international relations.* Oxford University Press, 2003.

Welsh, Jennifer M., and Maria Banda. 'International law and the responsibility to protect: clarifying or expanding states' responsibilities?' *Global Responsibility to Protect* 2.3 (2010): 213–231.

Wheeler, Nicholas J. 'Humanitarian vigilantes or legal entrepreneurs: enforcing human rights in international society'. *Critical Review of International Social and Political Philosophy* 3.1 (2000): 139–162.

Wheeler, Nicholas J. 'Legitimating humanitarian intervention: principles and procedures'. *Melbourne Journal of International Law* 2.2 (2001): 554–560.

Wheeler, Nicholas J. 'Pluralist or solidarist conceptions of international society: Bull and Vincent on humanitarian intervention'. *Millennium* 21.3 (1992): 463–487.

Wheeler, Nicholas J. *Saving strangers: humanitarian intervention in international society.* Oxford University Press, 2000.

Wheeler, Nicholas J. 'The humanitarian responsibilities of sovereignty: explaining the development of a new norm of military intervention for humanitarian purposes in international society', in Jennifer M. Welsh, ed., *Humanitarian intervention and international relations.* Oxford University Press, 2003.

White House. *National security strategy of the United States of America,* December 2017. Available at https://www.whitehouse.gov/wp-content/uploads/2017/12/NSS-Final-12-18-2017-0905.pdf (accessed 20 October 2019).

Wight, Martin. 'Why is there no international theory?' *International Relations* 2.1 (1960): 35–48.

Williams, Paul D., and Alex J. Bellamy. 'The responsibility to protect and the crisis in Darfur'. *Security Dialogue* 36.1 (2005): 27–47.

Wyndham, John. *The day of the triffids.* Penguin, 2001.

Zahar, Marie-Joëlle. 'The (in)efficiency of mediation in contemporary conflict: a question of design?' Annual John Burton Lecture, delivered at University of Kent, 12 November 2018.

Bibliography

Žižek, Slavoj. 'Are we in a war? Do we have an enemy?' *London Review of Books* 24.10 (2002): 3–6.

Žižek, Slavoj. *Like a thief in broad daylight: power in the era of post-humanity.* Penguin, 2018.

Žižek, Slavoj. 'NATO, the left hand of God', *Nettime*, 29 June 1999. Available at https://www.lacan.com/zizek-nato.htm (accessed 13 July 2018).

Zounmenou, David. 'The National Movement for the Liberation of Azawad factor in the Mali crisis'. *African Security Review* 22.3 (2013): 167–174.

Zuckerman, Ian. 'One law for war and peace? Judicial review and emergency powers between the norm and the exception'. *Constellations* 13.4 (2006): 522–545.

Index

Index

Index

Index

Index